Dams, Migration and Authoritarianism in China

Past studies on the Chinese state point towards the inherent adaptability, effectiveness and overall stability of authoritarian rule in China. The key question addressed here is how this adaptive capacity plays out at the local level in China, clarifying the extent to which local state actors are able to shape local processes of policy implementation.

This book studies the evolution of dam-induced resettlement policy in China, based on extensive fieldwork conducted in Yunnan Province. It shows that local governments at the lowest administrative levels are caught in a double bind, facing strong top-down pressures in the important policy field of hydropower development, while simultaneously having to handle growing social pressure from local communities affected by resettlement policies. In doing so, the book questions the widespread assumption that the observed longevity and resilience of China's authoritarian regime is to a large extent due to the high degree of flexibility that has been granted to local governments in the course of the reform period. The research extends beyond previous analyses of policy implementation by focusing on the state, on society and the ways in which they interact, as well as by examining what happens when policy implementation is interrupted.

Analysing the application of resettlement policies in contemporary China, with a focus on the multiple constraints that Chinese local states face, this book will be of interest to students and scholars of Political Science, Chinese Studies and Sociology.

Sabrina Habich is a Postdoctoral Fellow at the University of Tübingen, Germany.

Routledge Studies on China in Transition
Series Editor: David S. G. Goodman

Dams, Migration and Authoritarianism in China
The local state in Yunnan

Sabrina Habich

Routledge
Taylor & Francis Group

LONDON AND NEW YORK

First published 2016
by Routledge

2 Park Square, Milton Park, Abingdon, Oxfordshire OX14 4RN
711 Third Avenue, New York, NY 10017

Routledge is an imprint of the Taylor & Francis Group, an informa business

First issued in paperback 2018

British Library Cataloguing in Publication Data
A catalogue record for this book is available from the British Library

Library of Congress Cataloging-in-Publication Data
Names: Habich, Sabrina, author.
Title: Dams, migration and authoritarianism in China : the local state in
    Yunnan / Sabrina Habich.
Description: New York, NY : Routledge, 2016. | Series: Routledge studies
    on China in transition ; 49 | Includes bibliographical references and index.
Identifiers: LCCN 2015026638 | ISBN 9781138934931 (hardback) |
    ISBN 9781315677637 (ebook)
Subjects: LCSH: Yunnan Sheng (China)—Politics and government. |
    Local government—China—Yunnan Sheng. | Authoritarianism—
    China—Yunnan Sheng. | Forced migration—China—Yunnan Sheng. |
    Hydroelectric power plants—Political aspects—China—Yunnan Sheng. |
    Dams—China—Yunnan Sheng.
Classification: LCC JS7365.Y852 H33 2016 | DDC 307.2—dc23
LC record available at http://lccn.loc.gov/2015026638

ISBN: 978-1-138-93493-1 (hbk)
ISBN: 978-1-138-60902-0 (pbk)

Typeset in Times New Roman
by Apex CoVantage, LLC

Contents

Figures

Maps

Tables

Acknowledgements

Throughout my educational journey and especially while finishing this manuscript, I have received help and support from a great number of individuals and institutions. I should like to take this opportunity to express my gratitude to a few in particular.

I would first like to thank my advisor, Wang Jenn-Hwan, who set me on the path towards studying dam-induced resettlement in Yunnan and has provided me with invaluable academic advice throughout the entire research process. I am also grateful for the unstinting support offered by my committee members, Leng Tse-Kang, Tang Ching-Ping, David Holm, and Chien Shiuh-Shen, who provided me with patient advice and guidance.

Individuals from the China Studies Center and the International Doctoral Program in Asia-Pacific Studies (IDAS) at National Chengchi University have helped with various aspects of this monograph. Lee Ching-Chian, Wang Lin-Zi, Angel Li, and Ray Hsieh provided me with much needed assistance in dealing with various administrative issues related to my studies. I would also like to thank the former IDAS director, Kuan Ping-Yin, for his support.

My thanks also go to everyone who participated in the meetings for postgraduate students and research groups organized by Professor Wang. This network for mutual support and assistance had an immensely positive impact while I was preparing my dissertation. Huang Shuwei and Shih Yijen served as shining examples, helping me to navigate through the oftentimes tiring process of graduation.

During my field research phases, I received support and advice from scholars at the Yunnan University of Finance and Economics in Kunming and Hohai University in Nanjing. Professor Shi and Professor Chen deserve special mention. I was also fortunate enough to have the opportunity to spend a week at the Universities Service Center for China Studies at the Chinese University of Hong Kong, which served as a valuable resource pool. I would furthermore like to express my gratitude to the interview partners with whom I had valuable discussions throughout my field research. Although they must remain unnamed here, I would like to offer them special thanks for being so ready to share their knowledge with me and to contribute to my research. I am also exceedingly grateful for the unwavering support and advice provided by Z. Huan, without whom much of my fieldwork at the very local level would not have been possible. Chou Muyi was of tremendous help with regard to getting in touch with relevant interview partners in Beijing. My thanks also go to Jean-François Rousseau for providing support when data collection was not going at all well.

Throughout my studies, the National Science Council of Taiwan, the Ministry of Education, National Chengchi University, and the Mainland Affairs Council have provided vital funding. In addition, portions of Chapters 5 and 6 are based on material from my 2015 "Strategies of Soft Coercion in Chinese Dam Resettlement," *Issues & Studies, 51*(1), 165–199.

As a Visiting Junior Scholar at the Institute of Political Science at Academia Sinica, I was provided with generous financial support and an excellent environment for conducting research. I would especially like to thank Wu Yu-Shan, Hsu Szu-Chien, Chung Yousun, Tsai Wen-Hsuan, Shirley Shen, and Christina Chen for the invaluable advice they gave me during the final stages of my dissertation. I am grateful to David Goodman who encouraged me to turn my dissertation into a book manuscript, and offered tremendous support during this process. I also thank two anonymous reviewers whose insightful advice has helped me to significantly improve this book. Among the many other scholars who have helped me, Andrew Mertha, Janet Sturgeon, Jean-Marc F. Blanchard, Lin Kun-Chin, Bettina Gransow deserve special mention. Further, I would like to thank Rebecca Lawrence and Stephanie Rogers at Routledge for their support during the production process and Anna Mackay for her excellent proofreading of the manuscript.

My community at the University of Tübingen has provided me with sage counsel when finishing this book manuscript. I thank Gunter Schubert for his guidance, and for inviting me to come to Tübingen in the first place. I also thank Franziska Plümmer, Ailika Schinköthe, Andreas Sobiegalla, Martin Fricke, and Teresa Fay for providing me with indispensable support, and making my return to Germany all the more worthwhile.

Finally, I would like to extend my heartfelt thanks to my family and friends who have provided me with unconditional support and love. Despite being baffled at times by the path that I have chosen, they have been there for me always. Anja, Martin, and Jens made sure that I had everything I needed while studying abroad. Sebastian Biba has offered guidance and constant encouragement. My parents, Christine and Werner Habich, have been my greatest supporters since I first made the decision to study Chinese. This dissertation is dedicated to them.

Despite the enormous number of individuals who have contributed to this dissertation, I am solely responsible for any errors in the work.

Abbreviations

BNSC	Building a New (Socialist) Countryside
CCP, CPC	Chinese Communist Party/Communist Party of China (used differently, according to the official usage in the relevant sources)
EIA	Environmental Impact Assessment
FA	fragmented authoritarianism
GONGOs	government-operated nongovernmental organizations
GDP	gross domestic product
MEP	Ministry of Environmental Protection
MLR	Ministry of Land Resources
MWR	Ministry of Water Resources
MWREP	Ministry of Water Resources and Electric Power
NDRC	National Development and Reform Commission
NEA	National Energy Administration
NGO	nongovernmental organization
NZD	Nuozhadu Dam
Powerchina	Power Construction Corporation of China
PRC	People's Republic China
RMB	*Renminbi* (currency of the People's Republic of China) [€1 = RMB6.93 – as of June 2015]
RMRB	*Renmin Ribao (People's Daily)*
SPCC	State Power Company of China
TVEs	Township and Village Enterprises
UNESCO	United Nations Educational, Scientific and Cultural Organization

1 Introduction

Authoritarianism, policy, and dams

The longevity and continued stability of the People's Republic of China (PRC) has spurred a lively debate about the necessary ingredients for authoritarian regimes to be resilient. What kind of foundation does a Communist single-party system need in order to successfully adapt to changing social, political, and economic circumstances? And how much adaptability is possible without causing damage to the main pillars upon which the authoritarian state system has been built? In the early 1990s, China's one-party system not only survived the collapse of communism in the Soviet Union but remained stable to the extent that impressive social and economic development was achieved. Rather than being inherently static, the Chinese political system features a dynamic adaptive capacity. Although some parts of the system are continuously evolving and adjusting to the changing national and international environment, new conflicts along ethnic, economic, and social lines have emerged, which bring into question the continued resilience of the Chinese political system.

The possibilities for political renewal on the one hand and the threat of Communist decay on the other have prompted a lively debate among scholars focusing on China's political development. In the special issue, *China's Changing of the Guard*, which was published by the *Journal of Democracy* in 2003, Nathan introduced the term "authoritarian resilience" into the discussion on China's political evolution. In general, two main positions are found with regard to the future of Communist rule in China. According to one school of thought, the power of the Chinese Communist Party (CCP) is expected to decline (e.g., C. Li, 2012; Pei, 2006), but advocates of the other position argue that a Leninist system is resurfacing in China (e.g., D. L. Yang, 2004). However, the majority of studies have come to an ambiguous conclusion, placing an emphasis on the "atrophy and adaptation" of the CCP (Shambaugh, 2008).

From a macro-level perspective, the Chinese party-state has so far proven to be sufficiently responsive to societal demands so as to stay in power. Continuous institutional change and political performance represent what has been referred to as adaptive authoritarianism – a concept first applied by Samuel P. Huntington (1970) to describe the process of change that revolutionary one-party systems undergo, namely, transformation, consolidation, and finally adaptation. The latter refers to institutional adaptation and a redefinition of the role of the party, which the CCP has arguably been doing in various fields including ideology (see, e.g., Shambaugh, 2008: Chapter 6; Holbig, 2013); propaganda (see, e.g., Brady, 2012); organization (see, e.g., Gore, 2011; Shambaugh, 2008: Chapter 7); and administration (see, e.g., Christensen, Dong, & Painter, 2008).[1]

In 2011, Sebastian Heilmann and Elizabeth Perry made an important contribution to the discussion on how and why the CCP is still in power today. In the book entitled *Mao's Invisible Hand*, the two authors expressed concern with regard to the ability of the Chinese political system to cope with serious crises, such as the Asian financial crisis, the SARS epidemic, and the global financial crisis. They provided an analysis to explain how and why the system continues to survive and, in particular, described the mechanisms that underpin its survival. At the core of their explanation lies the ability of Chinese decision-makers to flexibly adapt policies in an uncertain national and international policy environment.

Dam-induced resettlement is one of the policy fields that demonstrate the adaptive capacity of the political center in Beijing. This book studies the consequences of authoritarian adaptability at the central level for local policy implementation. It will be shown that, first, an analysis of authoritarian adaptability has to differentiate between administrative levels and should not assume the existence of adaptive capacity on all levels. In the present case, while the center has proven its ability to adapt, the local level – while attempting to creatively implement central policies – has been tied to hierarchical structures and public demands that taken together limit the local state's ability to adapt flexibly. Xi Jinping's twin campaigns of anticorruption and recentralization of state control will reinforce this situation and mostly likely enhance inflexibility in other policy fields.

China's authorities claim that since 1949, more than 10 million people have been resettled in the course of water conservancy and hydroelectric projects; independent observers, however, estimate the number to be much higher (Heggelund, 2004: 62). For the largest hydropower project in the world alone, the Three Gorges Dam, approximately 1.24 million inhabitants of Chongqing Municipality and Hubei Province were displaced (Xinhua, 2011). Studies on resettlement processes in China indicate that involuntary resettlement all too frequently causes chronic impoverishment among the displaced people, which poses a serious threat to social stability in areas with a high concentration of resettled people (Jun, 2000). For several decades now, in order to safeguard the country's hydropower development strategy as well as social stability, the State Council and China's resettlement bureaucracy have been actively designing a regulatory framework for resettlement.

The construction of the Three Gorges Dam since the 1980s, in particular, has drawn the attention of scholars and bureaucrats to the problem of resettlement induced by large hydropower projects spurring the development of new resettlement regulations in recent years. These new regulations are in line with the new focus of the central government on social development, which has found expression in development paradigms that have surfaced during the Hu-Wen era such as the concept of building a "socialist harmonious society" and the "scientific development concept" (see, e.g., Holbig, 2007, 2013). These new concepts indicate a shift that is taking place – at least at the central government level – away from the traditional development paradigm with its mere focus on economic growth towards a more balanced approach to social and economic development (Lam, 2006). Recent policy decisions, including the "Decision on Major Issues Concerning Comprehensively Deepening Reforms" adopted at the Third Plenary Session of the Eighteenth CPC Central Committee in November 2013, indicate a continued focus on social development under the new administration led by Xi Jinping. The introduction of more socially oriented resettlement policies after 2006 has to be regarded in this context.

This new regulatory framework for resettlement is one example of the institutionalization of the CCP regime, in particular of "the differentiation and functional specialization of institutions within the regime," regarded as one major element of authoritarian resilience in China (Nathan, 2003: 7). However, implementation of these new policies does not occur at the political center in Beijing. Instead, as the most recent central-level resettlement regulations state, governments at the county level are responsible for organizing resettlement work in their jurisdiction while the provincial level is responsible for overall guidance and monitoring of policy implementation (State Council, 2006a). This is in line with the principle of "adjusting measures to local conditions" (*yindi zhiyi*) that Han Dynasty (206 BC–220 AD) historian Zhao Ye had already brought up in his *History of the Southern States Wu and Yue* and which remains an important concept in the Chinese policy process. Therefore, the consequences of this new regulatory framework are primarily observed at the local level. In the words of Shambaugh (2008: 104), the changes that have been taking place in the realm of resettlement policy have "triggered certain consequences (some expected, others unexpected) that in turn cause readjustments and further reforms." These unexpected consequences are currently being dealt with primarily by local governments who have to resettle communities under these new conditions brought about by said reforms.

A common theme in much of the literature on the local state is its flexibility and strategic agency. No matter if these two characteristics lead to "irresponsive image-building" (Cai, 2003), "factionalism" (Hillman, 2014), or "gangster capitalism" (Le Mons Walker, 2006), or whether they result in "effective policy implementation" (Ahlers, 2014; Ahlers & Schubert, 2015) and local economic development (e.g., Edin 2000; Oi 1992, 1995), scholars of the Chinese local state agree that local cadres in contemporary China are relatively autonomous in the way they implement central-level policies.

It goes without saying that a thorough understanding of the consequences of local state flexibility is of central importance to the study of contemporary China. Nevertheless, in order to discern different varieties of policy implementation that undoubtedly exist in a vast country like China, it is equally important to look for sources and results of inflexibility in the policy process. Since the beginning of the reform process in 1978, the Chinese state has undergone several phases of decentralization and recentralization that have, through different means, strengthened or loosened the knot between the political center in Beijing and its localities across the country (Burns, 1994; Landry, 2008; D. Yang, 1996). Recent reform initiatives announced by the Xi-Li administration indicate another round of recentralization that is likely to further reduce local state flexibility.[2]

This book studies the evolution of dam-induced resettlement policy in China and shows how bureaucratic structures, as well as the underlying distribution of power together with the introduction of more socially oriented resettlement policies, limit local state agency and produce new forms of state-society relations at the grassroots level. The state is no longer dominating society; instead, the empowerment of migrant communities brought about by the introduction of new resettlement regulations contributes to a more equal relationship that, together with the hierarchical nature of the resettlement bureaucracy, limit local state flexibility. Although this study only analyzes one policy field, it is to be expected that recent attempts of institutional recentralization and increased party dominance by the new leadership under President Xi Jinping will produce similar situations in policy fields other than dam-induced resettlement.

Bureaucracy and resettlement

The key question of this book is how adaptive authoritarianism works at the local level in China. This question is analyzed by looking at the ways in which policy changes at the central government level in the field of dam-induced resettlement impact on the ongoing processes of local policy implementation. This central line of inquiry leads to a series of questions: First, what is the structure of the Chinese resettlement bureaucracy, and what types of actors are involved in policymaking and implementation? Second, how have the resettlement regulations changed in the course of "reform and opening up," and how feasible is the idea of implementing them within the current structure of the Chinese resettlement bureaucracy? How do the current institutional arrangements foster or obstruct local policy implementation? Third, what do these policy changes and local cadres' subsequent attempts to implement them mean for state-society relations on the ground? Fourth, how is the local state adapting to newly introduced central-level policies that require increasing attention to be paid to social rather than economic aspects of development? And, finally, what does this analysis reveal about processes of adaptation at the national level as well as its potentials and limits?

It might be assumed that central-level policy changes introducing higher compensation standards, improved consultation with affected communities, and, in general, more "human-oriented" resettlement processes would be highly skewed by local cadres during the implementation processes. According to O'Brien and Li (1999), the incentive structure created by the central government caused local cadres to implement policies that had hard and quantifiable targets rather than soft and nonquantifiable policy targets. Although resettlement regulations stipulated the amount of compensation to be paid to migrants as well as the way that resettlement was to be planned and carried out, they did not stipulate any quantifiable policy target. Instead, hard targets specifying the number of migrants to be resettled within a specified timeframe were set according to resettlement plans designed for each hydropower station. It seems likely then that local governments, although eager to fulfill the hard targets set by resettlement plans, are more flexible and selective when it comes to attaining the loftier goals stipulated by the new resettlement regulations introduced by the State Council in 2006.

On the other hand, the resettlement bureaucracy functions as an appendix to the influential hydropower bureaucracy in China, with resettlement policymaking and implementation being driven by the need to construct hydropower stations and implement China's ambitious plans for reducing carbon emissions and ensuring energy security. Furthermore, the construction of hydropower stations is highly favored by local governments who are eager to attract investment. As a result, local cadres employed in the resettlement bureaucracy are not only driven by the general incentive to fulfill policy targets set by their superiors but are crucial actors within the hydropower strategy that is considered highly important by the central government as well as by each of the government departments responsible for economic planning at the local level. The pressure to complete relocation plans in a timely fashion is therefore even higher and has the potential to undermine the "human-oriented goals" set out in the new regulations.

Moreover, during the entire resettlement process, local governments retained a firm grip on resettlement communities in order to ensure the smooth attainment of planned targets and to prevent any instances of social instability. As Mertha (2008) showed, civil society is sometimes able to prevent the construction of dams, but in order to ensure the smooth progression of construction after the government has decided on a project, local communities are generally given little opportunity to hinder the implementation of resettlement plans or to influence policy implementation in any other way. It is therefore to be expected that, due to the increasing economic and political clout of energy companies, local governments are pressured to implement construction projects in such a way that the authoritarian nature of political rule is enhanced rather than weakened. The following overview of the main arguments presented in this book takes these observations further.

This book argues that compared with policy initiatives, such as "Building a New Socialist Countryside," which, despite being centrally funded, are designed to foster local initiatives in the sphere of rural development. China's hydropower policy is a centrally mandated development strategy aimed at increasing clean energy provision. The hydropower bureaucracy is composed of powerful political actors, such as the National Development and Reform Commission (NDRC) and the Ministry of Water Resources (MWR), which are hugely in favor of large dams and work closely with equally powerful energy companies, which are increasingly being guided by market principles (Hensengerth, 2010; Mertha, 2008). At the same time, as will be shown in subsequent chapters, the central government has introduced a series of measures to improve dam-induced resettlement, one result of which has been to empower migrant communities.

Thus, this book studies a policy field in which local state agents are exposed to particularly strict policy demands from their superiors (including energy companies) and their local constituencies. When it comes to policymaking at the central level, the Chinese leadership and, in particular, the Ministry of Water Resources, have gradually, but continuously, improved and flexibly adapted resettlement policy in response to the constantly changing national and international environment for hydropower development, energy security, and social and economic development. The most significant improvements deriving from central-level policy change are the 2006 regulations and the subsequent accompanying measures and notifications, which required lower levels of government to pay more attention to resettlement issues and migrant communities.

The result of these improvements has been a much more regularized process of dam-induced resettlement. Nevertheless, at the current time, despite these changes, the organizational field of dam-induced resettlement in China is dominated by government agencies and industry representatives that are in favor of the construction of large dams rather than by departments that are genuinely interested in the protection of the dam migrants. In contrast to the organizational field of environmental protection, there is a lack of any independent ministry that is responsible only for resettlement. Thus, while the need to construct dams (as stated by the NDRC) has led the government to pay increased attention to resettlement in order to ensure the smooth running of the construction processes and to prevent social unrest, when it comes to deciding whether a controversial dam should be built or not, the decision will very likely be in line with the wishes of the project developers.

At the provincial level, the relevant government departments design resettlement policies for their jurisdictions based on the broad parameters provided by central policies and local circumstances, such as levels of social and economic development and the availability of land. In addition to these policies, provincial-level government departments, design institutes, and hydropower companies jointly formulate resettlement plans for each large hydropower station built within the province. These resettlement plans are again based on central and provincial-level policies and on the local circumstances of the region that is affected by the resettlement needed for the respective hydropower plant. Provincial governments, therefore, retain a certain degree of flexibility when it comes to formulating resettlement policies and plans. At the same time, they are embedded in the hierarchical government administration, which tends to limit this flexibility to some extent. The same applies as we move down to the prefectural level at which flexibility in terms of policymaking is further reduced and the impact of the hierarchical administration is enhanced.

Due to the fact that resettlement plans for large dams are fixed at the provincial level, the lower one moves within the administration, the less influence government actors tend to have on policy change and on negotiations with hydropower companies. The latter have the bureaucratic rank of vice-ministerial units (*fubuji*) and are therefore politically powerful actors. While being increasingly exposed to market principles, state-owned energy companies are largely insulated from those actors most impacted by their business operations – namely, county and township governments and resettlement communities. Instead, energy companies only negotiate with representatives of the central and provincial governments that promise to provide appropriate investment environments. The efficient removal of villages from project sites and resettlement communities that do not disturb project construction are both part of that environment. Ultimately responsible for ensuring part of this agreement are county and township governments. The latter are also the target of all petitions by local communities. Even those complaints originally directed at energy companies are forwarded to local cadres who are seen as part of the government bureaucracy, which had promised to provide an appropriate investment environment. As shown in Figure 1.1, county- and township-level governments have to face the majority of pressure by various groups of actors.

Although the Chinese bureaucracy allows for flexibility when adapting central policies to local circumstances, this is not possible in the case of resettlement because resettlement plans are firmly fixed at the provincial level by the provincial government, energy companies, and design institutes. Although prefectures have leverage over policy specifications, these are only flexible within the limited confines of overall resettlement regulations and the resettlement plan.

As I will show in Chapter 4, the larger the dam, the more top-down is the decision-making process. Moreover, with every increase in dam size, the number of dam migrants also increases, meaning that a strong negative correlation exists between the decision-making authority and the workload of governments at the county level and below. Although local Resettlement Bureaus (*yimin ju*) below the provincial level are consulted during the resettlement planning process, they nevertheless play a role as service providers for the hydropower industry. In this way, resettlement accompanies the construction process instead of shaping it.

The fact that county and township governments are left without any space to flexibly adapt provincial resettlement plans has a direct bearing on local processes of policy implementation. For county and township governments, their role as

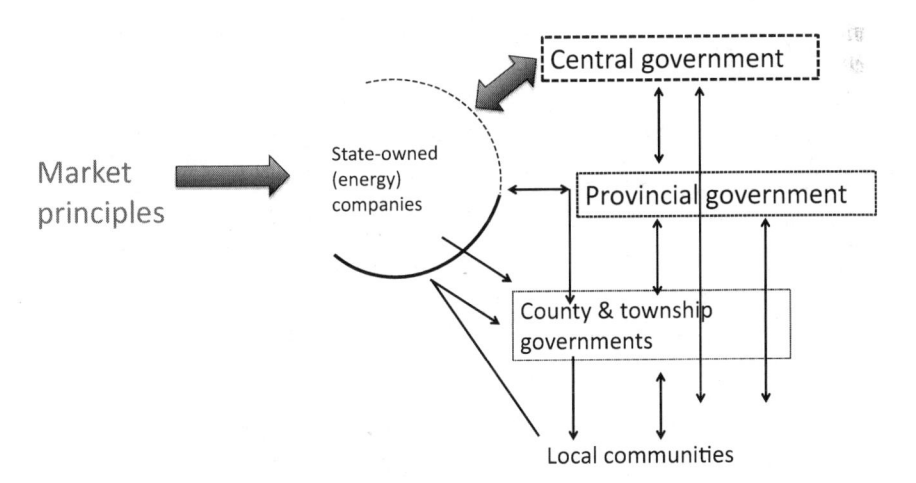

Figure 1.1 Structure of influence between actors in hydropower and resettlement bureaucracy

Source: Author.

service providers rather than active agents in the policy process causes them to lose authority in the eyes of the resettlement communities. The cases that will be presented in Chapters 5 and 6 show that, although before resettlement local cadres might serve as patrons whom the community trusts, after resettlement, the local government is more often than not regarded as a weak institution that is incapable of implementing the policy changes introduced by the center. The combination of flexible policy adaption at the political center and the hierarchical nature of the Chinese bureaucracy lead to the erosion of government resilience at the grass-roots level in resettlement villages. Thus, viewed from a macro perspective, the Chinese regime seems to be sufficiently responsive to societal demands. When tracing the consequences of pragmatic policy adjustments down to the local level, however, authoritarian resilience is far from view.

In Chapter 2, I suggest that the way in which the local state deals with this situation be entitled *fragmented mediation under hierarchy* (cf. Figure 1.2). Local governments agree to negotiate over policy implementation because they are caught in a double bind, between rising demands from local communities that could potentially threaten social unrest and the resettlement bureaucracy not allowing local cadres to flexibly adapt resettlement plans. Due to the introduction of more socially oriented resettlement policies, the local state at township and county levels is forced to consider and to try to reconcile diverging opinions and

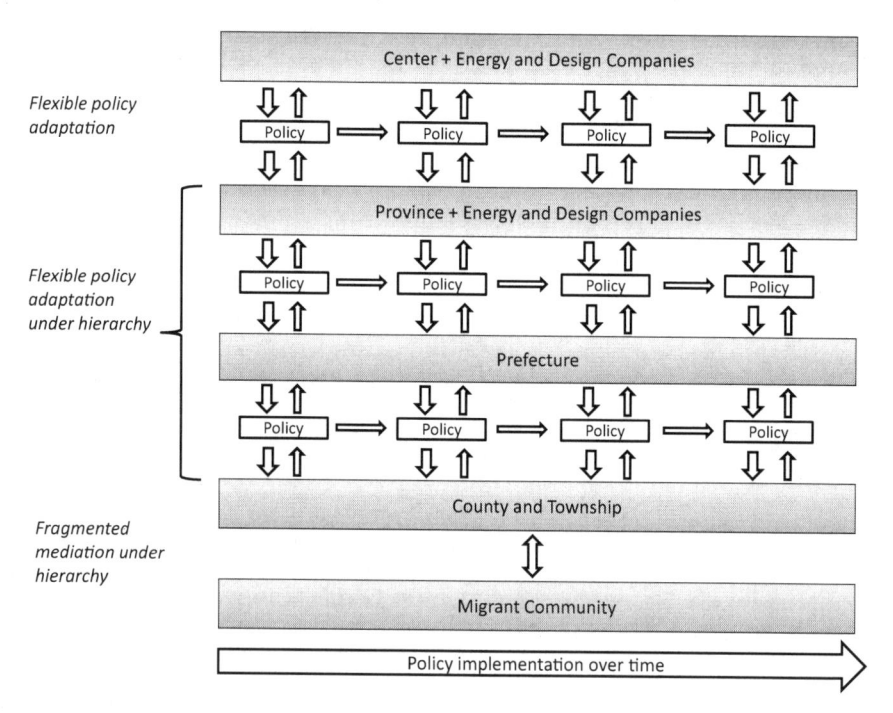

Figure 1.2 Actors and processes of dam-induced resettlement policy
Source: Author.

migrants' interests more than ever before, but these efforts are undertaken within a hierarchical structure that, at times, constrains the local state's ability to carry them through successfully.

Hence this book also deals with the question to what extent the local state has become more benign via-à-vis its local constituency, especially with regard to resettlement processes. While previous research has mainly dealt with the entrepreneurial nature of regional and local governments (e.g., Blecher, 1991; Oi, 1992, 1995; Walder, 1995; Blecher & Shue, 1996, 2001), this present study focuses on the way in which the local state (i.e., the county and township governments) deals with the social shift in central-level policymaking, including the introduction of the so-called "human-oriented" (*yiren weiben*) resettlement policies. It furthermore analyzes the extent to which the increasing attention paid to local communities is contributing to a change in the characteristics of the local state, which now does not have to merely increase economic growth but also has to accommodate the new societal demands deriving from these new central policies (see also O'Brien & Li, 2006).

Even a brief examination of the way in which local cadres prepare and propagate resettlement work reveals the direct impact of the newly introduced central-level resettlement policy on local policy implementation. The first principle of the resettlement regulations introduced in 2006 emphasizes the need for resettlement and compensation to be human-oriented and, furthermore, requires actors responsible for resettlement to "maintain . . . the legitimate rights and interests of migrants" (State Council, 2006a). Local governments, accordingly, are asked to provide future migrants with comprehensive information about the resettlement process and related policies, and this is seen as an integral part of the so-called foundation work for resettlement (*yimin jichu gongzuo*), which consists of publicizing policies and laws regarding resettlement and improving flows of information between the government and the people in order to guarantee the migrants' right to know, participate, and express their opinions (Pu'er Resettlement Bureau, 2011).

The lack of information provided for migrants on existing policies and on the way that their future lives might unfold has been criticized by nongovernmental organizations (NGOs) working in the field of resettlement. Villagers have frequently been left in the dark about the construction project for which they have to sacrifice their homes and land as well as about the way that resettlement is governed by official policies and laws (Interviews KM130222, BJ130309). Although, in both cases, local governments at and below the county level have provided abundant information for migrants, the type of information provided as well as the timing of its provision gives rise to the suspicion that giving information to the migrants served as an instrument of persuasion rather than as a means of protecting and enhancing the villagers' rights.

When informing migrants about the project, local cadres emphasize the scale of the dam project, its importance for China as a country, and the fact that the project has been initiated by the central government. In this way, local governments try to win the hearts of the migrants, in an attempt to make them feel as if they are part of a larger undertaking that is designed to further the nation's future development. It can be assumed that cadres deliberately stress the state's role in the dam project rather than that of the large energy corporations that are actually behind these schemes (Interview KM130222). By this means, cadres appeal to the migrants' identity as citizens of the PRC, which they are now given the opportunity to serve. Second, cadres are particularly careful to act in a friendly way with the villagers and to build up a good relationship with them, with the aim of increasing the trust of the people in the government, and to reduce the likelihood that villagers will resist resettlement and the accompanying government demands.

The question of local state behavior is directly related to central state capacity and the ability of higher state actors to steer policy implementation on the ground. While some scholars regard central control over local policy implementation as being limited, at least in certain policy fields (e.g., Alpermann, 2010b); others argue against the loss of control by central state actors (e.g., Edin, 2003; Landry, 2008). A third camp that has investigated central-local relations avoids the juxtaposition of central and local government actors so as to prevent an overemphasis on local noncompliance (e.g., Heilmann, 2008a, 2008b, 2009; Li, 2010). This third approach instead focuses on the policy steering process (see Göbel, 2011) as well as the intentions behind local state behavior rather than the degree to which central-level policies are implemented locally without distortions.

An examination of the policy steering process and the behavior of the local state lays bare the power structures within the hydropower and resettlement bureaucratic systems as a context to explain the local processes of resettlement implementation. Instead of analyzing the extent to which central policies are implemented at the local level, and whether there is any congruence between intention and policy outcome, this research details the processes of implementation in order to illustrate the strategies employed by local cadres as well as the ways in which central-level policy changes have interfered with the local processes.

Previous research on central-local relations in China has emphasized the importance of flexibility in local governments when adapting central-level policies to local circumstances. This research presents a new perspective on the element of flexibility in the Chinese policymaking process, namely, the flexible adaptation of (in this particular case, dam-induced resettlement) policies by the central state, which, in the present case, is paired with limited flexibility at the county and township government levels. This is a novelty in the literature on the Chinese local state, which, precisely because of its flexibility in policy implementation, has been perceived as the driving force behind the many changes that have been occurring in the People's Republic of China over the past few decades. In light of recent political developments in China under Xi Jinping that point to a recentralization of state control in various policy fields, the research presented here sheds light not only on local state behavior with regards to dam-induced resettlement. Instead, the study presents an example of what we are about to observe in other policy fields of local governance as well.

As past research has shown, it is not only the specific design of central policy that shapes local policy outcomes. In addition, local state agency is influenced by a diversity of factors such as local history, socioeconomic situation, policy training, political culture, the social and administrative structure as well as the cadre management system (see Ahlers, 2014: 10–14; Saich & Hu, 2012: 14). Apart from these factors, which are independent from the particular policy field under scrutiny, this book takes into account specific factors that constrain local state behavior prevalent in certain policy fields. Although these factors are context specific, they draw attention to the fact that local state behavior is embedded in and thus constrained by multiple bureaucratic channels, including those hierarchical structures that we find in China's hydropower and resettlement bureaucracies.

In contrast to Mertha (2008), this research is not on resistance against hydropower projects but instead examines what happens after a decision has been made to construct a power station and local governments have to implement related policy decisions, such as resettlement plans. Specifically, this study focuses on the strategies of local cadres to come to terms with newly introduced central resettlement regulations and local resettlement plans as well as growing demands by resettlement communities. The analysis of local policy implementation is thus confined to local cadres and their modes of interaction with resettlement communities during the processes of resettlement policy implementation. Such cases, although they sometimes involve resistance on the part of policy objects (i.e., local communities), also reveal the strategies employed by local communities who are more interested in influencing policy implementation rather than in actively trying to turn a policy around.

By juxtaposing flexible policy change at the central level and the lives of migrant communities as objects of this change, a simultaneity is introduced to the analysis of the policy process, which allows a more in-depth understanding of the impact of China's political structure on grassroots state-society interactions. This research therefore goes beyond previous analyses of policy implementation by focusing on the state, on society, and on the ways in which they interact during the resettlement processes, as well as by examining what happens when policy implementation is interrupted, that is, when the policy that is in the course of being implemented has to be modified.

Thus, the present research extends the current literature towards including two new groups of actors in the analysis of policymaking and implementation, first of all, the large hydropower corporations that are playing an increasingly important role in the way that resettlement policy is implemented. Past studies on the fragmented authoritarianism (FA) framework, rather than regarding the Chinese state as a monolithic entity, have highlighted the negotiating and bargaining processes during policymaking and implementation. Earlier works confined themselves to consensus building within the state (see, e.g., Lieberthal & Oksenberg, 1988; Lieberthal & Lampton, 1992; Shirk, 1993), and more recently, scholars have emphasized the role that civil society can play during the policy process (e.g., Mertha 2008), but these did not take into consideration the increasing power and influence of state-owned enterprises. As the present research will show, the growing strength of the latter has a direct bearing on policy formulation and implementation in the area of dam-induced resettlement.

Second, although Mertha (2008) highlighted the role that civil society and the media can play during the policy process, little attention has been paid to the potential influence of local communities in this respect: FA as developed by Lieberthal and others, for example, regarded policies as static constructions, placing the emphasis on the bargaining processes within the state, while Mertha's FA (also referred to as FA 2.0) highlighted the ways in which society informally influences the policymaking process. For this reason, in particular, this research examines the processual nature of public policies, paying particular attention to the negotiations over these formal policies that occur between state and society and to what extent these affect local state agency. The FA 2.0 framework is adapted to include instances of bargaining, not only between the state and NGOs, but also between local state agents and local communities.

Finally, this book studies the social consequences of infrastructure development and the efforts made by the Chinese government to limit the former in order to protect the latter. The forced or involuntary displacement of people by the state for development-related purposes has been taking place in developing and developed countries for several decades. These displacements have been aimed at settling both nomadic and semi-nomadic people to strengthen state control, or to make room for large infrastructure projects, such as dams or other hydroelectric projects in the name of the larger national interest. During the first 40 years of the Communist Party's rule in China, the government displaced, on average, 800,000 people every year (Robinson, 2003: 16). In the 1990s, resettlement for the largest hydropower project in the world, the Three Gorges Dam, began. By 2011, approximately 1.24 million inhabitants of Chongqing Municipality and Hubei Province were resettled (Xinhua, 2011), a number that, according to government estimations, will grow by another 4 million by 2020 (Oster, 2007). Studies on the resettlement processes in China have shown that involuntary resettlement frequently causes chronic impoverishment among the displaced people (Stein, 1997). Chau (1995) argued that around 30 percent of China's involuntary resettlement processes had failed.

Despite the negative social consequences, the Chinese government does not intend to give up large-scale hydropower development. Compared with conventional methods of electricity generation, hydropower has various advantages. In the context of the growing global population and the desire to improve peoples' livelihoods, dams have the potential to improve flood protection and control as well as to deliver clean energy, irrigation, and supplies of drinking water (World Commission on Dams, 2000). These are some of the reasons why China – despite the fact that the country already obtains more electricity from hydropower than any other country – intends to double its hydropower capacity by 2020 (EIA, 2010; Magee, 2006a). The 12th Five-Year Plan states that the development of hydropower resources has to be actively pursued (China New Energy Net, 2011).

Given the growing number of people who are having to be resettled as a result of China's hydropower development strategy, the ways in which the Chinese government deals with dam-induced resettlement is of immense importance, not only for the hydropower industry, but also for the Chinese Communist Party, because of the fear that if the resettlement work is not handled well, this could lead to social instability. This book bridges the gap between the studies that have merely focused on hydropower development and the decision-making related to China's energy politics and those that have only examined the social impacts attributed to infrastructure development. Additional information is also provided on the ways in which the Chinese government is attempting to ensure the continued growth of the hydropower sector and, more generally, to strike a balance between economic growth and the resulting negative social impacts.

Policy implementation in China

Western studies on policy implementation commenced with the work by Jeffrey Pressman and Aaron Wildavsky (1973), *Implementation: How Great Expectations in Washington Are Dashed in Oakland*. As the title of the book implies, the focus of the analysis was the discrepancy between the policy objectives and the actual results of implementation. More than a decade later, in 1987, David Lampton edited the book *Policy Implementation in Post-Mao China*, which shared some common features with the literature on policy implementation that followed Pressman and Wildavsky's work. The studies in Lampton's volume examined the unanticipated consequences of policy outputs in areas such as education, economic planning, and natural resources. Later studies on China's implementation process have had a similar emphasis in that they have tried to explain why certain policies do not bring about the expected results. The reasons cited for these deficiencies in policy implementation are conflicting policy goals (O'Brien, 1994) and their interaction with other policies (Lampton, 1987b); negative effects on the interests of targets (Manion, 1991); the "structural fracturation" of Chinese politics (Ding, 2010); or policy outcomes that cannot be measured in hard and quantifiable terms (Edin, 2003; J.J. Kennedy, 2007; O'Brien & Li, 1999; Smith, 2009).

In their analyses, scholars mainly follow one of two distinct approaches. One group of scholars views policy implementation as a top-down affair in which the central government attempts to impose its will on lower levels. These scholars attribute successful policy implementation to mechanisms that ensure organizational discipline; while policy failures are regarded as resulting from vague policy directives, discord among policy elites over the policy in question, or conflicts between policy goals and bureaucratic interests (Harding, 1981). Other scholars regard policy implementation as a bottom-up force by means of which local governments attempt to modify or sabotage policies designed at the top (e.g., Zhong, 2003).

A number of studies lay bare the strategies developed by local cadres to come to terms with a diversity of higher-level policy directives. Zhou (2010b) introduced the phenomenon of collusion among local governments as a reaction to higher-level government policies, while Kostka and Hobbs (2012), in their research on the implementation strategies employed by local governments in response to national energy efficiency targets, found that subnational governments employ "policy bundling" to link national objectives with local priorities. O'Brien and

Li (1999) presented an actor-centered analysis in their study on the behavior of street-level bureaucrats to show how central rules of cadre management interact with local incentive structures to mold policy outcomes. In a similar vein, Heberer and Schubert (2012) developed the concept of the "strategic group" composed of county and township cadres to explain local policy processes and implementation. They argued that members of this strategic group depend on each other and that "[s]trategic cooperation, if not collusion, is imposed on local cadres by their institutional environment and is further reinforced by a shared identity among county and township cadres that stems from a common habitus and 'esprit de corps'" (Heberer & Schubert, 2012: 245). A less actor-centered but more institutionalist approach is provided by Mertha, who, instead of scrutinizing the impact of power and bargaining among policy actors on policy implementation, analyzes functional bureaucracies and the rules that govern interactions between them to explain the dynamics of anticounterfeiting enforcement in China (Mertha, 2009).

Apart from the studies that differentiate between policymaking and policy implementation as two different stages in the policy cycle, focusing on either one of these, there are several studies that have acknowledged the linkages between the two. Heilmann (2008a, 2008b) introduced the Chinese experimentation-based policy cycle, which is characterized by selective policy implementation in a few localities in advance of legislation. These pilot efforts were led by local policymakers who aimed to resolve problems within their jurisdiction while, at the same time, advancing their careers. In order to do this, local officials sought the support of national policymakers who would endorse local experiments and encourage their introduction in a larger number of jurisdictions or into national legislation. Heilmann regarded this element of "experimentation under hierarchy" in the Chinese policy process as one of the keys to understanding China's reform experience. Combined with "long-term policy prioritization," policy experimentation makes up the formula for what Heilmann calls "foresighted tinkering," in the course of which long-term policy priorities are pursued by innovative policy instruments (Heilmann, 2009). S. Wang (2009) further developed this line of thought by introducing four models of policy learning that have allowed Chinese policymakers to constantly adapt to a changing environment by developing new policy priorities and tools.

Other studies that have acknowledged the linkage between policymaking and implementation are those that have developed the framework of fragmented authoritarianism. The latter does not only describe the bargaining process during policymaking in China but also how a variety of actors are able to exert an influence on policy implementation. Originally, fragmented authoritarianism meant that societal actors were excluded from the policymaking process (Lieberthal & Oksenberg, 1988; Lieberthal & Lampton, 1992; Shirk, 1993), but recent studies have shown that a new social dynamism has emerged from the reform process that has caused business associations (S. Kennedy, 2005; S. Kennedy & Deng, 2010), policy entrepreneurs (e.g., Nathan, 1976), think tanks (X. Zhu, 2011), and non-governmental organizations (NGOs) (Bragg, 2003; Mertha, 2008; X. Zhu, 2008) to actively shape policy outputs.

Mertha (2008) described this new phenomenon within the framework of "fragmented authoritarianism 2.0," which pays attention to the roles and policy preferences of societal actors who were previously excluded from the Chinese policymaking process. This body of research illustrates the sociological shift in the field of China studies that were formerly dominated by studies on the political elite. Under the heading of "state-society relations," works in this new sub-field do not only document the social changes brought about by reform and opening, but also the consequences of these changes for the Chinese policy process. A particular focus here lies on the activities of environmental NGOs (e.g., Büsgen, 2006; Cooper, 2006; Ho, 2007; Schwartz, 2004; Teets, 2014; G. Yang, 2005).

Governments at lower levels of the Chinese bureaucracy hold a crucial position in Chinese society. Acting as the nexus between state and society, local governments determine the way in which central policies are implemented at the grassroots level. Much of the behavior of local cadres depends on their institution's relationship with their administrative superiors and the way in which each local-level government department is embedded in the Chinese bureaucracy. This is why, in order to get a better grasp of China's ongoing transformation, scholars continue to focus on the relationship between local governments and the central government. In particular, due to the increasing influence and autonomy of provincial decision-making in the course of the reform and opening-up period, much of the research has focused on the way in which local governments, while still linked to Beijing through the nomenklatura system (Chan, 2004), have designed their own development strategies, independently of the political center. The majority of these studies had a provincial focus (Fitzgerald, 2002; Goodman, 1997; Hendrischke & Feng, 1999) or scrutinized the implementation of economic policies, such as decollectivization (Chung, 2000), tax collection (Remick, 2004), and investment (L.C. Li, 1998), in China's coastal provinces. The few works that were focused on China's west and on Yunnan, in particular, were mainly concerned with policies aimed at poverty alleviation and the impact of post-1978 development policies (d'Hooghe, 1994; Donaldson, 2011; Harwood, 2013; Hillman, 2014). Apart from the fact that most of these studies focused on the provincial state instead of county and township governments, there was also a paucity of studies that examined the implementation of policies directed at local communities and the way in which state-society relations evolve during these processes of implementation.

A number of studies on central-local relations have focused on the way in which the local state has responded to economic reform policies introduced by the central government during and after the 1980s. Montinola, Qian, and Weingast (1995) observed the development of Chinese-style federalism, which, in their view, has acted as the motor for China's rapid economic development. As a result of the devolution of authority over revenue to lower levels of government and the formulation of clearer property rights, local cadres have turned their attention to establishing township and village enterprises (TVEs), which have subsequently fostered economic growth.

In line with this development, a number of researchers have emphasized the role played by local government autonomy in developing the economy in their jurisdictions. Blecher and Shue, for example, distinguished between "developmental" and "entrepreneurial local states" (Blecher, 1991; Blecher & Shue, 1996, 2001), arguing that some local governments fulfill strikingly similar roles to those that have been identified among newly industrializing countries in East Asia. The local developmental state was perceived to focus on the creation of favorable conditions for economic growth, including "planning, bureaucratic co-ordination, arrangements of finance, procurement of inputs, development of infrastructure etc." (Blecher 1991: 267) as well as picking winners among private enterprises and navigating the development of particular industries (Blecher & Shue, 2001). In comparison, the entrepreneurial state engages in business activities on its own account, including investment and managerial decision-making. In a similar vein, Oi (1992, 1995) and Walder (1995) illustrated the ways in which local governments at the county-level function as corporate entities, a phenomenon that Oi has called the "local corporatist state." Wang et al. (2015) have extended this thesis to explain how the local state has dealt with the more socially and environmentally oriented policies introduced by the central state in recent years. In their analysis of small hydropower development in Yunnan Province, they suggested that local states, while trying to fulfill the requirement of poverty reduction and environmentally friendly electricity provision, follow an "environmentally bundled economic interest" approach in order to simultaneously develop the local economy.

Yang Zhong (2003) suggested that, due to the increased autonomy of the local state and the concomitant potential for discrepancies between central policy stipulations and local policy implementation, the center has to rely on Party organization and discipline in order to control possible centrifugal tendencies. Earlier research has shown that the cadre management system in China has led to two main developments: First, due to the fact that the assessments of achievements by local cadres are undertaken by higher government levels, the former tend to respond to the demands of their superiors rather than to local communities. Second, local cadres prefer to implement policies that have measurable (hard) targets, rather than nonquantifiable (soft) targets. Since the former mainly involve economic targets, local governments tend to implement economic policies instead of more socially oriented policies (O'Brien & Li, 2006). Edin (2003) and J.J. Kennedy (2007), however, also showed that soft targets can turn into hard ones, depending on the pressure emanating from the central government regarding policy implementation.

In contrast to these dualistic approaches to central-local relations, Li (2006) argued in favor of a "non-dualistic" approach that would emphasize the role played by central and local actors as "co-participants" in the policy process who, instead of working against each other, would share an interest in improving China's political institutions. Following a similar line, Heilmann (2008a, 2009) showed how local policy innovations are fed into the Chinese policy process, which should be regarded as an open-ended dialogue between central-level policymakers and local-level implementers rather than as a top-down flow of central directives that street-level bureaucrats are eager to evade. Finally, Göbel (2011) synthesized these nondualistic and dualistic approaches into a framework to explain how cooperation between government levels and resistance by local governments can foster policy change.

In the context of the relations between state and society during policy implementation, scholars have either focused on the state or on society; only a few researchers have paid attention to the mutual influences that are at work in state-society relations. One state-centered study by Y. Huang and Yang (2002) examined China's family planning policy and the way in which public administration can serve as an instrument of state power in relation to civil society. They showed that the relationship between bureaucratic capacity and state coerciveness is negative, meaning that a more capable and institutionalized family planning program is less likely to employ coercive measures during policy implementation. Following a similar strand of research, K. Chen (1998) looked at the way in which the state-induced policy shift in administrative decentralization had affected the potential impact of collective societal action on the state's decision-making processes. He showed that due to the change in the incentive structure, local officials had become much more responsive to political demands made by the local population.

Indeed, the pressures on the local states emanating from China's society are mounting. Studies on popular resistance have revealed the growing tensions between the state and society, highlighting either the strategies employed by society to resist state policies or the measures taken by the state to address social unrest (Deng & O'Brien, 2013; Diamant & O'Brien, 2015; L. Li & O'Brien, 2008; O'Brien & Deng, 2014; O'Brien & Li, 1995; Stern & O'Brien, 2011). Yongshun Cai (2008) focused on the state and examined the rationale underlying the local governments' use of suppression as a mode of response to popular resistance, showing that, on the one hand, local governments enjoy significant autonomy in dealing with resistance, which tends to make them use suppression mainly when local stability, policy implementation, or their image is threatened. On the other hand, the use of suppression has not yet succeeded in preventing people from staging resistance, a factor that is attributable to the relaxation of social control and to the central government's concerns over legitimacy (O'Brien & Deng, 2014).

In contrast, in order to examine the opportunities for undertaking successful collective action in China, F. Shi and Cai (2006) studied the strong resistance maintained by homeowners in Shanghai. They detailed the complex process of collective resistance, illustrating the way that the Chinese political system operates and investigating state-society relations at the local level. They argued that, due to the fragmentation of state power at the local level, opportunities for resistance arise and can even be successful, if the active participants are able to draw on social networks with officials or media workers.

Another sector of the studies on state-society relations in China has focused on the emergence of NGOs and their relations with the government. Since the 1990s, scholars have been debating on how best to conceptualize the newly emerging social groups that seem to challenge the Communist Party's monopoly on organization. While some have regarded this new phenomenon as the emergence of a civil society characterized by social interests that organize themselves beyond the realm of the state, others have employed corporatist models that show how the state has attempted to co-opt and control these new social organizations (see, e.g., Perry, 1994).

In recent years, a number of studies on state-society relations in China have revealed the oftentimes symbiotic and cooperative relations between the two spheres. This has fostered agreement among scholars that civil society organizations in China do not work in opposition to the Chinese state but, rather, collaborate with the state through various channels (see, e.g., Ho, 2001; Saich, 2000; Solinger, 1992). Although the state is dependent on civil society organizations in areas such as environmental protection, workers' rights, and cultural activities, the NGOs need financial support or, at least, the approval of the state in order to be able to carry out their work effectively.

In his study on environmental NGOs in China, Alpermann employed Migdal's state-in-society approach to show that processes of mutual accommodation are taking place between the state and social forces in China's environmental politics. Not only is society fragmented, as evidenced by the existence of various types of unconnected organizations, such as officially registered NGOs, unregistered environmental groups, and individual advocates, but also the state itself is fragmented and being pulled in different directions. While parts of the state form ties with one segment of society, other state actors join forces with different societal actors (Alpermann, 2010a).

Although these studies have provided us with valuable insights into the increasing pluralization of the Chinese policy processes, the literature nevertheless has one major limitation. Although existing studies document the increasing activism on the part of civil society and explain how this activism impacts on certain state projects, such as dams (Mertha, 2008; Mertha 2009; Schwartz, 2004), the analyses are mainly focused on a single point in time. For example, in the case of the Dujiangyan Dam in Sichuan Province, the plan to construct the dam was abandoned when policy entrepreneurs, together with the media and several government officials, successfully reframed the issues surrounding hydropower development and mobilized the public against the project (Mertha, 2008). The analyses have certainly helped to explain how, in an authoritarian regime, the long-standing policies of the state can be reversed by societal actors, but such studies have not taken into account the broader implications of policy reversals such as these on the hydropower sector in China. Beyond the fact that the Chinese policy process in the area of hydropower development seems to be more pluralized than in the past, we are not able to anticipate the direction that the industry might take in the future nor to learn about past trajectories; we are limited to noting the factors that have led to policy change on a single occasion.

The study presented here is aimed at extending research on the local state and policy implementation as well as the fragmented authoritarianism model by analyzing the impact of the institutional environment of dam-induced resettlement on local cadres and processes of resettlement policy implementation. Apart from examining upper-level demands, this research highlights the ways in which local communities perceive and react to policy implementation and sometimes engage in lengthy bargaining processes in an effort to influence the latter. This book also builds on previous research on the Chinese local state and, in particular, on the ways in which local governments implement central policies. With only a few exceptions, earlier research focused on the ways in which local cadres had adapted economic reform policies to local circumstances; this study takes a different perspective, to look at the ways in which the local state has had to adapt in the face of the more socially oriented policies mandated by their superiors at the central and provincial levels. The introduction of "human-oriented" resettlement in 2006 has been a fundamental policy change in this regard, the implementation of which has so far not been analyzed by the aforementioned studies.

Dam-induced resettlement in China

A few scholars have already studied policy change in the field of dam-induced resettlement. Due to the importance and scale of the project, the Three Gorges Dam has received widespread attention in the literature on dam-induced resettlement in China. Heggelund (2004) examined the decision-making process surrounding the project in general as well as the resettlement process. Other scholars examined the socioeconomic impact of the dam on the displaced people (Brown, Magee, & Xu, 2008; H. Li, Waley, & Rees, 2001). Jackson and Sleigh (2000) conducted an analysis in the light of China's transition to a market economy and showed how this transition had exacerbated the social problems of the people after they had been resettled, while Tan, Hugo, and Potter (2005) highlighted the difficulties of rural women who had been displaced by the dam. More recently, Wilmsen, Webber, and Duan (2011) have investigated the situation of dam migrants who were dependent on land before being resettled, but had to move to cities due to the lack of land available to them afterwards. Jun (2000) examined resettlement policies in the context of their historical evolution and the impact of the policy reforms that were introduced in the 1980s. Finally, Brian Tilt provides an excellent analysis of hydropower development and resettlement along the Lancang and Nu Rivers in Yunnan as well as the interests pursued by various constituent groups in implementing and influencing dam construction (Tilt, 2014).

Scholars have also paid attention to the resettlement processes resulting from other dam projects. Hensengerth (2010) looked at the reforms in China's resettlement policies and the impact of domestic and external actors on Chinese legislation. He paid particular attention to the dams that were going to be constructed along the Nu River in Yunnan Province and the Xiaolangdi project along the Yellow River in Henan Province. In a similar vein, P. Guo and Li (1998) examined the positive impact that World Bank resettlement policies had on resettlement work in Yunnan.

A number of Chinese scholars have focused on the various risks posed by resettlement. Several Chinese scholars employed Cernea's risk and reconstruction model, which anticipates major risks of displacement, explains responses by migrants, and guides reconstruction of migrants' livelihoods. While He (2011) examined migrants from mountainous regions in Yunnan, G. Shi, Su and Yuan

(2001) used the model to look at the resettlement experiences linked with the Xiaolangdi Dam. In addition, S. Chen, Han, Liu, and Zhao (1998) systematically analyzed the resettlement risks from political, economic, and environmental standpoints and came to the conclusion that dam-induced resettlement could create the following social problems: loss of land, unemployment, homelessness, insufficient means to make a living, illness, food insecurity, social disarticulation, and a breakdown in community services. One study, after investigating the resettlement processes of the Liangshanzhou Dam, drew similar conclusions but added marginalization, loss of access to public property and services as well as religious and cultural conflicts to the list of risks (D. Li & Bai, 2007). T. Wang and Guo (2006) went a stage further and categorized the above consequences into legislative risks, economic risks, social risks, and environmental risks. In their book, R. Zheng and Shi (2011) extended this line of research even further and developed a "risk warning indicator system" for dam-induced resettlement in western China.

Apart from studies that focused mainly on the risks incurred by resettlement, there are also several works that have investigated past and current resettlement policies in China as well as the conflicts of interest between the various parties involved in policymaking and implementation (Y. Wang, 2010; Zhou, 2010b; D. Zhu & Shi, 2011). Hensengerth (2010) explored the reforms in China's resettlement policies and the impact of domestic and external actors on Chinese legislation. In a similar vein, P. Guo and Li (1998) examined the positive impact of World Bank resettlement policies on resettlement work in Yunnan.

One essential feature is lacking, however, in all these studies on the politics of resettlement: a comprehensive analysis of the reasons for which resettlement policy undergoes change at a given moment in time, taking into account factors that have contributed to this change and how this change has affected resettlement policy implementation processes at the grassroots level. One of the few scholars who has dealt with grassroots contestation and resettlement implementation is Ying Xing (2005), but although his study provided in-depth empirical knowledge about the resettlement processes and the evolution of state-society relations in the course of the construction of a medium-sized dam in the 1970s, it did not consider the impact of policy change on local processes of policy implementation.

This research aims to make up for the above-mentioned lack and also to bridge the gap between the studies that merely focus on hydropower development and the decision-making processes related to China's energy politics and those that only examine the social impacts that are attributed to infrastructure development. Although those who are opposed to the construction of large dams draw on the negative social experiences of migrants to support their arguments, they do not provide us with analyses of the role played by resettlement work within the overall strategy of hydropower development. With the increasing importance of resettlement work for the successful implementation of China's ambitious hydropower development strategy, policies that ensure well-planned and regulated resettlement processes are just as important as industrial standards that are concerned with the overall quality of the dam project.

Past studies have provided us with in-depth knowledge about the decision-making processes surrounding China's hydropower policy (see, e.g., Magee, 2006b). However, here the resettled people were seen as only one of many variables influencing China's decision-makers. A close look at the ways in which the role of resettlement work has evolved over the past decades, particularly since the first regulations on resettlement caused by hydropower and water resource projects were published in 1991, and the revised version in 2006, will not only help to explain the attitudinal shift in China's development strategy but also, more importantly, the Chinese leadership's attempts to ensure the continuation of industrial development in the face of high human and environmental costs.

The Lancang River: local studies and local state agency

This detailed examination of the policy processes surrounding dam-induced resettlement in China focuses on the impact of central-level policy change on local implementation processes along the Lancang River in Yunnan Province. The key issue is the impact of flexible policy adaptation on dam-induced resettlement. In this study, the term "local implementation processes (i.e., resettlement)" is used to refer to the measures undertaken by local governments to promulgate and implement resettlement plans designed by upper-level resettlement organs, as well as the reactions of the local migrant communities to these measures. The implementation processes are therefore perceived as an interactive realm in which state and society meet, bargain, and negotiate to shape policy outcomes and future state-society relations on the ground. Instead of analyzing discrepancies between policy intention and outcome, this study highlights policy implementation as a process that is socially constructed by the policy itself as well as by local cadres and migrant communities.

Policy change in China involves complex interactions between policy actors at the political center in Beijing and between the central and local governments across the country (e.g., Heilmann, 2008b). The change in policy content represents one part of the analysis, but the interactions within the resettlement bureaucratic system and the way in which resettlement plans are implemented at the local level play an important role in this research. The aim is to present a solid description of these processes of implementation and the context in which these occur. Although quantitative analyses of policy intention and outcomes are able to show the extent to which a policy has failed or not failed, the present research lays bare the processual nature of public policy and explains what policy implementation, as a social phenomenon, means for grassroots state-society relations, local state authority, and community empowerment.

In the process, the analysis provides in-depth descriptions of resettlement implementation and the context within which it occurs. A detailed examination is undertaken of two processes of relocation in the course of the construction of the Nuozhadu Dam (NZD), which was constructed between 2004 and 2014. In terms of its core wall, the Nuozhadu Dam is the highest rock-fill dam in Asia, the largest hydropower plant in Yunnan Province, and the fourth largest dam among those that already have been or are currently being constructed in China. With a planned total installed capacity of 5,850,000 kilowatts, it is the largest dam in the Lancang River basin. Investment in the dam is estimated to amount to 50 billion yuan – the largest investment in a single construction project in Yunnan Province (Yunnan

Xinhua Net, 2011). The location of the dam spans two prefectures and one county. On the whole, it has been estimated that reservoir inundation will affect 2 cities, 9 counties, 32 townships and villages, and 597 villager small groups (*cunmin xiaozu*) – a total area of 329.97km². By 2013, a total number of 46,009 people were to have been resettled (Y. Xu & Li, 2005).

Yunnan and the Nuozhadu Dam were chosen as the focus of this research for several reasons. The Nuozhadu Dam is not only the largest hydropower station in Yunnan Province, involving the resettlement of more than 46,000 people, but was also being constructed during a period of major policy change at central and provincial government levels. One significant change in this respect was the 2006 amendment to nationwide resettlement regulations originally introduced in 1991, which led to an increase in resettlement compensation as well as to more consultation with resettlement communities, amongst others. Resettlement work for the Nuozhadu Dam began in 2004 and is still ongoing, a factor that provides an opportunity to examine the impact of policy changes on local processes of implementation.

Previous studies on dam-induced resettlement in China have provided rich empirical data of a range of issues that local communities face when being resettled (e.g., Tilt, 2014; Ying, 2005). The present study investigates the ways in which the local state deals with the complex task of resettlement and how local state agency is constrained by increasingly vocal communities and a growth-oriented hydropower bureaucracy.

Map 1.1 Pu'er in Yunnan Province
Source: Author.

Of particular interest to the analysis of these processes is the comparison of two resettlement villages established in the course of the construction of the Nuozhadu Dam. When selecting the resettlement villages to be studied more closely, I followed the most-similar-cases design originally developed by Przeworski and Teune (1970).[3] This design requires researchers to select two cases that are similar in as many independent variables as possible. Ideally, the two cases only differ in the dependent variable and one exogenous factor of interest to the analysis. The two resettlement villages selected for the present study have been resettled from the same home village (Old Tree) to two different resettlement villages (Green Mountain and South Stream) within the same county (Wild Grass). By selecting these two villages, the socioeconomic situation as well as the local cadres who have organized the move remain constants.

The difference between the two villages mainly involves the mode of resettlement: The inhabitants of Green Mountain were resettled in three stages over a period of seven years, and the inhabitants of South Stream were all resettled together at the same time. The comparison drawn between the two communities can help to explain the impact of flexible policy change on ongoing processes of local policy implementation and what this means for state-society relations on the ground. In detail, the two cases scrutinize resettlement processes in both villages, including the preparations for relocation, the actual relocation, and issues of contestation that ensued after the villagers had been resettled in their new homes. The major focus lies on the intricate relationship between flexible resettlement policy change at central and provincial government levels on the one hand and the detailed resettlement plan developed for the Nuozhadu Dam on the other.

Two cases of fragmented mediation under hierarchy are presented in this research. In one case (see Chapter 6), the local state entered into direct negotiations with the local resettlement community after the latter had protested against what they considered to be unfair policy implementation. This resulted in a compromise being agreed between the migrant community and the local government. Although successful in preventing any larger protests, the local government was

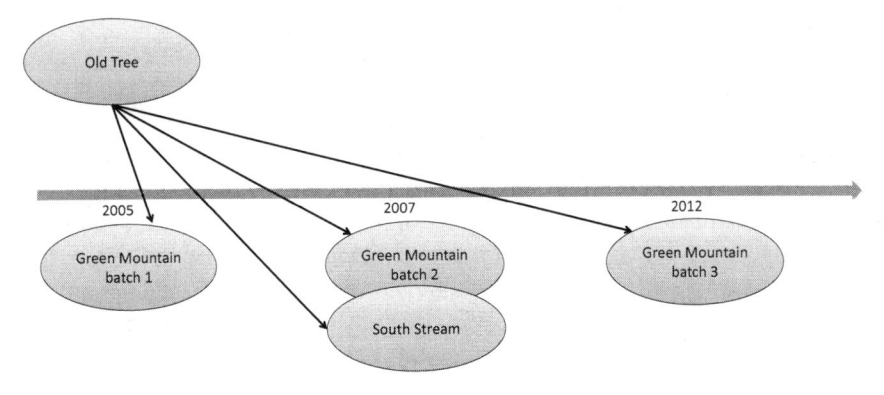

Figure 1.3 Two cases of resettlement in Pu'er

Source: Author.

exposed to repeated petitioning and resistance by the villagers. In the other case (see Chapter 5), the resettlement plan designed for the Nuozhadu Dam split the migrant community, which, on the one hand, prevented a concerted petitioning effort but, on the other, contributed to the further alienation of the local state and society, with the latter resisting any kind of mediating efforts made by the local state. Despite of the different outcomes in the two villages, the cases illustrate the limits to local state agency in implementing resettlement policy. Both cases highlight the ways in which local cadres attempt to come to terms with the task to adequately implement the plan in the face of heightened public demands and strict bureaucratic procedures.

Thus, in contrast with studies on "selective" or "effective" policy implementation (which acknowledge the existence of local state agency and street-level discretion), this research describes a case where the local state's room to maneuver during policy implementation is seriously limited, resulting in fragmented policy implementation. Effective policy implementation, as observed by Ahlers and Schubert (2014: 24), is the result of a

> three-level game played out between (1) centrally designed policies and institutional control mechanisms affecting all administrative tiers; (2) strategic agency on the part of local governments, most notably at the county level, which is able to transform institutional constraints in political resources, although unable to avoid or defy control by upper levels; and (3) public demands that cannot be ignored and that must be anticipated and accommodated.

Similarly, O'Brien and Li (1999) also regard the incentive structures of local cadres as being shaped by upper level demands and local circumstances. Both studies imply that local state agency is high. However, they differ in the observed consequences of local state agency. In O'Brien and Li's study, local cadres use their agency selectively, at times in favor of and sometimes against, higher-level requirements. In their view, social pressure has little impact on local state behavior. In contrast, Ahlers and Schubert come to the conclusion that the local state is embedded in a governmental bureaucratic system, which, with all its constraints, is conducive to achieving positive policy outcomes for the local population. In their view, government reforms have lowered insulation of local states from social pressure and have therefore realigned the incentive structure of local cadres.

Flexible adaptation of central-level resettlement policies and their subsequent reversal at lower levels leaves local cadres in a situation of policy overload. Meaning that while existing policies are being implemented for groups of migrants resettled before policy change, after a certain date, new policies have to be implemented either for all migrants or only for those resettled after the stipulated date. Such inconsistencies in policy design cause dissatisfaction among migrant communities, whilst also overstraining local Resettlement Bureaus. Thus, local cadres implement new policies only when these are deemed absolutely necessary, for example, in response to threats of protest action by the local community, or when they see fit. Therefore, top-down institutional constraints and "rightful resistance" in a contentious and simultaneously important policy field, increasingly infused with market principles, leads cadres to implement policies in a fragmented manner that is not necessarily effective. Fragmentation here is imposed on local cadres from above rather than a deliberate choice of the local state. This is a major difference from the concepts of selective and effective policy implementation. Both assume that the local state has enough room to make decisions and therefore, in the case of O'Brien and Li, "selects" to enforce mostly unpopular policies. In the present case, local cadres are pressed to implement resettlement policy unevenly.

Dams, migration, and the local state

After this Introduction, the book continues with a more detailed consideration of the interaction between fragmented authoritarianism and the local state. While central-level policymaking serves as one feature of these relations, the main focus, here, is on resettlement policy implementation at the local level in which local communities sometimes become involved as active agents. Elements of flexibility within Chinese policymaking at the central level are traced back to the concept of democratic centralism, revealing that episodic imbalances between democracy and centralism cause conflicts during grassroots policy implementation.

Chapter 3 then explains the changes that have been taking place in resettlement policymaking in China over the past six decades, showing how policy has evolved up to the present day and which policy entrepreneurs have been involved in these policy changes. Although significant improvements in resettlement policy have been achieved during this period of time, statist actors advocating hydropower development have continued to drive the most important decisions within the resettlement bureaucracy, which has limited the extent to which migrants' interests are represented.

Chapter 4 presents the Nuozhadu Dam project including its planning and construction as well as the administrative processes of resettlement. Particular attention is paid to the diverse range of actors at the central and provincial levels involved in the Chinese hydropower and resettlement bureaucracies. These include, not only political actors such as the NDRC and MWR, but also energy companies and design institutes, which increasingly operate under market rules and therefore influence dam-induced resettlement according to those rules rather than according to the specific socioeconomic conditions prevalent in migrant communities. The chapter illustrates the power structures underlying hydropower development and resettlement in China, providing a background against which subsequent cases of policy implementation can be analyzed. It is shown that the diverse responsibilities that local actors have to shoulder during dam construction and resettlement processes are not matched with the degree of authority that is necessary to ensure the smooth progression of resettlement policy implementation.

In Chapter 5, there is a detailed examination of the resettlement processes related to Green Mountain village, including the preparations for relocation, the actual relocation, and issues of contestation that ensued after the villagers had been resettled in their new homes. The analysis shows how these groups, which formerly saw themselves as parts of one large community, have been divided up into three different batches of migrants, causing social fragmentation and conflict, and, at the same time, a decrease in local state legitimacy.

Chapter 6 examines the resettlement processes of the South Stream villager small group. Compared with Green Mountain village, South Stream has been resettled in a unified manner, which has led to enhanced group cohesion and willingness to stand up against fragmented policy implementation by local cadres. The chapter highlights community reactions and the strategies that have been employed in response to policy change and local policy implementation. It is shown that resettlement policy change has, to some extent, empowered local migrant communities both by granting them more rights and by providing them with more information before relocation. This empowerment, however, has gone hand in hand with heightened requirements for local governments, which, not only have to deal with demands for the implementation of new and more challenging policies handed down from above, but also have to respond to the claims of the empowered migrants. This has, once again, led to a decrease in local state legitimacy.

Although the situations presented in Chapters 5 and 6 differ in the type of conflict and resistance on the side of the communities, yet, the reasons for these complex situations are the same in both cases: They result from a combination of hierarchical bureaucratic structures, market principles, frequent policy change, and increasingly vocal local communities. The behavior of local state officials in both of these cases can be described as fragmented mediation, a type of behavior that aims to come to terms with conflicting demands and interests of different actors and policy mandates.

Notes

1 For more studies on CCP reforms, see the edited volume by Y. Zheng and Brødsgaard (2006).
2 These reforms include, for example, the announcement at the Third Plenum to place Party discipline inspection committees under the leadership of the next higher administrative level rather than the Party committee at the same level (CPC Central Committee, 2013). Another example is the aim of the CPC Central Committee to assess local cadre interference in court cases, and to include these assessments in cadre evaluations (CPC Central Committee, 2014).
3 John Stuart Mill (1843/1974) was the first to develop methods of comparative case analysis. His "method of difference" is equivalent to what Przeworski and Teune call most-similar-cases design.

2 Fragmented mediation and the local state

The research presented here analyzes the impact that *flexible policy adaptation at the central government level* has had on *local processes of policy implementation* in the field of dam-induced resettlement, by examining the changes in resettlement policy that have occurred during the past three decades and the ways in which street-level bureaucrats in Pu'er have dealt with these changes in the course of the ongoing resettlement processes during the construction of the Nuozhadu Dam. More specifically, this research analyzes the extent to which the introduction of more socially oriented, central policies has shaped processes of resettlement policy implementation at the local level. Policy here is presented as a process that, at any one time, consists of policymaking and implementation. In the case of dam-induced resettlement, the processual nature of policy creates new fault lines and magnifies already existing fault lines between state and society, as well as within each state and society. Neither the former nor the latter can be regarded as a unified actor with the same interests. While each administrative layer and functional bureaucracy pursues different goals, resettlement policy change also physically and emotionally splits up local communities. Although Chinese society at large is denied a seat at the policymaking table, populations targeted by policies are seen as an important factor during the policy implementation processes and therefore have to be studied in that same context.

The analysis presented here draws on theories of central-local relations, policy experimentation, and democratic centralism, which help to explain the flexible nature of policymaking in China. While democratic centralism serves as an ideological background for the way in which the policy process is organized, instances of policy experimentation have been used to explain China's rapid economic growth since the beginning of reforms in the late 1970s as well as the continued resilience of the Communist Party.

Throughout the past thirty years, the usual way of explaining policymaking and policy change in China has been the fragmented authoritarianism (FA) model. This model focuses on "the structural allocation of authority and the behavior of officials related to policy process" (Lieberthal & Lampton, 1992: 8) by providing a framework that can be employed to identify the origins of the fragmented authority structures within the Chinese bureaucratic system, as well as the strategies and resources used by bureaucratic organs during the bargaining processes that are characteristic of decision-making within the Chinese polity (Lieberthal & Lampton, 1992: 10). The FA framework explains the fragmentation of the Chinese bureaucratic system along horizontal and vertical lines and therefore serves as a useful background against which the variety of interests represented in the hydropower and resettlement bureaucracies can be explained. However, in order for the model to remain applicable to contemporary Chinese politics, it needs to be adapted so as to reflect instances of bargaining, not only between the state and NGOs (Mertha, 2008), but also between local state agents and local communities. In the subsequent section, I therefore suggest a new approach to studying local policy implementation, which itself has to be viewed as a crucial part of the Chinese policy process.

This is followed by a detailed examination of the ways in which local cadres and resettlement communities have responded to newly launched and more socially oriented resettlement policies and how, within the institutional context provided by the hydropower and resettlement bureaucracies, this flexible policy change shapes state-society relations on the ground. Accordingly, the final section of this chapter introduces theories on the incentive structure of the Chinese local state as well as the responses of local cadres to central-level policy changes. Here, the results of research on the economic activism of the local state (Oi 1992, 1995; Walder 1995; Lin 1995) and the cadre management system (Chan 2004; Edin 2003; Landry 2008) are applied to explain the way in which socially oriented resettlement policies are implemented at the local level.

The fragmented structure of authority in central-local relations

The study of central-local relations focuses on "how policies decided at higher echelons of the formal system can possibly be implemented by the multitude of intermediary and local actors across the system" (Li, 2010: 177). The central question, therefore, is not whether local governments implement central policies or not, but rather how local actors adapt these policies to local circumstances and the extent to which original policy intentions are modified or even completely neglected in the course of these adaptations. According to a popular Chinese saying, "When policies are imposed from above, counter-strategies will emerge from below (*shang you zhengce, xia you duice*)." Especially those policies that leave much room for local flexibility bear the risk of being implemented in defiance of the goals that central-level policymakers originally had in mind. At the same time, if policies are too centralized and do not leave room for local experimentation, the diversity of the Chinese economy and society limit the applicability of central regulations over the vast territory that is China. Chung (2000) refers to this dilemma as the "centralizing paradox," in which the central government, while wanting to obtain the benefits of decentralization, also tries to retain central control over lower government levels.

One of the earliest models used to explain the fragmentation of authority between central and local government levels in China was the FA model. This was first developed during the 1980s and was based on elite-oriented rational actor approaches, in which the local state successfully blocked policy initiatives emanating from the center. Lieberthal and Oksenberg (1988: 3–4) explained policy outcomes in China as follows:

> Policy X resulted from a bargain among Ministries A, B, and C and Province D that was either 1. brokered by one or more top leaders, 2. arranged by coordinating staffs acting in the name of one or more top leaders, or 3. negotiated by the supra-ministry coordinating agency, and ratified through routine procedures by the top leaders. Disgruntled Ministries E and F, losers in the deal, planned to pursue strategies to erode the agreement. The bargain sought to reconcile the conflicting organizational missions, ethos, structure, and resource allocations of the ministries involved. Thus, policies are not necessarily coherent and integrated responses to perceived problems or part of a logical strategy of leaders or a faction to advance power and principles.

This paragraph shows that the Chinese political system is traversed by a number of fault lines causing power fragmentation. One of these fault lines runs between the political center and the localities (i.e., provinces, prefectures, and counties). The relations between the two are characterized by bargaining processes in which each party is forced to pay attention to the other's interests. While some provinces, due to favorable economic conditions, personal connections, or other strategic advantages, possess greater bargaining power than others, the extent of the control that the center can exert over the localities also varies (Lieberthal & Oksenberg, 1988: 138–139).

Another structural particularity of the Chinese bureaucratic system is the fact that it is highly fragmented along functional and hierarchical lines between different government agencies. In order to be able to rule as effectively as possible, there are both vertical (*tiao*) and horizontal (*kuai*) bureaucratic domains. The vertical lines of authority span various sectors reaching down from the ministries of the central government, while the horizontal level of authority comprises the territorial government at the provincial or local levels. The former coordinates according to function (such as the environment), and the latter coordinates according to the needs of the locality that it governs. Thus, a local Environmental Protection Bureau may have reporting responsibilities to both the provincial environmental protection department and to the government as well as to the party branch of the county in which it is located (Lieberthal & Oksenberg, 1988: 141–145).

There are various types of formal relations between different units in the Chinese bureaucracy. The two most important are "leadership relations (*lingdao guanxi*)" and "professional relations (*yewu guanxi*)." In the case of leadership relations, superior units have the authority to issue orders that are binding upon the lower unit, but professional relations only allow for the issuing of nonbinding regulations to subordinate organs. Although the latter have to pay attention to these regulations, they can be modified or even disregarded. While a unit may have professional relations with any number of other units, it can only have leadership relations with one unit, namely, the one that provides them with budgetary and personnel allocations. It should also be noted that "professional relations" are not confined to relations between superior and subordinate units; they define interactions between organs that are engaged in related issue areas, some of which are of hierarchical nature (Lieberthal & Oksenberg, 1988: 148–149; Mertha, 2005: 797).

The ways in which these different government agencies interact with each other is further defined by the ranks of both the agencies and the individuals who lead them. Every governmental, Party, or corporate unit in China is ranked and, by this means, integrated into the hierarchy of government levels from the villages up to the political center. One key rule of the Chinese system is that units of the same rank cannot issue orders that are binding upon each other. For example, since ministries and provinces have the same rank, they do not have formal authority over each other, and this means that a province may challenge, overrule, or ignore decisions made by a ministry. Because of this fragmented state of authority, resolving a matter below the political center requires discussion, bargaining, and finally consensus-building among an array of officials from an early point in the policy-making process. This means that many decisions are taken at relatively low levels in the national bureaucratic hierarchy (Lieberthal & Oksenberg, 1988: 148–149).

Due to the fragmented nature of China's authoritarian government, the processes for setting and implementing policies for a diverse range of policy problems are presented with many obstacles and barriers as the policies make their way downward from the top of the policymaking hierarchy. According to Lieberthal and Lampton, government actors below the top leadership level have become fragmented and policies have become incoherent because of decreasing political coercion, efforts to decentralize budgetary decision-making, the encouragement of bureaucratic entrepreneurship, and the weakened role played by political ideology in policy decisions since the start of Deng Xiaoping's reform initiatives. This fragmentation manifests itself both in the bureaucratic ranking system and in the functional division of authority, resulting in a political environment where no single governmental agency exercises complete authority and where policy formulation and implementation is dominated by negotiations, bargaining, exchange, and consensus-building (Lieberthal & Lampton, 1992).

In the words of David M. Lampton (1987), Chinese politics are a "bargaining treadmill" rather than a coercive apparatus. Bargaining is one of the central features of the Chinese polity and is mostly carried out by parties holding similar rank and power. The issues that underlie the bargaining processes are for the most part highly complex and require cooperation and trade-offs between the various actors concerned (Lampton 1992: 34–35). In more detail, bargaining

> [i]s a process of reciprocal accommodation among the leaders of territorial and functional hierarchies. Bargaining occurs because these leaders believe that the gains to be made by mutual accommodation exceed those to be made by unilateral action (if that were possible) or by forgoing agreement altogether.
>
> (37)

According to Lampton, the coercive abilities of the central government are limited, which is why higher authorities mostly confine themselves to noncoercive instruments, such as bargaining and consensus-building. This, however, weakens implementation, since local governments can increase their bargaining power by fulfilling a set of mandates such as birth control and tax collection. In this way, local governments have greater chances of being granted the tacit permission of the central government to avoid the implementation of other conflicting policies, such as environmental protection and public participation. Furthermore, vertical and horizontal government bodies tend to pursue their own interests, and these may diverge from or run counter to those of other ministries or administrative units, which makes bargaining and consensus-building essential decision-making tools (Lampton, 1987).

Lampton took water resource projects as an example to explain the bargaining processes that prevailed before and after the introduction of market reforms. In the cases of the Danjiangkou Dam along the Han River in Hubei, the Gezhouba Dam along the Yangtze in Hubei, and the Three Gorges Dam, he showed that intense processes of bargaining and negotiation accompany the planning and construction phases of water resource projects. This is because of the high number of functional and territorial actors involved who represent an array of conflicting interests that result from differences in organizational mandates and the effects that the water resource project has on them. For example, the water resource bureaucracy tends to focus on flood prevention and therefore advocated the construction of the Danjiangkou Dam mainly for the purpose of flood control. This was against the interests of the energy bureaucracy, which aimed to maximize power generation. Similarly, Henan and Hubei Provinces had to negotiate over the distribution of the costs and benefits of the project, since the displacement of people in the course of construction mostly occurred in Henan, while Hubei stood to gain the major share of the benefits with regard to electric power and flood control (Lampton, 1987b, 1992).

While the decentralization of decision-making after 1978 has stimulated economic development, it has also caused local protectionism as well as regional variations in policy implementation. In order to increase control of local cadre behavior and standardize policy implementation, the central government has centralized a number of key bureaucracies, including the statistical bureaucracy, administrative regulation, financial regulation, commodities management, and parts of the land bureaucracy. Under this approach of "centralized management" (*chuizhi guanli*), offices of certain bureaucracies are no longer controlled by their superiors in the local government (*kuai*-relations) but are beholden to their functional superiors within their bureaucracy (*tiao*-relations). This type of "soft centralization" in which relations are centralized from the county and township level to the province, while retaining decentralized relations between the center and the province, reshape political and economic incentives of local officials, thereby influencing local government behavior (Mertha, 2005: 792).

The role of society in policymaking

Since the beginning of China's reform era, the number of civil society organizations has increased rapidly. The number of NGOs registered with the Ministry of Civil Affairs grew from 4,446 in 1988 to 506,173 in mid-2013 (Spires, Tao, & Chan, 2014: 65). Due to the expansive and difficult registration process, an additional two to three million groups are registered as for-profit organizations (Teets, 2014: 157). In contrast to western nongovernment organizations, most of the Chinese NGOs are controlled by the Chinese government and are often referred to as GONGOs (government-operated nongovernmental organizations), which are embedded in the state and help to preserve social stability by representing large groups of society. The reason for the rapid increase in the number of NGOs since the 1990s is simple: they provide the social services that the state no longer provides.

During the Fifteenth Party Congress in 1997, the Communist Party announced the promotion of societal intermediaries that would be able to fill the social gaps created in the course of the reform and opening-up period. However, restrictive laws served to prevent any possibility of unrestrained organization and freedom of speech (Saich 2000: 126). The newly developed third sector has to operate in line with the ideological principles of the Communist Party, and each organization has to obtain governmental approval before it can start to carry out its work.[1] Thus, in order to maximize their influence within a regulative environment characterized by "a top-down style of state corporatism," Chinese NGOs have fostered closer ties with governmental actors at various administrative levels (Hsu & Hasmath, 2012: 3).

Nevertheless, during the 1990s and 2000s, civil society organizations have become increasingly vocal in defending the interests of the public against the coercive policies of the state or profit-seeking companies. Observers note an increase in oppressive measures and a tightening regulative environment exercised by the Xi administration towards civil groups (e.g., Cook, 2015; Wong, 2015). Oversight and control of NGOs has increased with a number of prominent crackdowns on civil society activism such as the arrest of five feminist activists (Jacobs, 2015). Furthermore, the second draft of the law on foreign NGOs in China, which is now open for public comment, is introducing a much stricter management and control of foreign civil society activity in China (National People's Congress, 2015). If introduced in the current form, the law is likely to limit, not only international NGOs activity in China, but also international funding for Chinese NGOs (M. Wang, 2015).

At the same time, Spires, Tao, and Chan (2014) have witnessed a growth in the number of grassroots NGOs in China and are expecting a further increase over the years to come. Moreover, Farid (2014) argues that although it is impossible to generalize about the impact of Chinese grassroots NGOs on the policy process, they have still been able to influence discourse on a number of social issues. In addition, the Chinese policy environment as one being characterized by policy flexibility and experimentation has allowed grassroots NGOs to influence policymaking by carrying out concrete programs that are subsequently taken up by local officials keen to gain political credit by innovatively solving governance challenges.[2]

J.C. Teets (2013, 2014, 2015) refers to the new model of state-civil society relationships in China as "consultative authoritarianism." In contrast to the purely corporatist model that has characterized the relation between state and society during the 1990s, this new model represents a combination of a more autonomous civil society with earlier mechanisms of state control found under corporatism. She bases her argument on recent changes in registration requirements, sources of funding, and the emergence of a system of positive and negative incentives designed to guide civil group behavior. Overall, these developments have fostered the shift from direct to indirect social control that has the potential to foster "professional, high capacity groups but at the expense of community-based organizations dealing with rights-based issues" (Teets, 2015: 175).

In China, environmental activism started in the 1990s, and since then, environmental activists and their organizations have monitored development and environmental projects.[3] One of these projects is the Three Gorges Dam, which – due to its huge impact on the natural environment and on the resettled people – has become one of the most controversial construction projects in China's history. According to Lin, the project has provoked the development of a number of environmental NGOs and has created environmental awareness among China's public (T.-C. Lin, 2007). Other reasons for the rapid rise in the number of environmental NGOs was the increasing environmental deterioration in China, the growing influence of international NGOs since the beginning of the reform era, the partial decrease in control exercised by the party-state as well as the overall diversification of Chinese society, and the willingness of newly emerging private entrepreneurs to contribute financially to the environmental cause (Bao, 2009; Tang & Zhan, 2008).

In 2008, 2,768 environmental groups were officially registered as NGOs (Bao, 2009: 2). Those previously involved in reshaping policies related to hydropower development in China include The Nature Conservancy (considered to be one of the more radical NGOs working in southwest China); the United Nations Educational, Scientific and Cultural Organization (UNESCO); Green Watershed; and Friends of Nature, China's first environmental NGO, established in 1994 by the activist Liang Congjie (Mertha, 2008).

As is the case in most policy fields in China, based on central-level laws, provinces have developed distinctive regulations suited for their respective jurisdictions. Accordingly, different social management models have evolved in different parts of the country. In Yunnan, the number of NGOs is particularly high. This is mostly due to the socioeconomic and environmental situation prevalent in the province: Yunnan is comparatively poor (third poorest province in terms of per capita gross domestic product [GDP] in 2010), it is very diverse both ecologically and ethnically and has a high number of people infected with AIDS. Therefore, many of the NGOs based in Yunnan are working in one or more of these issue areas. Due to the financial difficulties of the local government, the international funding received by civil society groups in Yunnan have been seen as a valuable asset in dealing with growing social problems, providing limited space for civil society groups to operate. In the course, the Yunnan model of social management developed, which is characterized by a heavy reliance on international funding and project-based cooperation between social groups and local government agencies (Teets, 2015).

In addition to civil society groups, the media have been actively exposing the unlawful behavior of local governments and business groups and, as a result, have started to play an increasingly important role in the Chinese policy process. Investigative journalism has been officially promoted since the late 1980s, when the Chinese government adopted the policy of "supervision by public opinion" (*yulun jiandu*). This allows the media to adopt a watchdog role over cases of power abuse by local governments. Another force that has been fostering critical and investigate journalism is the decentralization and commercialization of the Chinese media. This has led newspapers such as *Southern Weekend* to orient their articles according to readers' interests and to publish more critical analyses (Svensson, 2012).

Due to these developments, according to Andrew Mertha (2008), the FA framework, despite still being applicable to Chinese politics today, needs to be adapted to the increasingly pluralized Chinese policy process. In his analysis of hydropower politics in China, he argues that, as China's market has become increasingly complex, politics increasingly decentralized, and society increasingly multifaceted, the control and management of water is no longer merely an unquestioned economic imperative but a policy sphere dominated by bureaucratic infighting, societal opposition, and at times even open protest. Although bargaining has always been present in Chinese politics, the media, nongovernmental organizations, and other activists have started to become active players in the policymaking process.

Mertha draws on elements of the public policy literature in American politics, in particular, three critical dimensions, policy entrepreneurs, issue-framing and broad support for policy change, that allow him to show how political conflict and policy change intersect in Chinese hydropower politics. Mertha explores these three dimensions in each of his case studies in order to show how the FA framework has evolved since the 1980s. His main argument is that the fragmented structure of authority within the Chinese polity allows peripheral policy entrepreneurs to enter the policymaking scene without being coercively expelled from it. Specific characteristics (physical, jurisdictional, geographic) of the cases presented, the respective dominance of the issue frame developed by policy entrepreneurs, and the extent of public support as well as the characteristics and personal power of individual entrepreneurs constitute the main variables affecting the outcomes in the three cases analyzed in his work.

According to Mertha, these actors have been able to reverse policy decisions and reshape them in a way that supports their own goals. In the area of hydropower development, by means of demonstrations, investigative journalism, and at times violence, they have succeeded in reversing the decision to build the Dujiangyan Dam and have halted construction for the Nu River Project. This is why, according to Mertha, the fragmented authoritarianism framework needs to be revised. During the 1980s, when the framework was first developed, the policymaking process only involved governmental actors. Since that time, however, China's political decision-making has become less authoritarian and now allows formerly passive actors (the media, NGOs, and peripheral cadres) to become actively involved. To sum up, "while the fragmented authoritarianism framework continues to define the major contours of the policy-making process in China, the playing field is becoming increasingly crowded" (Mertha, 2009: 1012).

Limitations of the fragmented authoritarianism model

Both versions of the FA model have their limitations. The first version confines itself to the analysis of power configurations and bargaining processes within the state and therefore cannot account for the complex socioeconomic changes that have been occurring since the beginning of the reform era. As for FA 2.0, Mertha's updated FA framework argues that actors who were previously excluded from the policy process are now able to influence the policy process in substantial ways. The actors to whom the framework refers include "peripheral officials," NGOs, and the media. In order to succeed in their efforts at influencing policymaking and implementation, they need to garner broad-based public support. While this is arguably necessary in the case of large construction projects that enjoy strong political backing, this approach fails to shed light on the daily struggles surrounding policy implementation once the project has been approved and local governments are tasked with executing related policy decisions. Such cases, while at times involving resistance on the side of policy objects (i.e., local communities), reveal the strategies employed by local communities as attempts to influence policy implementation rather than as active efforts to turn policies around.

Another important group of actors that is neglected by FA 2.0 are state-owned enterprises (SOEs) – a group of actors that is increasingly contributing to the additional fragmentation of the Chinese polity. State-owned enterprises are important players within most of China's industries, but they are neither statist actors in the traditional sense of the word, nor are they societal actors. In his study on business group formation in China, Brødsgaard shows that state-owned enterprises in China possess both economic and political power. On the one hand, they reap

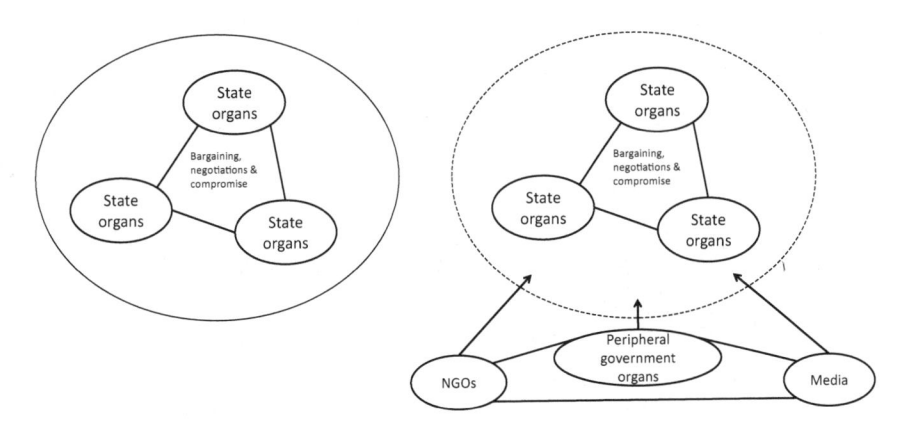

Figure 2.1 Fragmented authoritarianism 1.0 and 2.0

Source: Based on Lieberthal and Oksenberg (1988) and Mertha (2008).

huge profits from their operations, and on the other, they have in the past been able to prevent the creation of new ministries and regulatory commissions, which would have limited their powers (Brødsgaard, 2012). Hydropower development is one of the sectors in which state-owned enterprises play a particularly important role, not only during the construction process, but also during resettlement planning and implementation.

The study presented here moves a step beyond Mertha's research on resistance against hydropower projects to examine what happens after the decision has been made to construct a power station and local governments have to implement related policy decisions such as resettlement plans. Thus, while Mertha conceptualizes society as media, NGOs, disgruntled officials, and the general public at large, this study focuses on local resettlement communities and their daily struggles with local cadres during the process of resettlement policy implementation. Although it cannot be denied that the media, NGOs, and the general public might become involved in these struggles, the focus is nevertheless on resettlement communities, how these communities perceive policy implementation, and the strategies they employ to influence policy implementation. In this way, the bargaining and negotiations that were previously confined to statist actors at the central level (FA 1.0), and subsequently extended to civil society actors and peripheral officials at the local level (FA 2.0), have now been extended to the grassroots level and to processes of policy implementation that are shaped by interactions, negotiations, and bargaining (or the lack thereof) between the state and society.

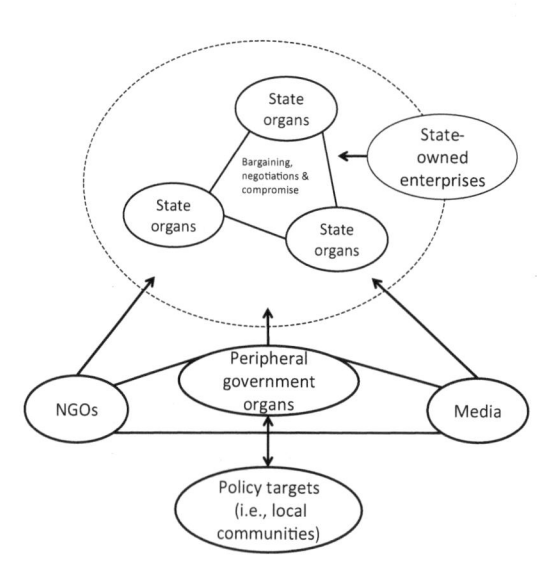

Figure 2.2 Adaptation of FA model for the research presented here

Source: Author.

A new approach to studying policy implementation

In order to understand the Chinese policy process, it is necessary to look beyond instances of bargaining and negotiation within the state and between state and society. What needs to be scrutinized is the impact that policy change has had on local resettlement processes within the contemporary Chinese political structure. In detail, this research presents an analysis of the changing role of the local state in policy implementation in the context of the more socially oriented resettlement policies introduced by the central state. Past studies have emphasized, first of all, the adaptability of central and local states in the process of economic development and, second, the ways in which local cadres have responded to the incentive structure that has been presented to them by their organizational environment. This research builds on these works to show how the organizational environment for local governments has changed in the course of the introduction of more socially oriented resettlement policies, and the increasingly rule-guided behavior of the Chinese hydropower bureaucracy.

As Lieberthal argues, since the beginning of reform and opening up, the Chinese polity has embarked on a transition process, moving on from a traditional hierarchical system toward a modern, market-oriented system. In the former, activities are shaped by traditional vertical relationships and informal connections, while in the latter, activities are primarily guided by market relationships and formal institutions, including official rules and regulations (Lieberthal & Lampton, 1992: 21–22).

The field of hydropower development represents one area in which the transition has begun but has not yet been able to achieve the previously envisioned goals of a purely modern polity. Although power sector reforms have introduced market forces into the field and big hydropower companies have started to operate more and more like modern corporations, market rules have certainly not taken the place of traditional hierarchical modes of governance. Instead, rule-guided market relationships and top-down bureaucratic interactions exist parallel with each other. This means that while certain areas of hydropower development are primarily governed by formal rules and regulations, others are dominated by informal patron-client relations, and the implications of this for resettlement policy implementation processes are at the center of this research.

The hybrid structure of the Chinese polity, consisting of traditional and market elements, serves as the context in which policies are formulated and implemented in China. While the previous section has introduced the fragmented nature of Chinese authoritarianism and the importance of bargaining during the policy process, the following section details one of the core features of the continued resilience of the Chinese political system, namely, flexible policy adaptation.

Democratic centralism and the Chinese policy process

Elements of flexibility inherent to the Chinese policy process are strongly connected to the CCP's ideology, in particular to Mao's idea of democratic centralism.

Originating from Russia and adopted as the guiding principle of the CCP in 1927, democratic centralism came to be understood and was defined by Wang Ming in the following way:

> The minority obeys the majority; party members have complete freedom to discuss and criticize before any issue is decided; after it is decided, everyone must implement the decision of the organization no matter what their view; the subordinate must implement the solutions and directives of the superior; if they have different views about the resolutions and directives of the superior, they may present their views to the superior, but they must still implement these resolutions and directives before they are changed by the superior.
>
> (quoted in Saich, 1996: 806)

The principle of democratic centralism as it was adapted to the Chinese polity by Mao was to harmonize the two conflicting concepts of democracy and centralism to limit the ineffectiveness of authority and allow for a discussion on how to find solutions to certain problems. Democracy was not regarded as an end in itself but rather as a means to promote initiative within lower levels of the hierarchy. Thus, democracy was subordinate to hierarchy and centralism and was to be limited by these two in order to prevent chaos (C. Lin & Lee, 2013).

Angle explains that democratic centralism can be viewed "as a dialectical combination of democracy and centralism, suggesting an ongoing dynamism or flexibility in the relation between the two poles" (Angle, 2005: 525). While democratic centralism primarily applies to the CCP itself rather than to the Chinese people at large, Angle suggests taking a look at the mass line in order to understand the role that society plays in the policy process. According to Mao (1943):

> In all the practical work of our Party, all correct leadership is necessarily "from the masses, to the masses." This means: take the ideas of the masses (scattered and unsystematic ideas) and concentrate them (through study turn them into concentrated and systematic ideas), then go to the masses and propagate and explain these ideas until the masses embrace them as their own, hold fast to them and translate them into action, and test the correctness of these ideas in such action. Then once again concentrate ideas from the masses and once again go to the masses so that the ideas are persevered in and carried through. And so on, over and over again in an endless spiral, with the ideas becoming more correct, more vital, and richer each time. Such is the Marxist theory of knowledge.
>
> (Mao, 1943: 119)

This quotation shows that Mao's ideology of the mass line had the aim of obtaining as much input from the masses as possible in order to solve policy problems in line with actual experiences on the ground. An inherent feature of this process was that policy needed to be revised frequently in order to keep up with local developments and to find the most appropriate instruments for solving policy problems.

Both democratic centralism and the mass line rely on processes during which a diversity of potentially conflicting opinions are collected and combined into a unified policy output by the political center. Subsequently, this output is again adapted to local conditions for implementation, and at the same time open to criticism, or further improvement. While during the first stage of policymaking, input from lower levels and society is both possible and welcomed, as the process moves on to policy formulation and adjustment, flexibility is limited, since this would pose a challenge to centralism. Accordingly, adjusting policies to local circumstances does not mean that local implementers are allowed to have a free hand. At the same time, adjustments and complaints cannot be allowed to dictate the process because this would mean that benefits accrued to those who complained the loudest (Angle, 2005: 528).

Reformers, such as Deng Xiaoping and Chen Yun, have taken up this approach to policymaking, advocating the need to "grope for stones when crossing the river (*moshi guohe*)" and to "seek truth from facts (*shishi qiushi*)" (Vogel, 2011). This approach has been particularly successful in the sphere of economic policymaking, since it has allowed the Chinese leadership to flexibly adapt to a rapidly changing domestic and international environment. Recent political developments under the leadership of Xi Jinping alter this gradualist approach to policymaking. The decision put forth in the course of the Third Plenary Session of the 18th CPC Central Committee calls for the establishment of leadership groups that implement reforms in a more coordinated and integrated manner than has been the case before (CPC Central Committee, 2013). At the same time, Xi has been attempting to increase Party dominance by reviving the mass line campaign as well as by introducing self-criticism sessions and educational campaigns (Martin & Cohen, 2014; Miller, 2014).

This section has provided an introduction to democratic centralism and the mass line, which serve as the ideological framework within which the Chinese policy process continues to be embedded. The following section presents details of the organization of the Chinese policy process and how it allows for the flexible adaptation of policies by the Chinese leadership.

Flexible adaptation of the Chinese policy process

In research on China, the most recent attempt to strike a balance between central-level policymaking and local policy implementation is found in the work of Heilmann and Perry (e.g., 2011). "Guerilla policy-style" rests at the core of their explanation as to why the CCP has remained in power until the present day, a policy style that originated in the Communist revolution in China and, in the authors' view, is still prevalent today. According to the authors, guerilla policymaking is a change-oriented "push-and-seize" style that contrasts with the stability-oriented "anticipate-and-regulate" norm of modern constitutional governments" and illustrates the system's preference for "agility over stability" (Heilmann & Perry, 2011: 13).

Heilmann (2008a, 2008b) furthermore shows that some parts of the features of the contemporary Chinese policy process date back to the Republican era and, in particular, to the revolutionary period of the CCP. One of the approaches used by the Communists for finding innovative policy instruments was policy experimentation. Policy experimentation, loosely defined, refers to the frequent reversals of policies that characterize all political systems when policies are considered unsuitable. A stricter definition refers to experimentation as part of the policy process in which different methods are tried out to find solutions for problems arising during experimentation. Policy experimentation is not equivalent to arbitrary trial and error but rather "a purposeful and coordinated activity geared to producing novel policy options that are injected into official policymaking and then replicated on a larger scale, or even formally incorporated into national law" (Heilmann, 2008b: 3).

If experimentation is planned and executed as part of pilot programs, these tend to be limited to a predefined set of measures and target groups and are mainly intended to adjust instruments of policy implementation rather than to design brand new policies. In contrast, experimentation aimed at transformation and reorganization is carried out in politically realistic environments characterized by uncertainty, fluidity, dynamism, and contestation. These experiments usually lack strict scientific analysis but may provide a comprehensive explanation of the impact of new policies on actors in the market, in society and in the administration (Heilmann, 2008b: 4).

Heilmann shows that there are three different types of experimentation at work in China today that have their origins in the revolutionary experiences of the Chinese Communist Party (2008a, 2008b): 1) "experimental regulation," 2) "experimental points," and 3) "experimental zones." Experimental regulation refers to interim rules that only become official law after ample information has been gathered on their impact during a trial period. Experimental points refer to demonstration projects that are carried out in a specific policy area with only a limited number of experimental units participating. Finally, experimental zones refer to a geographical area provided with discretionary powers by the central government to design and test new policies and institutions. All three experimental instruments have played and continue to play an important role in China's economic and social reforms (Heilmann, 2008b).

At the same time, experimental governance is deeply embedded in China's hierarchical political system, in which the central leadership promotes local initiative and at the same time limits those forces that might lead to extensive regionalization. Heilmann describes this type of "experimentation under hierarchy" as a "volatile yet productive combination of decentralized experimentation with ad hoc central interference, resulting in the selective integration of local experiences into national policy-making" (Heilmann, 2008a: 29). Such kind of "bottom-up diffusion pattern" is contrasted by the "central-down diffusion pattern" where the center initiates policies that are subsequently given to the provinces. J. Teets and Hurst (2014) identify two more diffusion patterns that lack central interference, illustrating policy diffusion from the provincial level down to counties and townships (i.e., "intra-provincial diffusion pattern"), and between subnational governments (i.e., "regional [or horizontal] diffusion pattern"). In short, since the beginning of reform and the opening-up, experimentation proved to be a viable means for policymakers at all levels to steer the economy in an environment of uncertainty, allowing the Chinese regime to flexibly adapt to rapidly changing economic forces.

Policy experimentation and flexible policy adaptation have not only been prevalent features in China's economic reforms but have also been employed in the field of resettlement policymaking. However, in these cases, it is not the economy that is steered but society. This study shows how policy flexibility by the center impacts on local processes of policy implementation and shapes state-society relations on the ground. Policy implementation "refers to the connection between the expression of governmental intention and results" (O'Toole, 1995: 42). Historically, two schools of thought have evolved among theorists who have examined the connection between the theory and the reality of specific policies. First, there are the top-down theorists who see policymakers at the central level as the key to policy implementation and focus, therefore, on the extent to which goals formulated at the center match with the actions of implementers and policy target groups. According to the results of their analyses, central government actors play the most important role in achieving the desired effects of a certain policy because they make the authoritative decisions that lower levels have to follow (Mazmanian & Sabatier, 1989; Van Meter & Van Horn, 1975).

Mazmanian and Sabatier (1989) further contended that the success of policy implementation depends on three sets of factors: the tractability of the problem, the ability of the statute to structure implementation, and the nonstatutory variables affecting implementation. In order to increase the chances of successful policy implementation, top-down theorists recommend setting clear policy goals, limiting the number of actors involved in implementation, minimizing necessary changes, and ensuring that responsibility for policy implementation lies with the actors who are committed to the underlying goals of the policy (Mazmanian & Sabatier, 1989; Pressman & Wildavsky, 1973; Van Meter & Van Horn, 1975).

Second, there are the bottom-up theorists who stress the importance of street-level bureaucrats and target groups for policy implementation. Policy implementation occurs at both the macro level and the micro level. In the case of the former, central planners devise a policy; in the case of the latter, local officials develop their implementation programs based on central-level policy. According to bottom-up theorists, the main problems during implementation arise from the interaction between central policy and local-level institutional settings, and central policymakers have limited influence on the latter. In order for policies to be implemented successfully, local officials need to be free to adapt central decisions to local environments (Berman, 1978).

However, in the cases presented below, local governments at county and township levels have not been able to freely adapt central decisions. Flexibility in adapting policies at the central level is not matched with an equivalent degree of flexibility during the local processes of policy implementation. This is not because local cadres forego flexibility but rather results from their being embedded in the administrative structure of hydropower development, which prevents them from flexibly implementing policies in line with local circumstances.

The Chinese local state and fragmented mediation under hierarchy

In order to understand local policy implementation, the incentive structure of local cadres as well as the activities developed within this structure need to be clarified.

During the 1980s, as a result of administrative decentralization, Chinese local leaders were given the power to extend their spheres of influence over economic sectors that were nonstatist and outside the plan. Local governments at each administrative level therefore started to pursue economic growth, which triggered more than three decades of rapid economic development (Qian & Weingast, 1996; Shirk, 1993). In their analyses of economic development in Chinese provinces, Blecher and Shue distinguished between "developmental" and "entrepreneurial local states" (Blecher, 1991; Blecher & Shue, 1996, 2001), pointing out that the latter engage directly in business activities, such as undertaking investments and becoming involved in managerial decision-making. Their findings came close to those obtained by Oi (1992, 1995) and Walder (1995) who highlighted the ways in which local governments at the county level functioned as corporate entities, a phenomenon that Oi called the "local corporatist state."[5]

In order to explain the period of rapid growth that started during the 1980s, Oi and Walder scrutinized China's local officials whose behavior, as agents, was influenced by incentives, constraints, skills, and resources to trigger growth, as well as the monitoring ability of the central state as the principal. Local officials in China are members of the official bureaucracy and therefore act as part of the administrative apparatus, but Oi's and Walder's analyses viewed local governments as distinct entities apart from the central state and society with their own interests and resources.

Oi argues that during the reform period, a form of local state corporatism developed in China, when local officials moved away from their focus on collectively owned enterprises towards the promotion of the private sector. She contends that *corporatism* denotes "a form of state-society relations where narrow interests within society are organized and integrated so as to achieve higher-order goals" (Oi, 1999: 12), whereas *local* and *state* refer to the fact that all this occurred at local government level, with local cadres rather than the central government coordinating and constituting this form of corporatism. Moreover, *corporatism* has both a "corporate" and a "corporatist" aspect: In the 1980s, local governments ran the companies under their administration as diversified corporations, with local officials taking up positions equivalent to those of a board of directors. In the 1990s, the corporatist aspect of local state corporatism in China became evident when local governments had to handle both privately and collectively owned firms and had to restrain the private sector from becoming an independent economic class. However, local officials did not only restrain the private sector, they also offered incentives, which has led to a type of synergy between state and economy, preventing the emergence of an independent – and potentially threatening – economic elite.

The local corporatist state is constituted of village-, township-, and county-level governments, which are all directly responsible for cultivating rural enterprises.

The performance of the latter determines the careers and salaries of officials at each local government level, and in return, each local government controls the profits accruing from local economic development. Oi describes the local corporatist state as follows:

> Somewhat akin to a large multi-level corporation, the county can be seen as being at the top of a corporate hierarchy as the corporate headquarters, the township as the regional headquarters, and the villages as companies within the larger corporation. Each level is an approximate equivalent to what is termed a "profit centre" in decentralized management schemes used in business firms. Each successive level of government is fiscally independent and is thus expected to maximize its economic performance.
>
> (Oi, 1995: 138)

What these past works on local economic development have shown is that the local state has been a crucial agent in flexibly adapting or even illegally modifying central-level reform policies for the benefit of local growth (see also Chien & Zhao, 2008; Liu, 1992). However, local states do not only foster economic growth. In their quest to fill local government coffers, many of these entrepreneurial states also revealed their predatory nature by indulging in activities such as grabbing land from peasants and engaging in corrupt activities (which sparked social unrest) (Cai, 2003; X. Guo, 2001; Hsing, 2010; Lü, 2000; O'Brien & Li, 2006). The Chinese leadership subsequently acknowledged the problems arising from the unfettered pursuit of economic growth and started to design more socially oriented development policies. In late 2000, China's leaders first mentioned the "threefold rural problem" that the countryside was facing. Two years later at the 16th Party Congress, Jiang Zemin's concept of the "Three Represents" was integrated into the party statutes. Among other things, this concept aimed to modernize agriculture and help farmers become part of the "moderately well-off society" that was to be created by 2020 (News of the Communist Party of China, 2006). In addition to narrowing the rural-urban divide, further government policies, such as the "Western Development Strategy (*Xibu da kaifa*)," aimed to reduce the inequalities between eastern and western provinces. Moreover, ideological reforms, such as the concept of building a "Socialist Harmonious Society (*Shehui zhuyi hexie shehui*)" and the "Scientific Development Concept (*Kexue fazhan guan*)," sought to limit general social disparities and promote balanced economic development (Holbig, 2007).

These ideological reforms indicate that a shift was taking place, at least at central government level, away from the traditional development paradigm with its focus on economic growth alone, towards a more balanced approach to social and economic development. The introduction of more socially oriented resettlement policies since 2006 should be viewed in this context. This gives rise to a number of questions, however, with regard to the implications of these socially oriented policies for the local state and the way in which they are implemented, particularly if policymakers make use of flexible policy adaptation, which entails the frequent updating of new policies and, consequently, of policy implementation.

The introduction of more socially oriented policies has had direct and indirect impacts on local policy implementation and the role played by the local state. As for the more immediate impacts, attention has already been drawn to the way that the CCP, through the cadre management system, ensures that central-level decisions are passed through the government bureaucracy and implemented by relevant government bodies (Chan, 2004; Edin, 2003; Heberer & Trappel, 2013). Local-level cadres are evaluated according to their performance in office, causing local governments to mainly implement those policies that have quantifiable, and for the most part economic, targets. With the introduction of more socially oriented policies, performance evaluation is slowly shifting from a focus on hard policy targets towards soft policy goals, including rural reconstruction and sustainable development (J.-H. Wang, Tseng, & Zheng, 2015).

This social turn in policymaking has also manifested itself in the field of dam-induced resettlement. As a result, local cadres are now required to increase consultation with local migrant communities throughout the whole resettlement process and to ensure the restoration of migrants' livelihoods after relocation. Although these newly introduced policy targets are difficult to measure, a stark increase in cadre training programs on "human-oriented" resettlement has raised awareness among local officials that military-style relocation campaigns are unable to contribute to successful resettlement results and that the social instability caused by dam migrants is a serious political issue (Interviews, NJ13030, SM110812).

Apart from these direct impacts on the work of local states in resettlement policy implementation, more socially oriented policies have also had an indirect impact on the role of local cadres – namely, the empowerment of local migrant communities. O'Brien and Li (2006) identified the phenomenon of "rightful resistance" as a consequence of the introduction of more socially oriented policies by the central government. They define rightful resistance as

> [a] form of popular contention that operates near the boundary of authorized channels, employs the rhetoric and commitments of the powerful to curb the exercise of power, hinges on locating and exploiting divisions within the state, and relies on mobilizing support from the wider public.
>
> (O'Brien & Li, 2006: 2)

Thus, in the course of these ideological shifts at the political center and specific policy changes regarding village election procedures, fee limits, and land use, Chinese villagers have gained space to raise their grievances and legally fight malfeasant officials. Chapter 6 of this book presents a case that supports these observations. However, these reactions from local communities are only part of the story. This research goes a step further to investigate what policy changes mean for local processes of policy implementation, which are regarded as being shaped by both the local state and local communities.

Previous studies have shown that local governments flexibly deploy a range of strategies such as "collusion" (Zhou, 2010b), "policy bundling" (Kostka & Hobbs, 2012), and neglect of formal directives in order to come to terms with the diversity of policies to be implemented simultaneously at the grassroots level and to accommodate the increasing demands of local constituents. The research presented here follows this line of inquiry but focuses more specifically on the introduction of "human-oriented" policies by the central government after 2006 and the interaction of this policy shift with the increasingly rule-guided nature of infrastructure development (here, hydropower).

My contention is that the introduction of more socially oriented resettlement policies with their direct and indirect impacts at local government level has caused the emergence of a phenomenon that can be termed *fragmented mediation under hierarchy*. In these cases, local governments agree to negotiate over policy implementation because they are caught in a double bind, with local communities threatening to obstruct project construction or even cause social unrest and the resettlement bureaucracy not allowing local cadres to flexibly adapt resettlement plans. Due to the introduction of more socially oriented resettlement policies, the local state at township and county levels is forced to mediate diverging opinions and migrants' interests more than ever before. However, this mediation occurs in a hierarchical structure that at times constrains the local state's ability to successfully implement policies. Similar to Heilmann's (2008b) conceptualization of "experimentation under hierarchy," local states are integrated in a hierarchical governance structure that requires them to fulfill policy targets set by higher levels. However, these levels no longer consist of government agencies alone. In the case of hydropower development, this hierarchy is infused by market mechanisms because large power companies, which are striving to increase their profits, negotiate with provincial governments over the details of project construction, resettlement, and related compensation.

In the local corporatist state, local cadres form part of the corporate structure and have the same interest in maximizing profit as their superiors and enterprise representatives, but in the case of resettlement policy, a diversity of interests exists with grassroots-level governments having to face the task of mediating them. While local cadres always have to represent the interests of their superiors at the provincial level who cooperate closely with the hydropower companies, they also have to represent the interests of migrant communities, who have the potential to challenge social stability. This clash of interests between society and industry occurs at the level of the local state (i.e., county and township governments) and places the latter under pressure to mediate these interests within the limits provided for by administrative hierarchies.

Mediation has been an important tool for resolving intra-societal conflict in China (P.C.C. Huang, 2009). In general, mediation refers to a strategy by means of which local communities or individuals seek the help of grassroots leaders to resolve conflicts that have arisen between two or more parties over property, interpersonal relations, or other personal matters (Read & Michelson, 2008). In this study, mediation does not refer to a strategy employed by local people but rather to the way in which local governments try to reduce the conflict of interests that exists between dam migrants, the hydropower and resettlement bureaucracies, and local cadres themselves.

Due to the fact that the local cadres are embedded in an organizational environment that limits the choices available to them with regard to policy implementation, these efforts at mediation are fragmented; they are only applied when deemed necessary. Zhou (2010) argues that cases in which local governments face the challenge of having to implement a diversity of policies with limited amounts of funding could be described in terms of the "flexibility of unintended design." However, a number of studies on the Chinese policy process have regarded flexibility as a positive attribute that has allowed both central and local states to navigate through economic and social development (Heilmann, 2008a, 2008b; Heilmann & Perry, 2011). For this reason, the term "flexibility" is not used in this research to refer to local state behavior. It is instead argued that local government flexibility is constrained by higher-level authorities to such an extent that local cadres have to muddle through the processes of resettlement rather than being able to deliberately apply specific tools of policy implementation. Applying the term "flexibility" to local state behavior would paint an overly optimistic picture of local government agency. Instead, I argue that the result of the organizational environment (here a combination of requirements imposed by the resettlement and hydropower bureaucracies, the government administration, empowered local communities, and more socially oriented central government policies) that local governments have to face is *fragmented* mediation. "Flexibility" in the policy process presented here only denotes the adaptation of central government policies in response to the constantly changing national and international environment.

The focus of this research takes the Chinese policy process as the context, and highlights processes of resettlement policy implementation at the grassroots level. As Heilmann (2008a, 2008b, 2009) has shown, the Chinese policy process continues to be defined by elements of democratic centralism, which allow the Chinese government to flexibly adapt policies to the constantly changing environment. While this form of democracy allows different voices to be heard and a variety of local experiences to be integrated into policy formulation, centralism confines potential centrifugal forces when it comes to adapting central policies to local circumstances. It could be argued, however, that in the case of dam-induced resettlement, this imbalance between democracy and centralism throughout the policy process gives rise to conflict at the grassroots level during policy implementation. This is because democratic centralism, while allowing for the active collection of different voices of opinion during policy formulation, insists on strict adherence to the formulated policy during later phases of the policy process, when policies are no longer allowed to be adapted to local circumstances. Instead, grassroots cadres act as service providers for large energy companies and China's national hydropower strategy. This inflexibility is enhanced by the increasingly rule-guided nature of planning and construction processes that, in the case of large dams, occur at the provincial level between the government and industry representatives. This process, in line with the findings of the FA model, is dominated by bargaining and negotiations that also serve to slow down potential flexible adaptation during policy implementation. In addition, as this research will show, there has been an increase in the number of strict construction rules, and these are not only too rigid for the constantly changing resettlement policies designed by the center but also clash with traditional village life that is affected by resettlement.

For county and township governments, their role as service providers rather than as active agents in the policy process weakens their authority in the eyes of the resettlement communities. The cases presented in this research show that before resettlement takes place, local cadres serve as patrons whom the community trusts, but after resettlement, this vertical relationship changes to horizontal in that the local government is regarded as an largely incapable institution that lacks the ability to implement the policy changes introduced by the center. The combination of flexible policy adaptation at the political center and the hierarchical nature of the Chinese bureaucracy thus cause the erosion of government resilience at the grassroots level in resettlement villages.

Although cooperating during resettlement work, Party and state organs each have specific tasks during resettlement processes that will be elaborated below. Party and government organs are thus treated separately when necessary. However, to increase readability, whenever a differentiation is unnecessary for the analysis, the terms "local state" and "local government" are used interchangeably, referring to government and Party organizations at county and township levels. These are the two lowest levels within the state bureaucracy that have been allocated a role in dam-induced resettlement processes by official resettlement regulations. They are also the lowest levels that have set up their own resettlement bureaucracies.

Centralism and localism

This chapter has synthesized theories on fragmented authoritarianism, policy experimentation, democratic centralism, and local state corporatism to show how the constant changes to resettlement policies that are carried out by the central level interact with the administrative structure of the hydropower and resettlement bureaucracies to shape local processes of policy implementation as well as the state-society interactions that evolve within them. Flexible policy adaptation refers to the policy revisions undertaken by central government officials that are based on the experiences with policy implementation at the local level. Policymaking and policy implementation can therefore be seen as two intertwined, rather than separate, processes in which street-level bureaucrats act as policymakers before the central leadership has even become aware of the policy problem to be addressed (see Kong, 2010).

The theoretical framework presented in this chapter builds on the theory of democratic centralism as the ideological context in which the Chinese policy process is embedded and extends the theory of local state corporatism to explain how the local state deals with policies that are socially oriented rather than purely economic central policies. The term *fragmented mediation under hierarchy* has been used to refer to the way in which the local state copes with this situation. In comparison with the local corporatist state in which local cadres are part of the corporate structure sharing with enterprise representatives and their superiors the interest of profit maximization, in the case of resettlement, a diversity of interests exist with grassroots-level governments having to face the task of mediating them. Thus, local governments are caught in a double bind in which they are forced to obey orders by superiors that are on the one hand increasingly benevolent towards migrant communities and on the other hand subject to the profit margins of hydropower companies. It is suggested that the local state attempts to mediate society in a way that prevents social unrest among dissatisfied migrants while at the same time fulfilling the requirements of resettlement plans fixed at higher levels of the government bureaucracy.

Political developments under Xi Jinping point to a further strengthening of hierarchical structures as well as the growing importance of market principles in other policy fields as well. First, recent efforts at institutional recentralization and increased Party dominance will increase pressure for local cadres to improve performance. Here, the announcement at the Third Plenary Session in November 2013 to place Party discipline inspection committees under the leadership of the next higher administrative level rather than the Party committee at the same level is of particular importance. Second, in the economic sphere, Xi aims to strengthen the state sector by exposing SOEs to increased competition (CPC Central Committee, 2013). This will in turn expose local governments to even stricter economic demands when cooperating with SOEs. Finally, while Xi anticorruption campaign has the potential to increase transparency in China's political system, it has the potential to further stifle flexible policy implementation in a regime firmly built on patronage networks (see Hillman, 2014). The concept of fragmented mediation under hierarchy, thus, does not only shed light on recent developments in the field of dam-induced resettlement but provides an outlook on developments to be expected in other policy fields of local governance.

Notes

1 In 1998, the Chinese government published the *Regulations on Registration and Administration of Social Organization*, which states that each organization has to gain the approval of an authorized department supporting the work of the organization. Only then can an organization register with the Ministry of Civil Affairs. Since many NGOs experience difficulty in finding a patron as well as in going through the subsequent registration process, many organizations are forced to register as profit-seeking companies or to pursue their work informally (Saich, 2000: 129). For further earlier literature on the development of civil society in China, see White, Howell, and Shang (1996) and Pei (1998).
2 For earlier discussions on the autonomy of civil groups in China, see Frolic (1997) and Chamberlain (1998).
3 For a study on how Chinese grassroots NGOs in Guangdong, Yunnan, and Beijing operate in issue areas such as HIV/AIDS, labor rights, environmental protection, and education, see Spires, Tao, and Chan (2014).
4 For a summary of the main points of criticism regarding the models presented by Blecher, Shue, Oi, and Walder, see Alpermann (2010b: Chapter 1).

3 Dam resettlement policy in China

China's rapid economic growth has led to a dramatic increase in the demand for electricity. Although the main share of this demand is still being met by the country's coal industry, China's central government has also been looking for alternative energy resources that have the potential to reduce environmental pollution. This is one of the reasons why hydropower is now playing a major role in China's energy sector strategy, turning Yunnan Province with its huge hydropower reserves into a crucial power supplier for the country's booming eastern and southern coastal regions (Magee, 2006b). Within the past two decades, large investments have been directed at the province's key industries and projects in the areas of infrastructure and hydropower development. However, Yunnan does not only have important mineral and water resources; China's most southwestern provincial-level unit is also the country's gateway to Southeast Asia and home to a high number of ethnic minorities who are mainly living in poverty. Hydropower development has the potential to improve social and economic development in Yunnan, but resettlement policymaking and implementation are of central importance, if this development is to be achieved in a sustainable manner. The changes that have taken place in resettlement policy since the CCP came to power in 1949 are a clear indication of the increased importance attributed to dam-induced resettlement by the Chinese government.

Studies on the resettlement processes in China have indicated that involuntary resettlement all too frequently causes chronic impoverishment among the displaced people (Stein, 1997). Nevertheless, as mentioned in Chapter 1, China intends to double its hydropower capacity by 2020. The world's third largest dam, the Xiluodu Dam, is currently under construction in Sichuan and Yunnan Provinces (Xinhua Net, 2014). As a result of the Communist Party's determination to exploit all possible avenues to ensure China's energy security, the number of dam-induced resettlement processes is continually rising. For several decades now, in order to be able to implement these processes in an orderly manner and to safeguard the Party's hydropower development strategy as well as social stability, the State Council and China's resettlement bureaucracy have been actively designing a regulatory framework for resettlement.

Although the government introduced its first resettlement regulations in 1953 (Xinhua, n.d.), resettlement before the 1980s has been regarded as an unsuccessful endeavor, even by Chinese officials (Heggelund, 2004: 62). Due to the lack of adequate planning and compensation mechanisms for development-induced resettlement, the living conditions of dam migrants have constantly remained precarious. This changed slightly after the reform and the opening-up period, when the problems associated with dam-induced resettlement started to become a strong focus of attention. Although resettlement still continued to serve to protect hydropower development, the planning and construction processes became less short-sighted and were now aimed at the long-term development of hydropower resources and reservoir regions (Jun, 2000; Heggelund, 2004).

Dam-induced resettlement started to draw even more attention when the government decided to design specific regulations to govern the resettlement processes resulting from dam construction. After these regulations were published in 1991, the problems created during previous unsuccessful resettlement work were acknowledged and addressed through several policies. This included the so-called left-over problems in reservoir areas as well as shortcomings in the planning and implementation processes of resettlement projects. Resettlement work was no longer confined to the relocation of people but was expanded to include pre- and post-resettlement phases. In 2006, the government published a revised version of the 1991 regulations, highlighting the continuing importance of dam-induced resettlement processes. Among other modifications, the new regulations raised the amount of compensation paid to resettled people, clarified the bureaucratic structure of resettlement administration, and introduced a more "human-oriented" resettlement system (State Council, 1991, 2006a).

In China, the social aspects of dam-induced resettlement have been attracting increasing attention among Chinese policymakers, and this development gives rise to several questions. First of all, given that China is governed by an authoritarian regime that does not necessarily respond to its citizens' needs, why did the Chinese government decide to introduce more socially oriented resettlement policies? If the new policies are not intended as a response to citizens' (or resettled people's) needs, towards whom (or what) are they directed? If the new policies are in fact designed to respond to resettled people's needs, do they represent a general shift within the leadership towards socially sustainable development, or is hydropower development a special case? If so, why? Second, how did the changes in policy come about, and what sort of actors took part in designing the new policies? Particularly during the planning and construction phases of the Three Gorges Dam in Sichuan, and projects such as the Manwan Dam in Yunnan, civil society organizations drew attention to the negative social and environmental consequences of large dam projects. In this way, NGOs, the media, and peripheral government officials managed to influence policymaking in the field of hydropower development, but the question remains as to whether they have had a similar influence on dam-induced resettlement policymaking. There have been indications, for several years now, that Chinese and international NGOs' engagement with the sensitive topic of resettlement has decreased, but if this is the case, why is the Chinese central government still seeking to improve the resettlement regulations?

By examining policy changes and the formation of an organizational field in the area of reservoir resettlement over the last six decades in China, the present chapter represents a first attempt to answer at least some of the questions posed above. It aims to show which actors took part in this process of policy formation and attempts to answer the question of why the Chinese government is increasingly developing more socially oriented resettlement policies. The present chapter aims to analyze the issues that have played a role in the formation of an organizational field of resettlement in China and the extent to which the composition of institutional entrepreneurs and other actors (i.e., field-makers and field-takers) has changed in the course of field formation. The present chapter therefore serves as background information to the chapters to come, providing an analysis on who drives dam-induced resettlement policy in China, and what changes these actors have brought about over the past six decades. The actors themselves, as well as the institutional structure underlying dam-induced resettlement, are introduced in Chapter 4.

The next section introduces four stages of organizational field formation in the area of dam-induced resettlement in China. The findings of this analysis are subsequently discussed and it is shown that, since the beginning of the reform period, dam-induced resettlement has become much more regularized. However, despite the huge improvements that have taken place, in China's resettlement policy, currently the organizational field of resettlement in China is dominated by state organs that are in favor of large dams, rather than by governmental actors with the mandate of protecting resettled people.

Evolution of resettlement policy

As of July 2006, a total of 25 million people had been resettled in the course of water resource projects in China, of whom 22.9 million were rural migrants. It was estimated that the dams being planned at that time would require the resettlement of another 600,000 people (Du et al., 2011: 6). China's authorities acknowledge that a great number of people have been resettled in an unsatisfactory way, mainly due to the fact that, traditionally, the construction phases of dam projects have been given more attention than resettlement processes (Heggelund, 2004: 62).

As Figure 3.1 shows, dam-induced resettlement policy in China has evolved in four distinct phases. The following sections discuss this evolution as well as the different issues at stake in each of the four stages identified and the various field-takers and field-makers involved.[1] In China, as in most other countries, there are great discrepancies between policy targets and policy outcomes. The titles of the four stages of organizational field formation[2] represent the focus of the policies introduced in each phase rather than the actual situation and results of policy implementation.

Stage one: construction (1953–1980)

In 1953, China's Government Administration Council introduced the first resettlement regulations, which stipulated that compensation must be paid for land

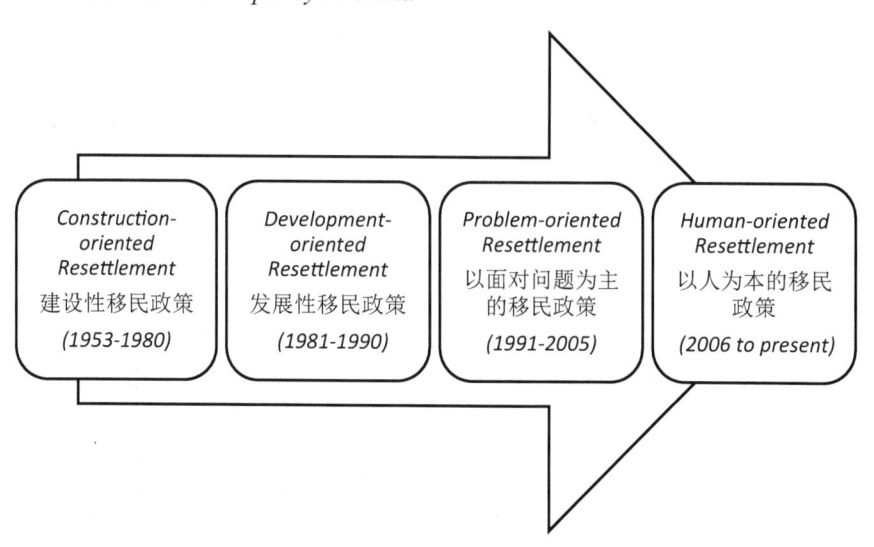

Figure 3.1 Evolution of dam-induced resettlement policy (1953 to present day)
Source: Author, based on Wang (2010).

appropriated for construction projects. First adopted in 1953, and then amended in 1958, the Measures for Land Appropriation in National Construction (*Guojia jianshe tudi banfa*) stipulated that the living standards of those who have to be resettled should not be worsened by resettlement and that compensation should be calculated according to the loss in land suffered by the resettled people as a result of inundation. The amount of compensation should be the average annual output value of the expropriated land for the three to five years preceding such expropriation. This was changed to two to four years in 1958. Another change concerned the ownership of land, which by then mostly belonged to the communes rather than to individuals. Individuals were to receive compensation only if the expropriated land belonged to them or if they, as members of the commune from which the land was taken, were directly affected by the expropriation (Xinhua, n.d.).

On the whole, during this first stage of resettlement policymaking, China's overall economic development model followed a pattern of short-term planning processes, which had a negative effect on resettlement communities. More than 20 reservoirs were built around this time, causing the resettlement of more than 30,000 people for whom, Wang reports, the compensation amounted to merely 100 to 300 yuan per person. Later, during the 1960s, compensation paid for individual property rose to between 300 and 500 yuan and reached about twice this amount (600 to 1200 yuan) during the 1970s (Wang, 2010: 78–79).

Apart from this regulation, resettlement before the 1980s has been regarded as an unsuccessful endeavor, even by Chinese officials (Heggelund, 2004: 62). Wang even argues that until the 1980s, China did not have any specialized resettlement rules or regulations or standards regarding resettlement planning, let alone any appropriate standard for resettlement compensation (Wang, 2010: 78).

The leading field-maker during that time was the State Council, while the field-takers were composed of the departments responsible for construction projects requiring resettlement as well as the local governments and People's Committees responsible for making the preparations for resettlement and abiding by decisions related to water resources development that were made at the center in Beijing.

During the time of the Great Leap Forward and the Cultural Revolution, the main purpose of resettlement was to remove people from the land needed for construction projects, without providing them with support to rebuild their livelihoods. The needs of the resettled people were not taken into consideration and resettlement funds were used for other purposes than resettlement compensation. One typical example was the Sanmenxia Dam on the Yellow River, which was completed in 1960 and led to 400,000 people being resettled without any compensation being paid to them (Heggelund, 2004: 62–63).

Due to the lack of adequate planning and compensation mechanisms for development-induced resettlement, the living conditions of the resettled people have constantly been precarious. This is why, after economic and political reforms were introduced in 1978, state organs started to consider introducing measures that would ameliorate the situation.

Stage two: development (1981–1990)

During the 1980s, China was not the only country that ramped up its dam-building activities. Dams and other large-scale infrastructure projects were built all over the world, causing scholars and social activists to refer to the 1980s as a "decade of displacement" (Dwivedi, 2002). The World Bank has long been one of the major donors to these large-scale infrastructure projects and, as a result, has been able to influence the way in which aid recipients carry out project design. In the context of resettlement, the World Bank began to work on and formulate a policy on involuntary resettlement in the 1980s (World Bank, 2012), and this influenced resettlement policymaking in China. According to its own reports, the World Bank has cooperated with Chinese organizations in planning and implementing resettlement since 1984, when the Lubuge hydropower project was approved. Subsequently, World Bank policy papers on resettlement were translated into Chinese and used in training workshops (World Bank, 1993: 188).

In addition to these international influences, policy decisions at the national level and developments at the local level in China have also spurred the formation of an organizational field in dam-induced resettlement. At the domestic level, the resettlement problems caused by the Sanmenxia hydropower project became apparent. Throughout the 1980s, villagers from Shaanxi, who had been resettled in the course of dam construction, moved back to the Sanmenxia reservoir area, because the water level of the dam was lower than had originally been planned. On their way back, the villagers had to face police blockades and the military as well as state farms, which by then had occupied their former land. In official terms, these events were referred to as the "reverse flow of reservoir resettlers (*shuiku yimin daoliu*)" (Jun, 2000).

Against this background, the State Council, together with related ministries including the Ministry of Finance and the Ministry of Water Resources and Electric Power, began to design policy frameworks for dam-induced resettlement. A notification (*Guanyu cong shuidian fadian chengben zhong tiqu kuqu weihu jijin de tongzhi*) issued in 1981 by the Ministry of Electric Power Industry and the Ministry of Finance stipulated that all hydropower stations have to allocate 0.001 yuan per kWh for a so-called reservoir maintenance fund, which was to improve living conditions in reservoir resettlement areas and prevent social instability (Ministry of Finance and Ministry of Electric Power Industry, 1981).[3] Furthermore, in 1982, the State Council announced the "Regulations for Land Appropriation in National Construction (*Guojia jianshe zhongyong tudi tiaoli*)," which led to two major changes for people being resettled in the course of hydropower development: First, with regard to the standard for land compensation, the regulations stipulated that the compensation for land would be three to six times the average annual output value of the expropriated land for the preceding three years. In addition, resettlement compensation was now to be paid in addition to compensation for land. The former would be two to three times the average annual output value per *mu* for the three years preceding expropriation. Second, the regulations stipulated that the Ministry of Water Resources and Electric Power (MWREP)[4] and the state organs responsible for land management would have to jointly formulate the "Measures for Land Appropriation and Resettlement Induced by Large-Sized and Medium-Sized Water Conservancy and Hydropower Projects (*Dazhongxing shuili shuidian gongcheng jianshe zhengdi buchang he yiminanzhi banfa*)" (Law110, n.d.). This was the time when a specific resettlement policy began to emerge.

In 1984, the MWREP established new reservoir resettlement design requirements (*Shuili shuidian gongcheng shuiku yanmo chuli sheji guifan*), which asked planners to minimize resettlement, maintain the real income of resettled people, compensate lost assets at replacement cost, pay attention to the special needs of resettled minorities, and design housing that conformed to local styles. Furthermore, the regulations required that resettlement planning and project design should take place simultaneously.

Until then, central government policies had mainly paid attention to reservoirs and their maintenance. It was not until 1985, when the Central Finance Leading Small Group held a conference on reservoir resettlement problems, that resettled people themselves began to occupy a central position in policies (Zhang, 2008). Subsequent policies by the MWREP, such as the "Report on Paying Close Attention to Handling the Resettlement Problems Induced by Reservoirs (*Guanyi zhuajin chuli shuikuyimin wenti de baogao*)," announced in 1986, demanded that projects include resettlement costs in the overall project budget and stipulated that any project design not containing appropriate resettlement plans should not be approved. The regulations also clarified and determined the responsibilities of the different state organs in resettlement work (Heggelund, 2004: 64; Wang, 2010: 82).

In additional regulations, such as, the "Detailed Rules Regarding the Investigation of an Index for Objects Inundated by Water Conservancy and Hydropower

Projects (*Shuili shuidian gongcheng yanmo shiwo zhibiao diaocha xice*)" and the "Measures for Cleaning up the Reservoir Area (*Shuiku kuqu qingli banfa*)," the MWREP further regulated the planning and analysis of the reservoir area as well as resettlement work (Wang, 2010: 83). Research in the area of resettlement was also strengthened when, in 1987, the China Society for Hydropower Engineering (*Zhongguo shuili fadian gongcheng xuehui*) established the Reservoir Economics Committee (*Shuiku jingji zhuanye weihuanhui*), responsible for research on resettlement policy, environmental capacity, enterprise development, and rural resettlement standards (China Power, 2007). Still today, with members from academia, design institutes, the government, and industry groups, this society continues to serve as an unofficial exchange platform that investigates all steps in the resettlement process and proposes policy recommendations accordingly (Interview, NJ130305).

All in all, during the 1980s, the resettlement problems caused by reservoirs and hydropower stations began to draw increasing attention from central and local governments. In 1986, the MWREP acknowledged that since 1949, the construction of more than 80,000 large, medium-sized, and small dams had caused the resettlement of more than 10 million people. Furthermore, in 1989, the State Council Economic Development in Poor Areas Leading Group acknowledged that more than seven million of China's "reservoir resettlers" were living in "extreme poverty" (Heggelund, 2004; Jun, 2000).

Since the existing resettlement planning posed a threat to the livelihood of the settlers, to the construction projects, and to social stability, state organs came up with new and more socially favorable regulations. In addition, the main method of resettlement compensation, the so-called lump sum (*yicixing*) compensation, was turned into more development-oriented compensation (*kaifaxing yimin fangzhen*). The former "lump sum" form of compensation consisted of an amount of money being given to the peasants according to the value of the land and house they had lost during resettlement, but the latter required that economic development plans be included in resettlement strategies and therefore also took into consideration the lives of the people after resettlement. This change to the way that the payment of compensation was made took place during the debates surrounding the Three Gorges Project and was mainly triggered by earlier negative experiences with resettlement schemes in China. What is more, for the first time in China's resettlement history, the issue of post-resettlement support was addressed by relevant regulations (Heggelund, 2004: 65–67).

In organizational terms, a resettlement bureaucracy began to emerge in which the responsibilities of the various actors were clearly defined. Policy implementation, since that time, has been taking place at different administrative levels, and specific offices have been established to undertake reservoir resettlement at all levels. However, most of the detailed work takes place at county, township, and village levels (Jun, 2000).

Whilst, during the first stage of resettlement policymaking in China, the actors responsible mainly focused on the construction processes and protection, during the 1980s, resettled people increasingly became the focus of attention. Although resettlement still continued to serve to protect hydropower development, the planning and construction processes were less short-sighted, now aimed at the long-term development of hydropower resources and reservoir regions. The 1981 regulations that apply to the setting up of the reservoir maintenance fund, for example, state that reservoir maintenance is necessary in order to "spur the development of the hydropower sector, strengthen reservoir protection, and solve remaining problems in the reservoir area" (Ministry of Finance and Ministry of Electric Power Industry, 1981).

As a result of a more developmental approach being adopted for resettlement and reservoir management, the focus of the organizational field changed during the 1980s. Not only this, apart from the regulative aspect of improved policies, a normative system of resettlement began to emerge when the Reservoir Economics Committee was set up and tasked with research related to hydropower development and resettlement. As far as the field-makers (or institutional entrepreneurs) are concerned, however, few changes could be observed since the leading field-makers and field-takers remained the same. Policies and regulations were still developed by the State Council and relevant ministries, while according to the new Water Law, local governments were responsible for policy implementation (National People's Congress, 1988).

Stage three: problem-specific (1991–2005)

During the 1980s a basic framework for reservoir-induced resettlement compensation was already being developed, in the form of the first specific rules on resettlement planning, implementation, and compensation: the "Regulations for Land Appropriation and Resettlement Induced by Large- and Medium-Sized Water Conservancy and Hydropower Projects (*Dazhongxing shuili shuidian gongcheng jianshe zhengdi buchang he yiminanzhi tiaoli*)." The State Council announced these regulations in 1991, which marks the beginning of the third stage of resettlement field formation in China (State Council, 1991).

At the international level, the 1990s have been described as a "decade of popular resistance to displacement" in contrast to the decade of displacement during the 1980s. Resistance to displacement and large construction projects that neglected social issues intensified, causing the World Bank to undertake a review of involuntary resettlement in projects that the World Bank supported and to publish a report on involuntary resettlement in China (World Bank, 1993). World Bank policy had an influence on the way that Chinese actors designed resettlement policy during the 1980s. This was even more marked the 1990s, when China became the world's largest recipient of World Bank aid for dam construction. For example, in 1991, the World Bank agreed to partly finance the Xiaolangdi hydropower station along the Yellow River. In return, the World Bank asked the Chinese government to introduce elements of the bank's own resettlement policies into Chinese regulations (Webber & McDonald, 2004: 676). One of these elements was the third-party monitoring of resettlement processes, which was first applied during resettlement for the Xiaolangdi Dam and has since become an official requirement for all resettlement processes in China (Interview, NJ130305).

At the national level, resettlement policy and related activities in the field of dam-induced resettlement were mainly focused on the Three Gorges Project, which was approved in 1992 (Xinhua, 2003). In April 1993, the State Council set up the Three Gorges Construction Committee (*Sanxia gongcheng jianshe weiyuanhui*), which was the decision-making organ for the Three Gorges Dam at the central level. A few months later, in August, the State Council published the Resettlement Regulations for the Yangtze-Three Gorges Construction Project (*Changjiang sanxia gongcheng jianshe yimin tiaoli*) that governed the resettlement work of the project until 2001, when the regulations were amended (Heggelund, 2004).[5]

Government agencies not only strengthened the existing regulative framework by designing new policies but also further developed the normative aspect of resettlement by improving research and training in the field of dam-induced resettlement. In 1992, the State Council published "Opinions on Strengthening Reservoir Resettlement Work (*Guanyu jiaqiang shuiku yimin gongzuo de ruogan yijian*)" and the Ministry of Water Resources (MWR) opened the National Research Center for Resettlement at Hohai University in Nanjing. Since then, the center has been advising the State Council and leading ministries on resettlement work in construction projects and has been undertaking theoretical and practical research in the field. In addition, the center has introduced master's and doctoral programs on "resettlement science (*yimin kexue*)" (Hohai University, 2012; State Council, 1992). Graduates from Hohai University can be found among the resettlement officials at central government level, within the resettlement offices of the big hydropower corporations and design institutes as well as in international organizations, such as the World Bank and the Asian Development Bank (Interview, NJ030304).

Also in 1992, the MWR and Shaanxi Province jointly established the Cadre Training Center for Reservoir Resettlement (*Shuiku yimin ganbu peixun zhongxin*). Previously, resettlement officials were recruited among former members of the Chinese military. These officials were placed in their new jobs without any kind of training and themselves regarded resettlement as an easy job that mostly involved drinking with dam migrants in order to persuade them to move. At times, dam migrants were more familiar with the resettlement policies than the cadres themselves. During the resettlement preparations for the Three Gorges Dam, the government realized that better trained local resettlement cadres were needed, and for this reason, the Cadre Training Center was tasked with "responsibility for implementing development-oriented resettlement and for educating cadres in the areas of economic development and the commodity economy, in order to ensure that the resettled people can become wealthy (*zhifu*)" (Interview, NJ130304; Xinhua, 1992). Governments at each administrative level, from the provincial level downwards, provide funds for training cadres either in Shaanxi or at Hohai University in Nanjing. Training courses are organized according to local cadres' needs. At Hohai, there are courses on specific topics, such as resettlement policy implementation, international resettlement experiences, best practices from within China, and communication strategies with dam migrants, among others. In addition, Hohai offers more general classes on resettlement policies and the overall resettlement management system. The latter are necessary because the fluctuation of resettlement cadres is high, and new cadres from various bureaus enter the system without becoming familiarized with it first (Interview, NJ130304).

The new millennium began with the announcement of the Western Development Strategy (*Xibu da kaifa*) by the central government. The aim of this strategy, which was introduced in 2000, was not only to develop China's western provinces, but also to promote the transfer of energy from the oil- and water-rich west to the industrialized east. The strategy of sending energy from west to east (*xidian dongsong*), therefore, became an important project within the Western Development Strategy (People, 2001). This entailed the need for actively developing energy resources in the west, including establishing the right conditions for this development. By 2001, the MWR had realized that past resettlement processes had caused problems that needed to be addressed in order to continue hydropower development, and this resulted in the ministry introducing the "10th Five-Year Plan Reservoir Resettlement Work Goals (*"Shiwu" shuidian yimin gongzuo mubiao*), which included the handling of "left-over problems of reservoir resettlement (*shuiku yimin yiliu wenti*)" (*Renmin Ribao*, 2001). This new focus on "left-over problems" was also reflected in subsequent policies published by various ministries (Q. Wang & Li, 2011).[6]

The emergence of these policies was accompanied by several incidents at central and local levels. First of all, in 2003 and 2004, Yu Xiaogang of the Kunming-based NGO Green Watershed together with the Green Earth Volunteers organized villagers to voice their grievances about the planned Xiaowan Dam and the Nu River Project in Yunnan. The NGO complied a report on the social consequences of the Manwan Dam[7] for the resettled people, in order to raise awareness among the people to be resettled in the course of future dam projects as well as the central government (Interview, TP122903). Second, in 2004, the biggest demonstrations after Tiananmen took place in Sichuan where the people organized their own demonstrations against the planned Pubugou hydropower project. Finally, also in 2004, Wen Jiabao ordered the suspension of the Nu River Project due to shortcomings that became evident in the required environmental impact assessment of the dams (e.g., Mertha, 2008; Mertha & Lowry, 2006).

In the course of this increasingly successful activism by NGOs, representatives of the hydropower and resettlement bureaucracy have become suspicious about the work of NGOs and their involvement with local communities. Advocates of dam construction projects do not only fear an increase in the costs of resettlement, if civil society groups continue to unveil the negative effects of resettlement and the need for higher amounts of compensation: They are also afraid that the NGOs will drive a wedge between the local cadres and the migrant communities, inciting the latter to resist resettlement (Interview, NJ130304). Officials also argue that since government policies towards dams are frequently improving, the work of NGOs is becoming redundant. In the past, resettlement processes caused many problems due to the lack of adequate legislation and the inability of local cadres to deal with resettlement issues, but now, the resettlement bureaucracy has introduced a number of policies that protect the rights of migrant communities while at the same time constantly improving the capabilities of local resettlement cadres.

In general, the period between 1991 and 2005 saw the strengthening of the organizational field of reservoir resettlement. The above-mentioned policies increased the compensation for loss of land that was paid to migrant communities and improved the organizational structure of the resettlement bureaucracy. In particular, the 2002 "Notification on the Distribution of the Provisional Measures Governing Land Appropriation in the Course of Hydropower Construction Projects (*Guanyu yinfa shuidian gongcheng jianshe zhengdi yimin gongzuo zanxing guanli banfa de tongzhi*)" published by the State Planning Commission clarified the distribution of responsibilities among government and construction agencies. According to this notification, the government at different levels is responsible for managing and implementing resettlement work, while project developers are required to take part in the work. Developers have to set up resettlement plans and cooperate with the resettlement bureaucracy during the various stages of implementation and supervision (State Planning Commission, 2002).

This meant that field-makers during this third stage of resettlement field formation changed only little. The State Council and relevant ministries were still implementing the policies, although now the State Planning Commission and the State Economic and Trade Commission also played a role until their tasks were taken over by the National Development and Reform Commission (NDRC) in 2003. In addition, civil society organizations, through their involvement in protests against dam projects, pressured the government to design better policies directed at resettlement work. As a result, however, these same organizations have been discredited by representatives in the field, making it more difficult for NGOs to gain a seat at the policymaking table. Field-takers remained the same, with local governments and resettlement offices at county, township, and village levels undertaking resettlement implementation and project developers taking part in resettlement work. However, each of their tasks was now spelled out more clearly.

Another new attribute of this third stage was that, from the 1990s onwards, not only the resettlement process itself was governed by respective policies. The problems created during previous unsuccessful resettlement work were now acknowledged and addressed through several policies. This included the so-called left-over problems in reservoir areas as well as shortcomings in the planning and implementation processes of resettlement schemes. Resettlement work was no longer confined to the relocation of people but was expanded to include pre- and post-resettlement phases.

In 1996, moreover, the Resettlement Bureau of the Three Gorges Project introduced a list of prohibitions for departments involved in resettlement work and called for improvements in resettlement supervision, particularly the appropriate usage of resettlement funds (RMRB, 1996). A framework for research and teaching in the field was also introduced. As already mentioned, resettlement work was regarded as a scientific and technical undertaking that mainly involved economic rather than social factors.

Stage four: people-focused (2006–present)

One critical event that marks the beginning of stage four in resettlement field formation was the publication of the amended resettlement regulations from 1991. The new regulations, which were published by the State Council in 2006, included most of the policy inputs published during the 1990s, reflecting the problems related to resettlement that had previously been identified. Compared with the 1991 regulations, the new policy went into much more detail regarding resettlement planning, post-resettlement support and the monitoring process. There was a separate section for each of these topics in the regulations, highlighting the importance of the pre- and post-resettlement phases today (State Council, 1991, 2006a).

The principles governing compensation and resettlement work changed during the fifteen years after the first regulations for reservoir resettlement were published. While the 1991 regulations focused on the state, demanding that "the resettlement community and the host community have to conform to the way that interests are arranged in the state as a whole" (State Council, 1991: Section 1, Article 4, No. 1), the 2006 regulations focused on the resettled people themselves, stating that "resettlement and compensation shall be human-oriented [*yiren weiben*]" and that "the legitimate rights of the resettled people have to be guaranteed and their livelihood and development needs satisfied" (State Council, 2006a: Section 1, Article 4, No. 1). The third principle of the new regulations, in addition, required that the scale of resettlement should be controlled – a demand that was lacking in 1991.

Regarding the organizational framework of resettlement and the allocation of responsibilities within the bureaucratic system, the new regulations includes those already introduced in the 2002 "Notification on the Distribution of the Provisional Measures Governing Land Appropriation in the Course of Hydropower Construction Projects," which lent them even greater legal validity. According to the new regulations,

> [t]he State Council administrative framework of water resources and hydropower project resettlement is responsible for the nation-wide management and supervision of resettlement work induced by large- and medium-sized water resources and hydropower projects. County-level governments and higher-level local governments are responsible for organization and leadership of resettlement induced by large- and medium-sized water conversancy and hydropower projects in their respective administrative regions. Resettlement mechanisms stipulated by provinces, autonomous regions and by municipalities directly under the supervision of the central government are in charge of managing and supervising resettlement caused by large- and medium-sized water conversancy and hydropower projects in their respective administrative region.

> (State Council, 2006a: Section 1, Article 5)

Other changes included the amount of compensation paid for land, which was increased from three to four times the average output value of the land to sixteen times its average output value during the three years prior to the land being expropriated. Furthermore, specific standards governing the maximum amount of compensation to be paid to the resettled people were removed from the new regulations in 2006.

As already mentioned, the new regulations included a separate section regulating post-resettlement support. In 2006, in order to further strengthen post-resettlement support and integrate the different policies that had governed "left-over problems" until then, the State Council published the "Opinions on Improving Post-Reservoir-Resettlement-Support Policies (*Guowuyuan guanyu wanshan shuiku yimin houqi fuchi zhengce de yijian*)." As of July 2006, resettled people who had been resettled before that date, as well as newly resettled people, would be entitled to 600 yuan resettlement support each year for twenty years. Officially, the aim of this financial support is to "lift resettled people out of poverty, foster economic development in the reservoir and resettlement regions, guarantee the healthy development of the water resources and hydropower sector, build a socialist harmonious society, and improve post-resettlement support for large- and medium-sized reservoirs" (State Council, 2006b). In subsequent years, the NDRC, the MWR, and the Ministry of Finance published a series of policy papers, supplementing the new post-resettlement support policy and clarifying its financial and practical implementation (see Wang, 2010).

Apart from strengthening post-resettlement support, in this fourth stage of resettlement field formation, the State Council and related ministries increasingly paid attention to pre-resettlement work as reflected in the 2010 "Provisional Measures on Pre-Resettlement Work of Large- and Medium-sized Water Resources and Hydropower Projects (*Dazhongxing shuili shuidian gongcheng yimin anzhi qianqi gongzuo guanli zanxing banfa*)" published by the MWR (Wang, 2010).

Another critical event that occurred during this fourth stage was the State Council's official acknowledgement of the problems caused by the Three Gorges Dam. After a cabinet meeting held in May 2011, the government released a statement promising to increase efforts to reduce the negative environmental and social impacts in areas affected by the dam, offering assurances that the government would undertake efforts to curb water pollution, promote biological diversity, and raise the standard of living of relocated residents, by "stick[ing] to the principle of putting people first and promoting sustainable development in post-construction work" (Xinhua, 2011). It is likely that this statement has further triggered policy efforts that have come to the fore over the past years. One of these efforts is the "Notification on the Tasks Surrounding the 'First Resettle then Construct' Effort of Hydropower Construction Projects (*Shuidian gongcheng xian yimin hou jianshe youguan gongzuo de tongzhi*)" published by the NDRC in February 2012. The new policy includes demands to

> treat resettlement from beginning to end as an important part of hydropower projects; make resettlement work a priority; carry out resettlement according to the previously worked out resettlement plan and coordinate the resettlement process with project construction; guarantee the lawful rights and

interests of the resettled people and, under the premise of completed resettlement work, actively achieve hydropower development.

(National Development and Reform Commission [NDRC], 2012)

The policy therefore aims to give resettlement a prominent position within the hydropower construction process, which could be seen as a response to former dam projects that treated resettlement as a troublesome byproduct of hydropower development and did not pay sufficient attention to its successful implementation. In order to better monitor resettlement work, the MWR has additionally published the "Provisional Measures on Managing the Inspection of Resettlement Processes in the Course of Large- and Medium-sized Hydropower Construction Projects (*Dazhongxing shuili shuidian gongcheng yimin anzhi yanshou guanli zanxing banfa*)" (Xu & Mu, 2012).

Since 2006, the State Council and the leading ministries acting as field-makers have stepped up efforts to improve resettlement planning, implementation, post-resettlement support, and monitoring. Although pre- and post-resettlement support already played a role in stage three of resettlement field formation, it has now been granted a more prominent place in the respective policies, which also provide a more detailed account of how to carry out the planning, implementing, and monitoring of resettlement work.

During stage three, policymaking agencies in Beijing were influenced by World Bank resettlement policies, but China is now funding its own dams. Resettlement policies are therefore not based entirely on requirements issued by the World Bank or other international development agencies but rather based on China's own experience in dam construction and resettlement. Past failures, particularly problems related to the Three Gorges Dam resettlement work, are constantly spurring policymaking. In addition, a number of high profile protest cases in the course of dam-induced resettlement as well as the large number of people that have to be resettled for single dam projects have caused the water conservancy bureaucracy to improve resettlement regulations. Although other infrastructure projects also cause resettlement, so far, on the national level, there are no other resettlement regulations that specifically cover these projects. As a consequence, resettlement for other development projects is governed by the less specific Land Administration Law (*Tudi guanli fa*) and the less authoritative Guiding Opinions on Improving Land Requisition Compensation and Resettlement (*Guanyu wanshan zhengdi buchang anzhi zhidu de zhidao yijian*) issued by the Ministry of Land and Resources.[8]

The Chinese hydropower bureaucracy has not only been undergoing continued policy learning processes, Chinese experts in dam-induced resettlement have in recent years also begun to disseminate the country's experiences with dam building to international organizations. During conferences held jointly by the World Bank and national government bodies like the NDRC and the Ministry of Land and Resources, domestic resettlement experts report on their experiences with implementing World Bank resettlement policies and raise suggestions on how to improve them. Thus, over the past years, policy learning has turned into a mutual learning process in which both international policies are integrated into national policymaking and Chinese experiences are built on to improve international resettlement policies (Interview, NJ130304).

In the context of the organizational structure, the fourth stage has not seen any substantial changes so far. The State Council together with the NDRC and the MWR are still the leading field-makers. With regard to field-takers, local governments, and resettlement offices at county, township, and village levels remain responsible for undertaking resettlement implementation and project developers are required to take part in resettlement work. The new resettlement regulations introduced in 2006, however, now differentiate between the sending governments and the host governments in the resettlement process, acknowledging the fact that resettled people do not only have to be relocated from a certain place but also integrated into a new one.

One notable difference between the third and fourth stages is the lack of NGO involvement. Although previously active NGOs still engage in activities concerning dam building such as study tours to resettlement regions, they do not organize any projects that directly involve resettled people and also refrain from visiting dams and villages in the vicinity of those dams that are guarded by military personnel (*wujing*) such as the Nuozhadu Dam.[9] This is due to the sensitive nature of dam-induced resettlement, which has been perceived to be higher in recent years after activists had successfully challenged hydropower development and after violent protests had erupted in the course of the Menglian incident (see Chapter 5) (Interviews, BJ130903, KM130222).

In the course of the successful activism by NGOs during stage three, representatives of the hydropower and resettlement bureaucracy have become suspicious about the work of NGOs and their involvement with local communities, which is why, over the past years, NGO representatives have been under strict government supervision both in the cities where their representative offices are located as well as in resettlement villages (Interview, KM120707). Advocates of dam construction projects fear an increase in the costs for resettlement, if civil society groups continue to unveil the negative effects of resettlement and the need for higher amounts of compensation. In addition, local cadres fear retribution, if the problems surrounding resettlement work in their jurisdictions are exposed. Accordingly, after Green Watershed had conducted a social impact assessment of the Manwan Dam, the provincial government announced a ban on any future assessments. This was because the report prepared by the NGO revealed that about 2,500 people had not received appropriate compensation, forcing the government to spend an additional amount of 800 million yuan on the resettled people (Interview, KM120707).

The mutual mistrust and lack of understanding between industry representatives and NGOs becomes apparent during interviews with both parties. Each party accuses the other of pursuing their own material interests to the detriment of the resettlement communities. Industry representatives frequently claim that NGOs' understanding of existing laws and policies is insufficient, which is why they cannot stand in for the resettled people in any adequate manner. Officials also argue that, since government policies towards dams are frequently improving, the work of NGOs is becoming redundant. In the past, it is argued, resettlement processes caused many problems due to the lack of adequate legislation and the inability of local cadres to deal with resettlement issues, but now the resettlement bureaucracy has introduced a number of policies that protect the rights of migrant communities while at the same time constantly improving the capabilities of local resettlement cadres (Interviews, NJ130304, NJ130305, BJ130307).

Future policy change

All in all, resettlement policy has undergone significant changes over recent decades (cf. Table 3.1). Since the last major policy change in 2006, the central government has continued to update its regulations on dam-induced resettlement. At the same time, the MWR has been undertaking investigations during ongoing resettlement processes to identify the current problems in policy implementation, and to prepare for another round of policy updates. MWR officials take part in study tours to resettlement villages all over the country in order to find out exactly how policy is implemented on the ground as well as the problems that occur. In addition, the ministry holds conferences at the central level to discuss policy issues with the hydropower and land bureaucracies (Interview, NJ130304, Ministry of Water Resources 2013).

These conferences at the central level are at the top of a hierarchy of conferences held at each administrative level all the way down to county level. During each of these conferences, all related departments with a stake in hydropower development and resettlement take part to identify and discuss policy problems. Once the problems have been identified, the conference participants work together to design research projects that take these problems into account, find ways to resolve them, and formulate specific clauses for policy amendments. Every participating department is subsequently responsible for different parts of the research project.

For example, one problem that has been identified in the 2006 resettlement regulations is the requirement to maintain or increase migrants' standard of living after resettlement. While this is a goal to be strived for, the actors responsible for resettlement have experienced difficulty in carrying out an appropriate assessment of the standard of living of migrant communities. The policy does not stipulate whether the standard should be based merely on financial means or whether other social and psychological aspects should also be referred to. And, even if it were based only on the financial means of resettlement communities, would a per capita increase in income of only 1 yuan per month count as an increase in the standard of living? Policymakers have been discussing this issue and, as a result, have designed a research project that analyzes standards of living in resettlement communities. Other problems that have been identified during recent rounds of conferences is the limited availability of land for migrant communities, the protection of minority cultures in the course of resettlement, and the provision of social security. After the government departments responsible

Table 3.1 Changes in Chinese resettlement regulations after 1978

Year	Legislation	Content
1981	Reservoir Maintenance Fund	0.001 yuan per kWh cash compensation, infrastructure (drinking water, transport)
1982	Regulations for Land Appropriation in National Construction	Compensation standard increased and divided into compensation for land and for resettlement as such; specific regulations for resettlement and land appropriation in the course of dam projects to be set up
1986	Reservoir Construction Fund	0.004 yuan per kWh = 240 million yuan per year for people resettled before 1985
1986	First Land Administration Law, which contains Resettlement Regulations	Establishment of resettlement offices
1991	Regulations for Land Appropriation and Resettlement Induced by Large- and Medium-Sized Water Conservancy and Hydropower Projects	Post-relocation support and income generation (5–10 years)
1996	Post-Relocation Support Fund	0.005 yuan per kWh for projects in service and approved between 1985–1995
1998	Land Administration Law amended through ADB Technical Assistance	More transparency and compensation
2006	1991 Regulations updated	Monitoring and evaluation; post-relocation support fund: 600 yuan per year for 20 years
2006	Opinions on Improving Post-Reservoir-Resettlement-Support Policies	Migrants entitled to 600 yuan of annual post-resettlement support for 20 years
2012	Notification on the Tasks Surrounding the 'First Resettle then Construct' Effort of Hydropower Construction Projects	Resettlement receives prominent position in construction process; resettlement prioritized
Under consideration	Amendment of Land Administration Law	Flexible compensation criteria to improve implementation and compensation
Under consideration	Amendment of 2006 Regulations	In accordance with new Land Administration Law, specification of migrants' standard of living; resettlement without provision of land; unification of compensation standard for different construction projects

Sources: Hensengerth, 2010; Interview, NJ130304; National Development and Reform Commission (NDRC), 2012; State Council, 2006b.

for the investigations into these problems have achieved results, the conference participants come together again to discuss and to summarize policy recommendations for higher levels of government (Interviews, NJ120813, BJ120817, NJ130304, BJ130307).

Policymakers are currently working on another amendment for central-level resettlement regulations, and in the course of this work, officials from central-level departments have to travel to various areas to study the local processes of policy implementation. At the same time, further investigations are being conducted at each government level, and reports are being submitted by lower levels of government to the upper levels. In these reports, the local cadres sum up the specific problems that have been noted during policy implementation. The results of these reports are not only fed into central-level policies, but the departments responsible in each province collect information from the prefectures and counties within their jurisdiction in order to refine local resettlement policies and bring them into line with the more general central-level regulations.

Authoritarian government and socially responsible policies

In this chapter, the policy changes in the area of reservoir resettlement have been examined that have taken place during the last six decades in China, and this has shown that policymaking has evolved in four main stages, each of which has been marked by critical events and related trajectory activities that have contributed to the formation of an organizational field of resettlement. Over the past six decades, field definitions have changed according to new issues that have emerged in China's local, national, and international environment.

At first, China aimed at fast-paced development that neglected resettlement communities. Until the 1980s, a regulative framework for resettlement was basically lacking. During the second stage, new policies for resettlement were developed in line with World Bank requirements as well as with national developments in China, in particular the planning of the Three Gorges Dam and local incidents related to the Sanmenxia hydropower project. Not only did a regulative framework begin to emerge, but slowly also a normative system involving research on resettlement issues. During the third stage, institutional entrepreneurs within the field of resettlement began to focus on the problems that had arisen as a result of previous resettlement processes, further developing a regulative and normative framework for dam-induced resettlement. Resettlement was seen as the cause of both economic and social problems that had to be managed scientifically. In order to prevent these problems from arising in the future, the fourth stage of policymaking has concentrated on preventive measures by improving pre- and post-resettlement work as well as monitoring processes. The focus is now on the people themselves rather than only on hydropower development and reservoir maintenance.

Therefore, along with China's overall development, resettlement policy has made great strides over the past decades. In contrast to these changes and this regulative and normative evolution, however, institutional entrepreneurs in the field of resettlement have stayed the same. Brint and Karabel argue that organizational fields become "arenas of power relations" in which a variety of actors compete over issue definition (1991: 355). In the case of environmental protection, for example, the State Environmental Protection Agency has gradually become a full-fledged ministry. Although the Ministry of Environmental Protection is still weak, it is nevertheless able to pursue its own beliefs and values related to environmental protection (Child et al., 2007).

In the case of resettlement, there is no such independent organization. Resettlement Bureaus are under the authority of the Ministry of Water Resources, which is hugely in favor of large-scale dam projects (Mertha, 2008). While this might lead the ministry to improve resettlement policymaking and implementation in order to safeguard hydropower development, when it comes to deciding whether a controversial dam should be built or not, the decision will almost always be made in favor of project developers. There is no organization that exists solely for the purpose of resettlement that has the potential to limit the impact that various policies (no matter how advanced they are) have on actual resettlement practice in China.

In the early 2000s, the NGOs and the media exposed some of the problems that were arising during the resettlement process, which led the government to publish a more socially oriented resettlement policy in 2006. Although this process confirms the finding that the Chinese policy process has become increasingly pluralized, developments since 2006 counter this finding. In the field of dam-induced resettlement, the incentives for the Chinese government to design socially responsible resettlement policies have changed; previously, international donors, NGOs, the media, and peripheral officials put pressure on central government agencies to limit dam projects, but today, the imperative to construct large dams has become a generally accepted fact among the majority of policy actors. The Chinese government is therefore working towards creating an environment conducive to its hydropower development strategy. By designing socially responsible resettlement policies, conflicts that have the potential to jeopardize dam construction can be prevented. Instead of conflict-ridden negotiations, the policy process in the field of dam-induced resettlement is characterized by the general agreement of policy actors on the necessity of hydropower development. The work of the actors who are cooperating to design new policies therefore runs smoothly. In return, NGOs previously active in protecting the rights of resettled people are slowly being pushed out of the policy process, first, because government actors are taking on the task of improving resettlement policies on their own and, second, because several large protests related to resettlement work have led the government to frame dam-induced resettlement as an issue directly affecting social stability. NGOs have therefore become increasingly cautious when dealing with resettlement issues.

Notes

1 Field-makers are institutional entrepreneurs – which through rule-making, issue definition, and other activities – influence the formation of an organizational field. Other

actors are in the position of abiding by these rules and implementing established practices. The latter may be named "field-takers" (Child, Yuan, & Tsai, 2007).

2 Hoffmann argues that an organizational field does not necessarily develop around common technologies or industries but is "formed around the issues that become important to interests and objectives of a specific collective of organizations" (Hoffman, 1999: 352). Further, according to Scott, the notion of field "refers to the existence of a community of organizations that partakes of a common meaning system and whose participants interact more frequently and fatefully with one another than with actors outside the field" (1995: 207).

3 In 1986, this figure was increased to 0.004 yuan per kWh for all reservoirs and hydropower stations directly subordinate to the central government (Wang, 2010: 83).

4 In 1982, the former Ministry of Water Conservancy and the former Ministry of Electric Power were merged to become the Ministry of Water Resources and Electric Power (MWREP). Although the Chinese name continued to employ the term *shuili*, the official translation of the ministry changed from Ministry of Water Conservancy, to Ministry of Water Resources and Electric Power (Lieberthal & Oksenberg, 1988: 95–96).

5 For an in-depth analysis of the decision-making surrounding the Three Gorges Project, see Heggelund (2004).

6 In 2001, these ministries published the "Opinions on Quickly Resolving Left-over Resettlement Problems Caused by Projects of the Central Government" followed by "Regulations on Planning and Implementing the Handling of Left-over Resettlement Problems Caused by Projects of the Central Government" in 2003, and, finally, the "Provisions on Managing Training and Planning Fees for Handling Left-over Resettlement Problems Caused by Projects of the Central Government" (Wang, 2010).

7 The Manwan Dam was the first large dam to be constructed in Yunnan Province. Construction began in 1986.

8 Resettlement and land compensation for such projects are lower than for hydropower and water resources projects. According to Article 47 of the Land Administration Law, compensation for expropriated land shall be six to ten times the average annual output value of the expropriated land, calculated on the basis of three years preceding requisition, while resettlement compensation shall be four to six times this value (National People's Congress, 2004).

9 In fact, as I had been doing research in resettlement communities in Yunnan, when conducting interviews with NGO representatives, I was regarded as one of their informants for many developments on the ground rather than vice versa.

4 Hydropower development, resettlement, and the Nuozhadu Dam

The Nuozhadu Dam (NZD) is located along the lower reaches of the Lancang River[1] in Yunnan Province (see Figure 4.1). The project falls within the borders of the prefecture-level city of Pu'er. The dam represents the fifth of the originally planned eight-dam cascade along the Lancang River. In terms of its core wall, the Nuozhadu Dam is the highest rock-fill dam in Asia, the largest hydropower plant in Yunnan, and the fourth largest dam among those that have already been constructed or are currently under construction in China. With a planned total installed capacity of 5,850 megawatts,[2] it is the largest dam in the Lancang River basin. Investment in the dam is estimated to amount to 50 billion yuan – the largest investment in a single construction project in Yunnan (Yunnan Xinhua Net, 2011).

This chapter introduces the main features of the NZD project, including the planning and construction processes as well as the administrative processes related to resettlement. A special focus is placed on the various actors involved in these processes as well as on the accompanying regulations that govern resettlement in the NZD case. In this way, attention is drawn to the multiplicity of responsibilities that have to be shouldered by local actors once the decision has been made to construct a dam in their locality. At the same time, it is shown that these responsibilities are not matched with the authority required to guarantee the smooth progression of resettlement policy implementation.

The outline of the chapter is as follows: First, there is a brief description of the Chinese hydropower bureaucracy, including the most important actors involved in making decisions on the industry's development trajectory. This serves as a background for the second section, which introduces the Nuozhadu hydropower project as one part of the Lancang River dam cascade in Yunnan Province. This dam is not only important for Yunnan as a major energy generator in China, but also – and even more so – for the country's manufacturing base along the east coast (Magee, 2006b). The subsequent section introduces the Chinese resettlement bureaucracy with its various actors at different levels of the Chinese administrative hierarchy, including their respective roles and responsibilities, illustrating the top-down nature of resettlement planning that is also prevalent in hydropower development in general. The fourth section examines the situation of dam-induced resettlement in Pu'er, with a special focus on the Nuozhadu Project. This is followed by an

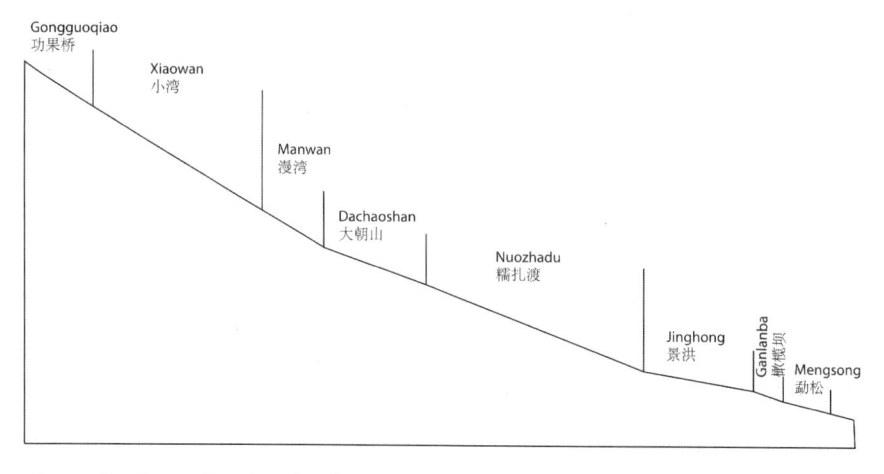

Figure 4.1 Comprehensive plan for hydropower development along the Lancang River
Source: Author.

analysis of the challenges faced by local governments in the context of resettlement policy implementation in recent years.

The Chinese hydropower bureaucracy

At the central level, the National Development and Reform Commission (NDRC) is responsible for assessing China's economic development and energy situation to decide whether dams should be constructed. In addition, the Ministries of Agriculture, Land and Resources, Environmental Protection, and Water Resources have to approve prefeasibility and feasibility studies, design plans, and a project application report for each dam project. Depending on the size of the project, the approval of the Water Resources Bureaus at different administrative levels is also required (Hensengerth, 2010: 4).[3]

At the central level, the seven basin commissions under the Ministry of Water Resources are responsible for managing river projects in China when these involve the major rivers that cross provincial boundaries. The commissions develop basin plans, including assessments of their hydropower potential. The reformed Water Law of 2002 requires project developers to submit their project plans to the appropriate commission in the region in which the dam is to be constructed. Since 2002,

Table 4.1 Decision-making authority of local governments

Government level	Wall height	Reservoir volume
Provincial Water Resources Bureau	More than 50 meters	10 million cubic meters
Prefecture Water Resources Bureau	30–50 meters	1–10 million cubic meters
County Water Resources Bureau	15–30 meters	100,000–1,000,000 cubic meters

Source: Based on Hensengerth (2010: 4).

five state-owned companies (China Huadian Group, China Huaneng Group, China Sanxia Group, China Guodian Group, and China Datang Group) have had the right to construct hydropower stations along China's major rivers. Their plans for hydropower development have to comply with the basin plans drawn up by the basin commissions, and the approval of the latter is also required. After deciding whether to approve a plan, the basin commission submits a report to the NDRC for further approval (see Mertha, 2008).

Once a project has been approved, the energy companies employ one of the design institutes belonging to the China Hydropower Engineering Consulting Group (Hydrochina) to develop a detailed plan for the dam, including the dam site and size as well as the details of resettlement. At the same time, the energy companies hire agencies to carry out the feasibility studies, which have to contain information on the technological, economic, environmental, and social aspects of the project. After these studies have been approved, the company compiles the project application report, including the environmental impact assessment (EIA) Report, which is compiled by a certified EIA agency (Mertha, 2008).

Apart from the NDRC, the major actors within China's hydropower bureaucracy who are also in favor of dam construction are the Ministry of Water Resources, with its seven water commissions, and the corresponding local-level Water Resources Bureaus, the local-level Development and Reform Commissions, and the above-mentioned five big power generation companies, which own majority stakes in companies responsible for hydropower development on China's major rivers (see Figure 4.2).[4] These were established in 2002, when the State Power Company of China (SPCC) was disbanded and its shares redistributed among the five power generation companies, two power grid companies (National Power Grid and China Southern Power Grid), and four auxiliary companies (see Mertha, 2008). These actors share the responsibility for planning and implementing projects along China's major rivers.[5]

When it comes to deciding whether or not large dams should be built, the conflicting views that exist within the government are clearly revealed. These are mainly due to the various organizational mandates that are imposed on the different state actors. The NDRC, for example, aims for fast-paced economic development without paying much attention to micro-level conditions for this sort of short-term growth, while China's Cultural Relics Bureau, Bureau of Seismology, infrastructure bureaucracy and especially the Ministry of Environmental Protection (MEP), are generally opposed to dam construction. Although similarly conflicting views are also found in other countries, the advocates of large hydropower projects, such as the NDRC, enjoy a higher standing within the Chinese bureaucracy than, for example, the MEP. Moreover, since the State Council controls the power companies through the State-Owned Assets Supervision and Administration Commission other ministries find it hard to regulate them. The companies' leadership is often staffed with influential people who have good connections within the government. For example, the former general manager of China Huaneng Group was Li Xiaopeng, the son of China's ex-premier, Li Peng, who has been an ardent supporter of the Three Gorges Dam (Hensengerth, 2010: 5–6; Mertha, 2008).

In order to better coordinate the different mandates of the actors involved in energy policy, in 2010, the State Council established the National Energy Commission (*Guojia nengyuan weiyuanhui*). The commission functions as an interministerial body made up of high-ranking officials from the State Council and all other ministerial-level actors involved in the energy bureaucracy. Currently, Premier Li Keqiang and Vice Premier Zhang Gaoli serve as the commission's director and deputy director, respectively. By establishing such a high-level body, the State Council can circumvent long-drawn negotiations between individual ministries and more effectively coordinate energy policy. Formerly, this task belonged to the less powerful National Energy Administration (*Guojia nengyuan ju*) – a vice-ministerial unit (*fubuji*) that now serves as the office (*bangongshi*) of the commission.

The Nuozhadu Dam

The preparatory work for hydropower development along the Lancang River was carried out during the 1950s, when the Chinese government started to explore the river's potential for electricity generation. In 1957, the Kunming Institute for Hydropower Survey and Design (*Kunming shuidian kance sheji yanjiuyuan*; hereafter, the Kunming Institute) dispatched an investigation group to undertake a general survey of the river's hydropower capacity. In 1979, the Ministry of Power Industry (*Dianli gongyebu*) added the Lancang River to its list of China's ten big hydropower construction bases. Six years later, the Yunnan provincial government established the Lancang River Basin Planning Commission (*Lancang jiang liuyu guihua weiyuanhui*) and after a further three years, in 1986, the Kunming Institute completed the "Planning Report for the Lower and Middle Reaches of the Lancang River." Finally, in 1987, plans were made to build a cascade of eight dams with a total installed capacity of 1,505 megawatts (Simao Water Resources & Hydropower Bureau, 1997).

In a 1981 report that dealt with the lower reaches of the Lancang River, the Kunming Institute recommended the area of Nuozhadu Township in present day Pu'er[6] as a suitable site for dam construction. Ten years later, in 1991, the Department of Energy, the National Energy Investment Company, and the governments of Guangdong and Yunnan signed an agreement to jointly fund and construct three dams along the Lancang River: the Dachaoshan Dam, the Xiaowan Dam, and the Nuozhadu Dam (Simao Water Resources & Hydropower Bureau, 1997: 243).

Figure 4.1 shows the original outline of the so-called "comprehensive plan" for hydropower development along the lower reaches of the Lancang River. At present, five out of the eight dams originally planned have been completed. The first hydropower plant constructed in Yunnan was on the Manwan Dam along the Lancang River, which was completed in 1995. This dam has been severely criticized for its negative social and environmental impacts, which have included the impoverishment of resettlement communities, a lack of consideration for the dam's ecological impact, and the failure to transfer part of the dam's generated electricity to local grids (Magee, 2006b: 136–139). The experience gained during the construction of the Manwan Dam was instrumental in the building and completion of the Dachaoshan Dam (the second completed dam in the cascade), which was fully operational by 2003, and this was followed by the completion of the Jinghong and Xiaowan projects in 2009 and 2010 respectively (Yunnan Daily, 2009; Yunnan Net, 2010). Taken together, the Xiaowan, Jinghong and Manwan Dams, located along the middle and lower reaches of the Lancang River, account for 26 percent of Yunnan's daily electricity generation (Yunnan Xinhua Net, 2011).[7]

The smallest projects in the cascade are also those intended to be constructed furthest north and south along the Lancang River, namely, the Gongguoqiao, Ganlanba, and Mengsong Dams. The Gongguoqiao Dam was completed in June 2012 (Sinohydro, 2012), but the Ganlanba Dam is currently still in the planning stages with no dates set for completion of the project (Jinghong Government, n.d.). Finally, the construction of the Mengsong Dam, which was to be located furthest to the south along the Lancang River, was canceled in 2010 in order to "prevent abnormal downstream water-level fluctuations caused by power plant operation" (Liang, 2010).[8]

The Nuozhadu Project is the fifth of the eight-dam cascade, the construction of which is planned for the middle and lower reaches of the Lancang River. While the dam is mainly being constructed for the purpose of electricity generation, it is also designed to prevent floods, improve irrigation, and attract tourists to the region. The reservoir has a total storage capacity of 23.7 billion cubic meters and a regular water level of 812 meters. With a total installed capacity of 5,850 megawatts, the power station is guaranteed to generate 2,406 megawatts of electricity, increasing Yunnan's hydropower-generated electricity from 5,533 to 6,123 megawatt hours (China Huaneng Group, 2011).

The Nuozhadu Dam is the most prestigious of all the hydropower projects and even of all the construction projects that have ever been undertaken in Yunnan. The dam is not only the fourth largest hydropower station in China, but is also the highest rock-fill dam in Asia – two facts that are both frequently stressed by the advocates of the hydropower station. The director of the Chinese Academy of Engineering, furthermore, described the Nuozhadu Dam as "a construction project that challenges the world's problems, a construction project that climbs to the peak of technology, [reflecting the spirit of] feeling the rocks as one crosses the river!" (cited in China Huaneng Group, 2011).

The energy companies employ one of Hydrochina's design institutes for the planning stage of the dam projects. In the case of the Nuozhadu Dam, Hydrolancang entrusted the Kunming Institute with the research and design work for the Nuozhadu Dam. By 1998, the Kunming Institute had completed the prefeasibility study, which was then granted official approval. Subsequently, Hydrolancang and the Kunming Institute signed an agreement detailing the institute's responsibilities during the feasibility study phase of the Nuozhadu Dam (Hydrolancang, 2001a). According to the schedule set by Hydrolancang, the Kunming Institute was to submit the feasibility report for the dam by June 2003, and subject to discussion and revision, approval would finally be granted by the end of the same year (Hydrolancang, 2001b).

The Kunming Institute duly submitted the feasibility study for the Nuozhadu Dam in June 2003, as agreed with Hydrolancang. During a conference held in October 2003, fifty experts, including representatives from the NDRC, the National Energy Administration (NEA), the MWR, the Ministry of Land and Resources, the State Administration of Work Safety, China Huaneng Group, Hydrochina, the Yunnan Provincial Government, Hydrolancang, the Chinese Academy of Engineering, and the Chinese Academy of Sciences, reviewed the feasibility report and gave their general approval (Hydrolancang, 2003b).

Preparatory work for the construction of the dam began in April 2004, and the main construction phase commenced in 2006. In November 2011, the river's flow was stopped, and in September 2012, the first of the nine turbines started to generate electricity (Yunnan Net, 2012). Originally, the power station was expected to be completed in 2016 (Z. Yang et al., 2006), but during a conference held in 2006, Hydrochina announced that electricity would start to be generated two years ahead of schedule, which probably explains why the entire project was completed in 2014 instead of 2016 (CSHE, 2012; Pu'er Government, 2007).

Although the feasibility study for the dam was approved early on in the process, the construction project, as such, was only approved in March 2011. By that time, however, the construction of the dam and the resettlement work had already been going on for seven years. In fact, in 2012, only one year after approval was granted, the first of the nine turbines began to generate electricity (Hydrolancang, 2011b).

How was it possible for Hydrolancang to start work on the construction of the dam before official approval of the project had been granted? A company representative explained that between 2007 and 2010, Hydrolancang had submitted an application for project approval to the State Council on three occasions, but approval had not been granted. In one instance, the Nuozhadu Dam was listed as item number three on the agenda for a conference during which a total of five hydropower stations were to be granted approval. However, even the first power station on the list (the Jinanqiao Dam, planned for the Lijiang River) was rejected and, in the end, none of the five stations were approved. Hydrolancang was nevertheless able to start work on the Nuozhadu Dam because the company had been issued with a so-called "travel pass (*lutiao*)" by the NDRC and although this did not constitute official approval, it could be taken as confirmation that preliminary construction work could commence without risk of interference from the lawmakers. The major work on the dam, however, such as stopping the river's flow and building the embankments, would still need official approval (Sina, 2010).

The issuing of a "travel pass" for preliminary construction work has been made possible by the reforms carried out in 2004 by the Chinese investment administration. Before this time, all major investment projects were subject to an examination and approval process (*shenpi*). which meant that construction could only begin after the entire project had undergone several phases of investigation, but since then, in the case of projects that are not objects of state investment, only verification (*hezhun*) or reporting for the record (*bei'an*) has been necessary, depending on the area of investment. This new process is intended to streamline application procedures and ease the project application processes so that urgently needed infrastructure, such as power stations, can be constructed without delay. While the *shenpi*-process required a project proposal, a feasibility study report and a project launching report, *hezhun* only requires an application report that can be submitted to the state at a later stage after preliminary construction work has already begun (Sina, 2010).

On the one hand, this new application procedure for projects that do not involve state investment allows companies to speed up the construction and application processes, which has the potential to undermine social and environmental impact assessments; according to a Huaneng company representative, it also entails risks for project developers who tend to invest huge sums of money in preliminary construction and are subsequently dependent on state approval for the core construction phase (Sina, 2010). On the other hand, as has been shown in previous chapters, hydropower companies enjoy strong political backing from state agencies that are hugely in favor of large dams, most importantly the NDRC. Therefore, although there are official approval processes that involve several rounds of investigations for prefeasibility and feasibility studies for construction projects, these processes are undermined by the fact that powerful state agencies in favor of hydropower projects are able to make unilateral decisions and fast-track their favored projects through administrative procedures.

The Nuozhadu Project does not only involve a strong component of top-down decision-making, it serves as an example of the interprovincial energy geographies underlying Chinese hydropower development. As already mentioned, the Nuozhadu Project was based on a development agreement between the governments of Guangdong and Yunnan, indicating that project benefits do not exclusively accrue locally. In fact, the Nuozhadu Dam has to be seen as a national project by virtue of the fact that the central government's core strategy is to send electricity from western to eastern China (*xidian dongsong*), and from Yunnan to Southeast Asia (*yun dian wai song*)[9] rather than to provide electricity to localities in Yunnan (Magee, 2006b).[10] Between 1993 – when the strategy of sending electricity from east to west started – and 2012, Yunnan transferred 200.7 billion kilowatt-hours to Guangdong. The annual amount of electricity is going to increase further in the coming years, since China Southern Power Grid intends to install an 800-kilovolt high-tension power line from Nuozhadu Dam to Guangdong (Luo, 2013).

According to the "Yunnan Province Plan for Electric Power Development During the 10th Five-Year Plan and the Period Until 2015," only if construction on the Nuozhadu Dam commenced in 2005, would Yunnan be able to meet the target set for providing electricity to other provinces by 2014. This requirement was cited by Hydrolancang as one of the main reasons for the need to progress quickly with the preliminary construction work and it also led to the company's signing a liability statement with the Yunnan Province Western Development Leading Small Group for starting preconstruction work on the dam (Hydrolancang, 2001a).

Map 4.1 Dam projects in Pu'er
Source: Author.

However, the social and environmental impacts of the project are very much localized. On the whole, reservoir inundation is going to affect two cities, nine counties, 32 townships and villages and 597 villager small groups (*cunmin xiaozu*) amounting to a total area of 329.97 km² (Y. Xu & Li, 2005). Despite these huge losses of land, advocates of the Nuozhadu Dam have been promoting the project as one that fosters regional social and economic development. At the same time, it has been claimed that the dam will reduce coal-generated electricity consumption by 9.56 million tons annually, and that the risks of flooding along the lower reaches of the Lancang River will also be reduced by the regulating of the water flow (Hydrolancang, 2011b; Xu & Mu, 2012).

Furthermore, according to the Pu'er Resettlement Bureau, the Nuozhadu Dam will help the prefecture to become a clean energy base, foster investment in the region, spur economic growth, promote poverty reduction in the reservoir region and serve as a foundation for turning Pu'er into a model green economy region (Pu'er Resettlement Bureau, 2011). Although these statements on the importance of the Nuozhadu Project for both China in general and Yunnan in particular might be regarded as empty slogans used to try to justify the country's dam-building frenzy of recent years, they nevertheless illustrate the importance of the dam as a prestige project for Yunnan, as one of the poorest provinces in China, and Pu'er, as one of the poorest regions in Yunnan.

The Chinese resettlement bureaucracy

The dam-induced resettlement bureaucracy in China is governed by a multiplicity of actors. In line with past observations on the Chinese policy process, the resettlement bureaucracy is fragmented along horizontal and vertical lines. However, this fragmentation goes beyond purely statist actors. While central and local governments are at the core of the bureaucracy's administrative management, project developers, planning and design institutes, construction companies, and monitoring agencies play an important role in carrying out the resettlement work (Wang, 2010: 456–64). The various actors at different levels of the Chinese resettlement bureaucracy will now be introduced, including their respective roles and responsibilities, and with a particular focus on local-level actors at and below the county level directly responsible for undertaking resettlement work. Figure 4.2 presents an overview of the organizational structure of the hydropower and resettlement bureaucracy.

Central government

At central government level, resettlement work is governed by a multiplicity of actors, the most important being the Resettlement Development Bureau (*Yiminkaifa ju*) under the MWR. Apart from the Bureau, special commissions are responsible for resettlement in the course of large construction projects such as the Three Gorges Dam and the South-North Water Transfer Project, both of which have required the resettlement of particularly high numbers of people. In addition, the Joint Inter-Departmental Conference on the National Reservoir Post-Resettlement Support Policy (*Guojia shuiku yimin houqi fuchi zhengce buji lianxi huiyi*) under the NDRC[11], as well as the Ministry of Land and Resources, the NEA, and the resettlement office under the NDRC take part in resettlement policymaking (Interviews, BJ120817, BJ130307).

During the policy formulation stage for the 2006 regulations on dam-induced resettlement, the various actors at the central level that were concerned with resettlement agreed that in order to develop a clear command structure and to streamline resettlement work, a unified agency would be needed to replace the existing fragmented governing mechanism. This is why the 2006 regulations stipulate that resettlement work at the central government level is to be administered by the State Council Water Conservancy and Hydropower Project Resettlement Agency (*Guowuyuan shuili shuidian gongcheng yimin xingzheng guanli jigou*). More than

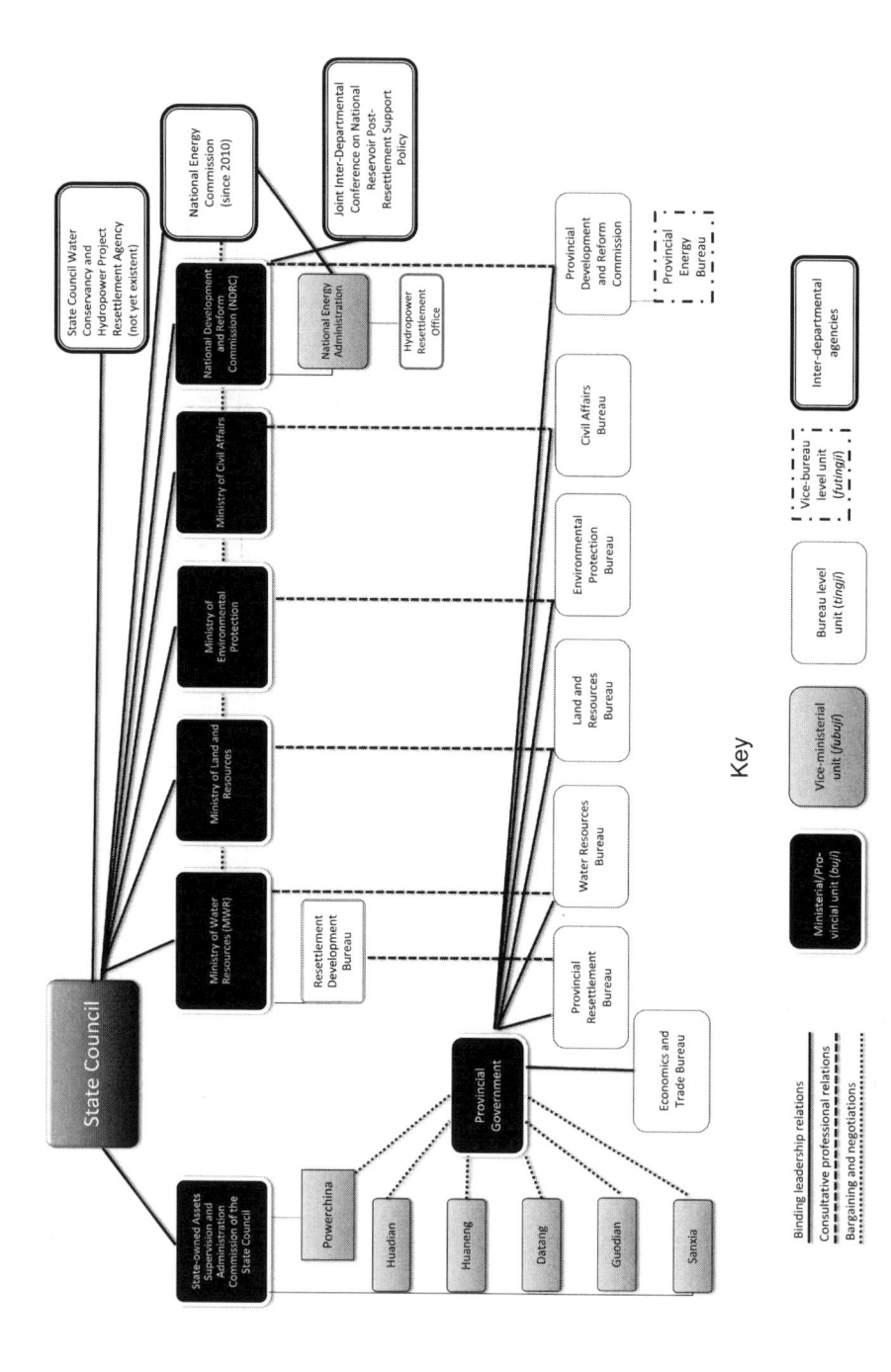

Figure 4.2 Organizational structure of hydropower and resettlement bureaucracy

Source: Author.

eight years have now passed since the regulations were published, but the resettlement agency has not yet been set up, and there is little reason to believe that it will be set up at any time in the near future. One reason for this is the limited usefulness of a unified resettlement actor in the view of the central leadership. The resettlement bureaucracy at both central and local levels has long wished for an end to fragmented leadership structures, but from a macro-level perspective, resettlement is still not regarded as important enough for the government to shoulder the administrative costs connected with establishing such an agency (Interviews, BJ120817, BJ130307).

Instead, an interdepartmental joint meeting mechanism has been set up to govern resettlement policymaking. Composed of 23 departments that meet twice a year to discuss the progress of annual national resettlement work, the mechanism is headed by the NDRC with MWR and NEA officials holding deputy leadership positions. In addition, there is the China Society for Hydropower Engineering (*Zhongguo shuili fadian gongcheng xuehui*), a not-for-profit academic organization that brings together experts on hydropower development, including members of every important Resettlement Bureau at the central level. In this way, although there is no unified institution to represent dam-induced resettlement in China, constant exchange through various channels still takes place (Interviews, BJ120817, BJ130307).

Nevertheless, the primary actor in resettlement work at the central level continues to be the Resettlement Development Bureau of the MWR. Established in 1984, the office was first called the "Resettlement Bureau (*yimin bangongshi*)." During the 1990s, when the central government introduced its new development-oriented resettlement policy, the office was subsequently renamed the "Resettlement Development Bureau (*yimin kaifa ju*). Its main task is to guide resettlement and post-resettlement support while water resource projects are being carried out. The bureau's nine departments draw up related policies and monitor their implementation, undertake research on water resource projects and poverty reduction policies, organize training courses, collect statistics and provide information on resettlement. The bureau also examines and approves resettlement plan outlines and resettlement plans for water resource and hydropower projects that are governed by the central government (Interview, NJ120815; MWR 2011).

In theory, the MWR Resettlement Bureau is responsible for resettlement work in the course of water resource projects only, while the NEA takes charge of migrants who are being relocated because of hydropower projects. In practice, however, since its experience of dam-induced resettlement reaches back into the 1980s, the MWR Resettlement Bureau plays a major role in policymaking and in distributing policies to lower levels of government. It regularly investigates resettlement villages, holds meetings with lower levels of government and receives reports from the latter in order to obtain their input for resettlement work. The MWR Resettlement Bureau is the main actor, in this respect, mainly as a result of past processes of administrative restructuring. The Water Resources Bureau and hydropower bureaucracy have been merged and separated several times, and the resettlement officials who were first employed during the 1980s stayed with the

MWR after the separations. Although the NEA now also has a separate Resettlement Bureau, the MWR continues to undertake the majority of policy research and formulation (Interview, BJ130307).

Governments at the provincial level and below

Resettlement Bureaus and related actors at the central and provincial levels are responsible for developing, supervising and managing the general outline of resettlement work arising from water resource and hydropower projects, whereas actors at the prefectural and county levels are concerned with the detailed management of resettlement planning and implementation (Wang, 2010: 460).

In line with the principle of "taking actions to suit local circumstances (*yindi zhiyi*)," the local government issues detailed resettlement regulations for its locality, based on central-level policies. Provincial cadres are furthermore responsible for signing resettlement agreements with the project developer, for supervising and organizing the utilization of resettlement funds, and – depending on the size of the dam project – for examining and approving resettlement plans. Finally, the province acts as the coordinating agency between project developers, design institutes, and monitoring agencies (Wang, 2010: 457).

The majority of the Chinese provinces have established a resettlement bureaucracy, which is as fragmented as its counterpart at the central level. In each province, there are eight departments involved in resettlement work: the Water Resources Bureau, the DRC and the Energy Bureau, the Land Resources Bureau, the Environmental Protection Bureau, the Office of the People's Government, the Bureau of Civil Affairs, and the Economics and Trade Bureau. This fragmented structure frequently leads to shortfalls in coordination with the result that each bureau tends to be more concerned with its own mandate than with harmonizing its work with the other actors involved (Interview, BJ130307).

As is the case at the central level, the bureau that bears most of the responsibility for dam-induced resettlement is the local Resettlement Bureau that, in the case of Yunnan, is a service organization (*shiye danwei*) that has professional relations (*yewu zhidao guanxi*) with the MWR Resettlement Bureau at the central level, but is administered by the provincial government.[12] This means that, although local Resettlement Bureaus are subordinate to the local government at the same level (i.e., the provincial Resettlement Bureau reports to the provincial government), when it comes to resettlement work, the bureau also reports to the Resettlement Bureau at the next highest level. These professional relations do not exist between the cadres who are responsible for resettlement work within, for example, the Energy Bureau. Although the latter has professional relations with the NEA under the NDRC, this work is not confined to resettlement. Thus, it is the water resources bureaucracy instead of the energy bureaucracy that governs resettlement for both water conservancy and hydropower projects. Although the NEA has set up a resettlement office, it merely serves to represent the energy bureaucracy in negotiations about resettlement policy change. Other than that the NEA has no further interest in dam-induced resettlement (Interview, BJ130307).

The rank of the Resettlement Bureau within the administrative hierarchy of the province depends on the prominence of resettlement in local politics. In the case of Yunnan, when the Resettlement Bureau was first established in 1990, it was a department-level unit (*zhengchuji*) under the purview of the provincial Land Management Bureau (*tudi guanli ju*). Back then it was called the Resettlement Office (*yimin banqian bangongshi*). In 2000, the Resettlement Bureau became a service organization under the newly established Land and Resources Bureau (*guotu ziyuan ting*). Two years later, the Resettlement Bureau, which now officially ran under the name of Resettlement and Development Bureau (*yimin kaifa ju*), was promoted to vice-bureau–level unit (*futingji*). Until 2004, it continued to be managed by the provincial Land and Resources Bureau. After that, while retaining the same bureaucratic rank, it became a service organization directly administered by the provincial government. Finally, in 2006, the Resettlement Bureau was promoted to bureau level (*zhengtingji*), which ranks a half-step above the provincial Energy Bureau. The continued increase in power and privileges of the Resettlement Bureau illustrates the growing importance of resettlement work in Yunnan (Yunnan Resettlement Bureau, 2012).

In addition to the above-mentioned bureaus involved in resettlement work, a resettlement leading small group has been set up at each level of the local bureaucracy. In Yunnan, apart from the leading small group set up at the provincial level, the government has called on all localities to strengthen leadership over resettlement work. Accordingly, Pu'er and all lower levels of government down to the township level have established groups composed of the leading personnel from the various government departments responsible for coordinating resettlement work at the respective government level (Pu'er Government, 2009).[13]

Project developer

Hydrolancang (*Huaneng Lancang Jiang Shuidian Youxian Gongsi*) is the project developer of the Nuozhadu Dam. As a subsidiary of Huaneng Group, the company is state-invested and was established for the purpose of developing large-scale hydropower stations along the Lancang River. In 2001, Hydrolancang was jointly established by the State Power Corporation, the Yunnan Electric Power Group, the Yunnan Development Investment Corporation and the Hongta Group, with an investment ratio of 27:29:24:20, respectively. At first, Hydrolancang was registered in Kunming as the Yunnan Lancang River Hydropower Development Company (*Yunnan Lancang Jiang Shuidian Kaifa Youxian Gongsi*). In 2002, in the course of China's power sector reforms, the company was reorganized and merged with the Yunnan Manwan Hydropower Company.[14] At the same time, ownership was transferred to the Huaneng Group, and the name was changed to Yunnan Huaneng Lancang River Hydropower Company (*Yunnan Huaneng Lancang Jiang Shuidian Youxian Gongsi*). In November 2008, the company was once more renamed, as the Huaneng Lancang River Hydropower Company (China Huaneng Group, 2011).[15] Although Huaneng is a state-owned company, in 2013, it was ranked 231st on the list of Fortune 500 companies (Huaneng, 2013).

According to the 2006 resettlement regulations, project developers are required to participate in resettlement work, for which reason, each project developer sets up specific bureaus that are responsible for resettlement work. In the case of the Nuozhadu Project, Hydrolancang has established the Nuozhadu construction management department (*Nuozhadu jianshe guanliju*), which in turn has its own land requisition and resettlement office (*Zhengdi yimin bangongshi*) (Interview, NJ120815).

Instead of working directly with county and township governments, however, to carry out the relocation tasks, the project developers cooperate with the provincial governments and the design institutes with whom they share responsibility for planning resettlement, formulating resettlement plans, and supervising the relocation process. They keep a close eye on the progress of the resettlement processes to ensure that the project is able to progress smoothly. The project developers are also required to participate in the procedures that have been established to deal with problems that arise in the course of resettlement and have to cooperate with local governments accordingly. In cases where the provincial government and the design institute decide that problems can only be resolved by increasing the resettlement budget, the project developer has to shoulder at least some of the extra costs (Wang, 2010; Interview, NJ130304).

Apart from these potential additional costs, the project developer pays all the compensation for the migrants, and a portion of the administrative fees accruing from resettlement work. The government calculates the administrative fees at the rate of four percent of the entire investment required for the project. In the case of large projects, such as the Nuozhadu Dam, the project developer transfers the money for the administration fees to the provincial government, which, after making a deduction, passes the money on to the prefecture, and so forth. The funds for compensation follow a similar route: The project developer transfers the money to the provincial government, and the provincial government passes the money on to the lower levels. Since the county government is responsible for paying out the compensation to the migrants (or the villager small groups), the provincial government, in some cases, bypasses prefecture-level governments, and transfers the money directly to the county government (Interview, NJ130305).

Hydrochina

Hydrochina (*Zhongguo shuidian gongcheng guwen jituan gongsi*), formerly known as the Administration of Water Resources and Hydropower Planning and Design (*Shuili shuidian guihua shejizongju*), was established in 2002, and provides technical services for hydropower, water resources and wind power development in China. The services offered by Hydrochina include design, consultancy, construction, evaluation and safety appraisal as well as the planning and supervision of resettlement in the course of energy projects (Hydrochina, 2012).[16]

Since 2011, Hydrochina together with Sinohydro Group Ltd., State Grid Corporation of China, and China Southern Power Grid, has belonged to the Power

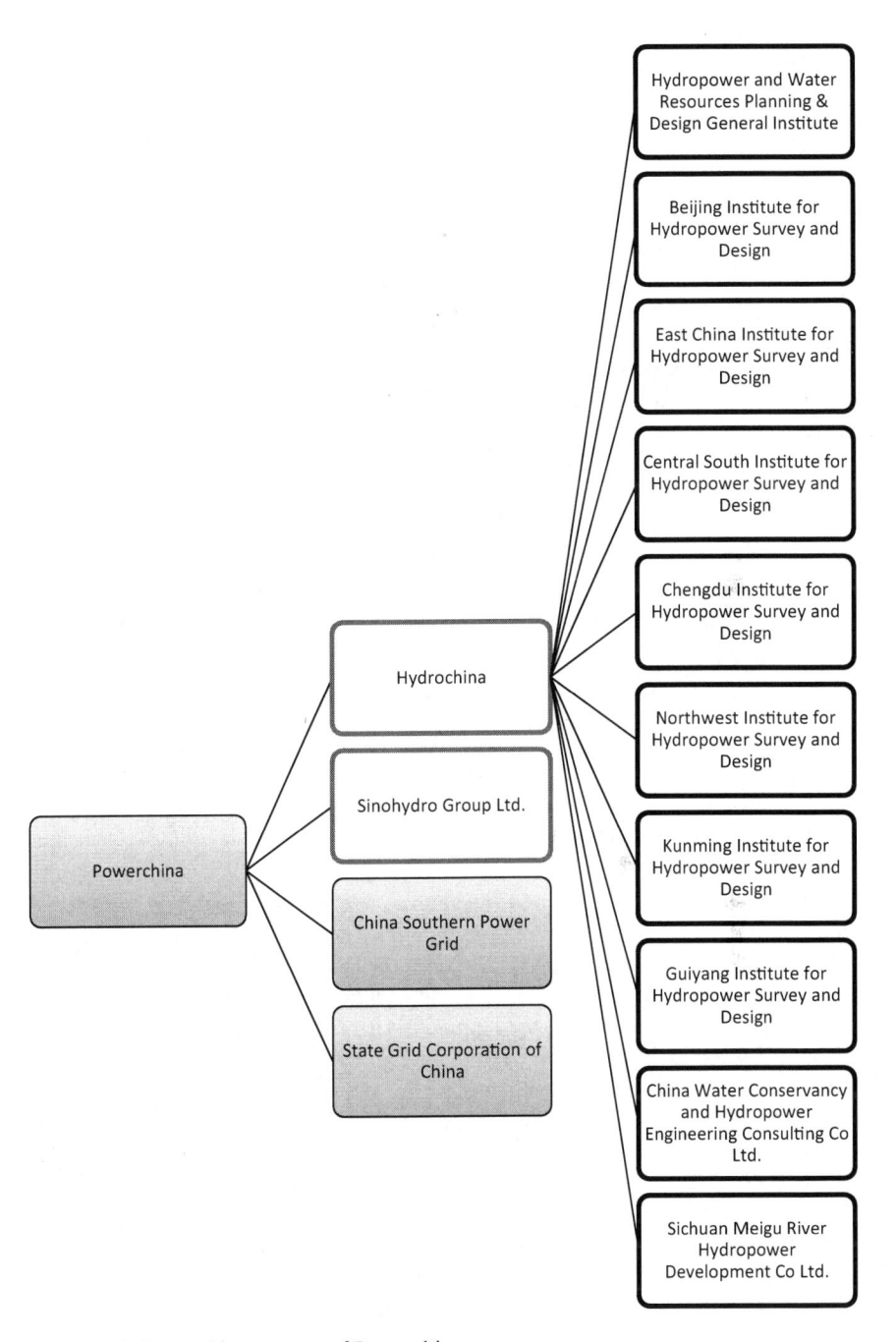

Figure 4.3 Ownership structure of Powerchina

Source: Author.

Construction Corporation of China (Powerchina). At the local level, Hydrochina is represented by seven research and design institutes that plan and design power stations in their respective regions as well as abroad, in line with the river basin plans put forward by the government (Interview, KM120827).[17]

As previously mentioned, the planning work for the Nuozhadu Dam was undertaken by the Kunming Institute, which covered all the aspects of construction, including the environmental and social impact assessments as well as resettlement planning and supervision. The institute is primarily involved in the preconstruction and pre-resettlement stages before a project is approved by the NDRC, and also when resettlement or construction plans have to be revised. In these cases, the design institute, the provincial government, and the project developer come together to undertake the necessary revisions (Interview, KM120827).

Technical experts at the various institutes and at Hydrochina are also the primary drafters of codes and standards for China's hydropower industry, including the specifications for resettlement planning and design published by the NDRC (e.g., National Development and Reform Commission [NDRC], 2007). They also provide important input for policy revisions. As explained in Chapter 3, design institutes take part in the major conferences that are held in the course of policy-making (Interview, NJ130304).

Complex governance of dam-induced resettlement

Resettlement in China is governed by a multiplicity of actors whose relationships with each other are not always clear-cut. The most ambiguous interactions are those between local governments and project developers (i.e., hydropower companies). The power sector reforms led to the end of the monopoly of the power sector and an increase in competition. Each of the five big power companies subsequently aimed to build up their businesses as quickly as possible. In order to achieve this, they looked first of all at the under-developed southwest regions of China, where local governments were eager for development.

Despite the fact that the State Council assigned the development rights for major river basins in the country's southwest to each of the five power companies, the precise distribution of these rights along each river is vague. The reason for this is that the State Council does not determine which power station is to be developed in each river basin and the authority to decide where power stations should be constructed rests with the provincial Development and Reform Commissions (W. Li & Wang, 2011). Huaneng and Huadian have been allocated the largest shares of development rights along the rivers in Yunnan, which has prompted the other companies to catch up as quickly as possible in dam construction. In March 2011, China Datang Group and the Yunnan provincial government agreed on a formula for strategic cooperation in the areas of hydropower and new energy resource development. The provincial governor, Qin Guangrong, has emphasized Datang's role in Yunnan's development and has promised to support the energy company by providing a friendly business environment and excellent services in exchange for Datang's investment (Yunnan Net, 2011).

Local cadres do not only aim to increase the local GDP, they are also motivated by the desire to see the investment that they have worked hard to attract bear fruit within their own terms of office rather than during those of their successors. Since a term of office usually lasts for about ten years, while dam construction generally takes a minimum of eight years, local cadres have tended to quickly approve several hydropower projects simultaneously, which has contributed to the unsustainable development rush that has been taking place in Yunnan during recent years (Li & Wang, 2011).

Local governments attempt to maximize the financial benefits that accrue from contracts with hydropower companies, but only those governments with which the development company has registered for a particular project are able to receive related taxes and fees, an issue that can become particularly complex, if the power station to be developed crosses regional boundaries. In these cases, local governments tend to compete for the company's registration (Q. Wang & Li, 2011).[18]

As long as the dams to be constructed are small enough to be controlled by local governments rather than by the NDRC, local governments have a certain amount of power over the project developers. If, however, the dams are large and centrally located, and provincial government levels set the tone, the local cadres at the county level and below have to follow suit. In these cases, provincial governments promise project developers an advantageous policy environment in return for their investments while frequently also acting as shareholders of these same projects. At the same time, the provincial Energy Bureaus and related design institutes have an active say in project planning processes. In contrast, county governments have neither the financial capabilities to become major project shareholders, nor the political clout to influence project design in other ways. Instead, when it comes to the resettlement process, the local government bureaucracy at and below county levels takes up service provider functions. This is particularly true for dams constructed by Huaneng and Huadian, which in terms of political clout and financial resources are the most powerful among the five energy companies. In their negotiations with provincial governments they easily take the upper hand when determining the resettlement budget and other stipulations related to dam construction. This is why it has been reported that resettlement conditions for hydropower stations under the purview of Datang are generally better than it is the case for stations built by Huaneng and Huadian. Datang is financially and politically weaker than the latter two, making it easier for provincial officials to broker better deals for the locality the reservoir is built in (Interview, KM150305).

The 2006 regulations on dam-induced resettlement further clarify the relationships between the various actors involved in resettlement work as well as their responsibilities. As previously mentioned, during the first stage of resettlement planning, the project developer employs one of Hydrochina's research and design institutes to work out the resettlement plan outline. The outline has to be based on previously conducted investigations on the objects to be inundated by the dam, on the economic and social situation of sending regions and host regions, and on the capacity of the natural environment. The main content of the plan outline includes an introduction to the basic duties of resettlement, the method of resettlement, an evaluation of the migrants' standard of living before relocation and the expected standard of living after relocation as well as post-resettlement support measures, and the impact that the dam will have on the region above the inundation line. The regulations furthermore stipulate that migrants' opinions on resettlement have to be sought, and a "hearing mechanism should be set up, if deemed necessary"[19] (State Council, 2006a).

The outline serves as the basis for working out the final resettlement plan, and has to detail the forms of resettlement intended for the project, the expected livelihood changes for the migrants, and the ways in which resettlement is to be integrated with other national and regional socio-economic development policies, among others. Although resettlement regulations stipulate that the county governments of the sending regions and host regions have to be consulted during resettlement planning stages, planning remains a top-down process that lower-level governments attend rather than shape. As already mentioned, the main actors involved in developing resettlement plans for each hydropower station are project developers and design institutes (Interviews, NE130218, SM130218).

Both the outline and the final resettlement plan have to gain the approval of the development and reform commission of the government level responsible for the general examination and approval of the dam. In the case of large dams, it is the central government which makes the decision. This means that although county-level governments do participate in resettlement planning, the larger the dam, the more top-down is the decision-making process. At the same time, with every increase in dam size, the number of dam migrants increases, meaning that there is a strong negative correlation between the decision-making authority and the workload of governments at the county level and below.

Before resettlement begins, the provincial government signs an agreement with the project developer, which sets out the general responsibilities of the government during the resettlement processes. The provincial government then signs an agreement with the next lowest level of government, which again does the same with the next lowest level. The lowest level of government that is required to sign an agreement with its superior is the county government. The latter, together with village and township governments, is ultimately responsible for implementing resettlement plans (i.e., carrying out relocation). In addition to the agreements signed before resettlement begins, the provincial government, the project developer, and the design institutes jointly formulate annual target agreements that stipulate the goals that are to be achieved regarding resettlement work within one year and that are again signed between each government level down to county level (State Council 2006a; Interview, NE120218).

Dam-induced resettlement in Pu'er

By 2010, 74,000 people had been affected by hydropower projects in Pu'er, the majority of whom had been displaced by four large dams: the Nuozhadu Dam (42,983 migrants), the Jinghong Dam (3,433 migrants), the Manwan Dam (2,814 migrants), and the Dachaoshan Dam (4,500 migrants).[20] Furthermore, 336 people have been resettled to Pu'er in the course of the construction of the Xiluodu Dam along the Jinsha River in Yunnan and Sichuan Provinces. Another 19,934 people were displaced by medium-sized hydropower stations (Pu'er Resettlement Bureau, 2011).[21] In addition, between 2011 and 2020, Pu'er will have to resettle another 42,149 people, half of whom will be displaced by hydropower stations located along the Jinsha River in northern Yunnan (Yang et al., 2006: 10–12).

At prefecture level, the Pu'er Resettlement Bureau (*yimin kaifa ju*) is responsible for resettlement work. Although the bureau has professional work relations with the MWR that is officially only responsible for resettlement work in the course of water resource projects, the local Resettlement Bureau in Pu'er undertakes resettlement work for both water resource and hydropower projects. Established in May 2003, the bureau first functioned at vice department level (*fuchuji*) agency but was upgraded to department level (*zhengchuji*) in 2006 (Na, 2010).

The bureau is subordinate to the Pu'er government. It functions as an intermediary between the provincial government, hydropower companies, and design institutes on the one hand, and county-level governments on the other. The bureau is responsible for passing down resettlement plans designed at the provincial level, and ensuring the plans' implementation by county and district governments. As each government level has to formulate its own annual resettlement plans, the prefecture-level bureau is responsible for developing its own plan as well as supervising and approving resettlement plans designed by county and district bureaus. At the same time, the bureau is tasked with the day-to-day work of the office of the Pu'er Government Resettlement Work Leading Small Group (Pu'er Government, 2010).

The institutional structure of Resettlement Bureaus in Yunnan is similar at each administrative level, with departments responsible for the administration of the bureau itself, financial affairs, policy-related work and post-resettlement support. At the prefecture level, the bureau is composed of six sections (*zhengkeji*), two of which are directly responsible for coordinating and monitoring the resettlement work for large, small and medium-sized dams. In general, twenty officials are employed in this bureau (Pu'er Government, 2010).

Due to the large numbers of dam migrants in Pu'er, all but one of the ten county-level governments had established Resettlement Bureau by the end of 2009. The county-level bureau responsible for resettlement work in the villages that have been selected as case studies for this research was established in 2003, one year after the pre-resettlement work for the Nuozhadu Dam had officially begun. Until then, the majority of the work related to resettlement at the county level had been handled by the local Land Resources Bureau (Interview, SM130218).

Although the majority of the work concerning dam-induced resettlement is managed by government organs, the Party itself has specific tasks in the process. The most important tasks that are primarily handled by the Party rather than the government concerns working with "the masses" (*qunzhong*). The county Propaganda Department and the United Front Department (*Tongzhan Bu*) as well as the Office of Receiving Complaints (*Xinfang Ban*) are all part of the Party apparatus that is responsible for propaganda and thought work (*sixiang gongzuo*) before, during and after resettlement when most of the complaints of migrants arise. As explained in Chapters 5 and 6, the government dispatches working groups to the villages to accompany villagers when settling into their new home, but also to handle potential conflicts and pacify disgruntled migrants. In addition, in 2012, the prefecture United Front Department has initiated its "With One Heart" campaign (*Tongxin gongcheng*) in the course of which Green Mountain became one of the first model villages, that is to receive financial support for poverty alleviation. Although the campaign is not directly related to dam-induced resettlement, the fact that Green Mountain is hosting a significant number of dam migrants has been the major reason for the Party to choose the village as a model (Interview, SM130218).

Resettlement during construction of the Nuozhadu Dam

Resettlement in the course of the Nuozhadu Dam construction was undertaken in different periods, depending on the progress of the construction. Villages that needed to be resettled therefore belonged to one of the following areas (Pu'er Resettlement Bureau, 2011):

1   The project construction area: required by the construction company to set up offices, store materials, construct roads leading to the dam, and so on.
2   The cofferdam area: required for the construction of the cofferdam as well as the area to be flooded due to its construction. This involved a region at an altitude of under 656 meters.
3   The area influenced by reservoir inundation: including areas that are permanently flooded below the altitude of 812 meters as well as regions that are only partly or temporarily inundated.

In 2002, the government began to compile a preliminary inventory of all the objects located and people residing[22] within the future construction and reservoir areas. Resettlement work for the construction of the dam began two years later, after the government issued an official ban on any new construction projects and any migration of people into future reservoir and constructions areas. This was done in order to control the amount of compensation that would have to be paid as a result of the resettlement processes. At the same time, between 2004 and 2006, a more detailed inventory was compiled in the construction area. This was followed by another two-year investigation of the reservoir region. The recording of both inventories was organized by county governments, which in turn ordered township and village cadres to undertake the survey work in their respective jurisdictions. Depending on property ownership, cadres had to sign an agreement with each household and village collective confirming the value of all objects to be compensated and the number of people eligible for resettlement compensation. After the government representatives at village and township levels had given their approval, the county government had to give its final approval of the investigation, and then submit the results to its counterparts at the prefecture and provincial levels. The latter then granted final approval of all the inventory reports and used these as the basis for future planning and design as well as for the resettlement budget (Pu'er Resettlement Bureau, 2011).

Although the resettlement of the people residing in the construction area began in 2004, the final phase of resettlement only commenced in 2011 when the dam was scheduled to be filled with water and all the remaining migrants within the inundation area were to be relocated. As explained in Chapter 3, during the last ten years, while local governments in Pu'er have been carrying out resettlement work, the resettlement policies designed in Beijing have been undergoing great changes, one of these being a substantial increase in resettlement compensation: The 1991 resettlement regulations stipulated an amount of compensation equivalent to three to four times the average output value of land during the three years prior to land requisition, but in the 2006 regulations, this amount was raised to sixteen times the annual average output value. Accordingly, those migrants resettled before the policy change in 2006 received lower amounts of compensation than their fellow migrants who were relocated after this date. The social and political consequences of this policy change are illustrated in Chapter 5; the consequences of this policy change for local policy implementation are examined in the following section.

Challenges for local government

The local resettlement bureaucracy faces a variety of challenges during policy implementation, which severely limit its ability to undertake resettlement successfully. These challenges range from the limited power of the resettlement bureaucracy itself and the top-down nature of hydropower and resettlement planning to the shifts in policy that have been taking place in the context of dam-induced resettlement in China in recent years.

Local Resettlement Bureau are mainly staffed with officials from other government departments related to resettlement. For example, one of the county-level Resettlement Bureaus interviewed for this research employs eight officials with backgrounds in agriculture, forestry, water resources, and poverty reduction. The majority of the officials were recruited from among the ranks of the employees of the county government, but none of the eight had had any experience of carrying out resettlement tasks when they first started to work in this Resettlement Bureau in 2003. Although the officials' backgrounds were in one or another way related to resettlement, none of the cadres was familiar with existing resettlement policies, or the way in which resettlement was to be prepared and carried out. One resettlement official reported that when he first took up his job in the local Resettlement Bureau, immediately after it had been established, the preparations for the construction of the Jinghong Dam were in full swing, and the bureau had to handle all the resettlement work affecting the district. Moreover, only one year after the Resettlement Bureau had been set up, the construction of the Nuozhadu

Dam began, which required the immediate relocation of five villager small groups (Interview, SM130218).

At the time, detailed resettlement regulations were lacking and the only policy that could be applied was based on the 1991 resettlement regulations designed by the central government. Specific regulations governing resettlement in Yunnan and Pu'er were only published when resettlement work was already ongoing. This has led to many conflicts. Although the 2006 regulations are better than the 1991 regulations, and have included many improvements for migrants, the differences in terms of the resettlement bureaucracy, the compensation standard, and policy implementation are stark, and serve to obstruct any chance of moving smoothly from one policy to the next. This problem is particularly prevalent in Pu'er, where most of the hydropower stations have been constructed while the policy changes were being implemented (Na, 2010).

However, despite the policy changes, the compensation standards for property, such as houses and infrastructure, are still below market prices, which presents problems for local governments who have to ensure that the migrants' new houses are the same standard, function, and size as their previous houses – a requirement that is listed in the new resettlement regulations (Na, 2010; State Council, 2006a).

Another problem that various officials from the local resettlement bureaucracy have reported refers to the post-resettlement support policy introduced by the central government in 2006, and subsequently specified by the Yunnan provincial government in 2008. The policy distinguishes between farmers whose homes needed to be relocated in the course of dam construction (*banqian renkou*), and those people who did not have to leave their homes, but whose land was flooded, and who were therefore allocated new land (*shengchan renkou*). The latter were only entitled to post-resettlement support to the annual amount of 600 yuan, if the hydropower station that had led to the flooding of their land had been approved and construction had started after July 1, 2006. If the hydropower station had been granted approval before that date, only those people who had had to relocate were entitled to post-resettlement support. In Pu'er, this policy decision has caused 16,000 people to be left out of the post-resettlement support scheme, causing conflicts between local communities and the government (Na, 2010; Interviews, SM130218, NE130218).

Other conflicts are caused by the fact that compensation standards for hydropower projects are higher than those for other construction projects, such as roads. However, in some cases, the construction of a hydropower station requires the construction of new roads that, in turn, necessitate the resettlement of local communities. Although dam migrants are compensated according to the standard set for hydropower stations, those people who reside in the areas needed for the new roads are compensated according to the lower standard set for roads and other construction projects (Na, 2010).

The limited availability of land also frequently leads to conflict. Since migrants are mainly resettled away from river banks with fertile land to regions with both limited land availability and land that is less fertile, it is difficult for them to maintain their former standards of living. Furthermore, the fact that the host populations usually have more land than the migrants leads to conflict between the two groups. For this reason, letters and visits to the local government by dam migrants account for about 17 percent of all letters and visits by the population (Na, 2010)

Cadres at the county level have the responsibility for dealing with most of the migrants' complaints but, for the most part, they do not have the authority to resolve the problems that are reported to them. If the solution to the problem requires a change in the resettlement plan (such as the adjustment of the compensation standard), the county has to report the problem to the prefecture, who report the matter to the province, if the prefecture-level cadres decide that it is worth reporting upwards. At the provincial level, the problem (again only when deemed urgent) is discussed by government representatives, the design company, and the project developer. If the three parties agree that changes to the resettlement plan are necessary, these are made and reported downwards. The result is that complex problems that might require additional investment are often only resolved after tenuous processes of reporting, investigation, and negotiation that can take up to two years and then only if all the involved parties agree that change is necessary. If not, the county is left to deal with the problem on its own (Interviews, SM130218, NE 130218).

In addition, the fact that the resettlement bureaucracy was understaffed made the efficient resettlement of the 50,000 people that was planned for the period between 2005 and 2010 extremely difficult: in Pu'er, there were only 130 officials involved in resettlement work at that time and this number might even decrease in the future, if upcoming rounds of administrative restructuring lead to the merging of county Resettlement Bureau with other departments (Na, 2010).

As can be seen from the preceding analysis, when it comes to resettlement, the pressure on local governments below the prefecture level is consistently high. During interviews, officials working in county Resettlement Bureaus have repeatedly emphasized the difficulties that arise when they try to reconcile the demands of higher-level governments with those of resettled people. This is further underlined by a Pu'er government report stating that the above-mentioned aim of allowing the Nuozhadu Dam to generate electricity two years ahead of schedule has placed the local government under additional pressure to resettle villagers on time (Pu'er Government, 2007).

Checks on flexibility

This chapter has introduced the Chinese resettlement bureaucracy as an appendix to the country's larger hydropower industry and, more importantly, the power structures underlying hydropower development and resettlement in China. Over the past three decades, China's reformed economy has been geared towards growth, a fact that is reflected in a large proportion of Chinese contemporary economic institutions. In order to keep the growth engine running, the political leadership in Beijing has been reforming its power sector in order to increase competition and streamline the industry. At the same time, the importance of energy security and the relative unimportance of the social implications are enshrined in the administrative structure of the hydropower and resettlement bureaucracies.

The major actors in China's power sector are large state-owned enterprises that enjoy strong political backing from Beijing when it comes to constructing large and oftentimes controversial power stations. Officially framed as a clean and efficient way to produce energy, hydropower is one area in which China's power companies have invested great sums to reap even greater benefits. Two major channels of power have been shown to be at work, illustrating which actors are allowed a seat at the decision-making table and which actors are merely responsible for policy execution.

First, as the decision-making processes linked with the Nuozhadu Project show, hydropower development involves a strong component of top-down decision-making with the NDRC and the MWR dominating the process of when and where large dams are to be constructed. Second, the Nuozhadu Dam is also a prime example of the interprovincial energy geographies underlying Chinese hydropower development. As Magee (2006b) has shown, this power station is a national project that is at the core of the central government's strategy to send electricity from western to eastern China, and from Yunnan to Southeast Asia.

When it comes to making decisions on the resettlement that becomes necessary in the course of dam projects, a top-down command structure can also be observed: the larger the dam, the more top-down the decision-making process. At the same time, with each increase in dam size, the number of dam migrants increases, meaning that a strong negative correlation exists between the decision-making authority and the workload of governments at the county level and below. Although local Resettlement Bureaus below the provincial level are consulted in the course of resettlement planning, they nevertheless play a role as service providers for the hydropower industry. Resettlement can therefore be described as accompanying the construction process rather than shaping it. In fact, it is the construction process worked out by the provincial government, the project developer and the design institute that determines when and how many migrants have to make way for the construction of a dam.

As explained in Chapter 2, since the beginning of reform and opening up, the Chinese polity has embarked on a transition process from a traditional hierarchical system toward a modern, market-oriented system. This chapter shows that although the transition has begun in the field of hydropower development, a purely modern polity has not yet been established. Instead, rule-guided market relationships and top-down bureaucratic interactions have come together to produce a situation in which local governments at county and township levels are unable to find appropriate solutions for the problems that arise during resettlement processes. Local governments are caught in a double bind in which they are forced to obey the orders issued by higher levels, which are, on the one hand (at least on paper), becoming increasingly benevolent towards migrant communities but on the other hand, subject to the profit margins of hydropower companies.

The Chinese bureaucracy allows for flexibility when adapting central policies to local circumstances, but this is clearly not possible in the case of resettlement, because resettlement plans are firmly fixed at the provincial level by the provincial government, energy companies, and design institutes. Although prefectures have leverage over policy specifications, these are only flexible within the limited confines of overall resettlement regulations and the resettlement plan.

This reflects a considerable tension between accountability and efficiency present not only in the Chinese system, but in public administration more generally. While in most policy fields, Chinese local cadres have been given a great room to maneuver when implementing policies designed by their superiors, in the present case, this preference for efficiency is offset by a strong focus on accountability. Interestingly, decision-making processes for hydropower stations reflect an opposite trend: In order to speed up the process, efficiency is favored and accountability suffers. This provides further evidence in support of the argument that current bureaucratic structures favor the efficient construction of large dams for a cost-conscious energy sector over the adequate implementation of accompanying resettlement processes. As Brian Tilt (2014: 48) has put it, "the convergence of capitalist development with the party-state's stronghold on political power is an incredibly effective way to fast-track large hydropower projects." Recent reform initiatives under Xi Jinping aimed at recentralizing policy control while simultaneously supporting the market by reducing government approvals for a number of economic activities will most likely lead to similar situations in other policy fields (Martin & Cohen, 2014).

Notes

1 The Lancang River is the name given to the upper Mekong River within China. The Lancang itself is divided into upper, middle, and lower reaches.
2 In comparison, the Three Gorges Dam has a full capacity of 22.5 gigawatts.
3 Exceptions to this rule are intercounty or interprefecture rivers, which require the approval of the next highest Water Resources Bureau. Decisions concerning dam construction on international rivers are made by the central government and, in these cases, input is only allowed from local actors (Hensengerth, 2010: 4–5).
4 Huaneng holds the rights for hydropower development along the Lancang River. It is also the biggest of the five companies. Huadian is responsible for the construction of the Nu River Project; Sanxia has been allocated the rights for dam construction along the lower reaches of the Jinsha River, while Guodian and Huaneng plan to construct hydropower plants along the upper reaches of the Jinsha. Finally, Datang's operations are focused only on the Guanyin Dam along the middle reaches of the Jinsha River within the "Three Rivers" region where all the other companies also operate (Z. Yang et al., 2006).
5 For thorough analyses of China's hydropower bureaucracy, see Mertha (2008) and Hensengerth (2010).
6 The entire prefecture governs nine counties (*xian*) and one district (*qu*).
7 In addition to the cascade planned and constructed for the middle and lower reaches of the Lancang River, planning for another eight-dam cascade along the river's upper reaches has been underway since 1996. The "Hydropower Development and Planning Report for the Upper Reaches of the Lancang River (*Lancang jiang shangyou shuidian kaifa guihua baogao*)" was published in 2003 and intends to provide for a total installed capacity of 9,400 megawatts (East China Investigation and Design Institute, 2006).

 8 For a more general analysis of the planning processes of the Lancang cascade and hydropower politics in southwestern China, see Magee (2006b). For studies on the impact of China's hydropower strategy on downstream countries, and the reaction of the latter to the former, see Cronin and Hamlin (2010), and Biba (2012).

 9 In 1998, China's Huaneng Group and Thailand's GMS Power Company signed a memorandum of understanding in which both sides set out their plans on cooperating in the area of hydropower development. According to the memorandum, Thailand intends to purchase 3000 megawatts of electricity from China by 2017. The Nuozhadu and Jinghong dams are at the core of the two companies' cooperative efforts (Hydrolancang, 2003a).

10 Magee (2006b: Chapter 6) undertakes an in-depth analysis of these policy frameworks.

11 The conference was established in 2006 with the tasks of communicating and implementing State Council decisions on post-resettlement support as well as approving related provincial-level policies. The deputy director of the NDRC functions as the conference convener while its members are made up of deputy ministers of all relevant ministries as well as deputy chief executive officers of powerful state-owned energy enterprises including the State Grid Corporation and China Southern Power Grid (State Council, 2006c).

12 Service organizations differ from other administrative organs (*jiguan*) in that they lack administrative authority over other units (Brødsgaard, 2002: 364). Due to them not pursuing profit, they have also been referred to as "nonenterprise public institutions" (Han, 2015).

13 In 2004, the prefecture government first set up the Hydropower Resource Development and Resettlement Coordination Leading Small Group (*Shuidian ziyuan kaifa ji yiminanzhi xietiao liangdao xiaozu*). In 2009, the resettlement leading small group was separated from this and set up as an independent group. At the same time, county-level governments belonging to the prefecture established their own leading small groups for dam-induced resettlement (Pu'er Government, 2010).

14 For details on China's power sector reforms, see Cunningham (2015); Amy McNally, Magee, and Wolf (2009); S. Xu and Chen (2006); and Yeh and Lewis (2004).

15 Hydrolancang was the third in a series of jointly invested companies established for the development of large dams along the Lancang River. The first such agreement was undertaken between the (at that time) Ministry of Water Resources and Electric Power and the Yunnan government, which jointly financed and built the Manwan Dam. Subsequently, while the Dachaoshan Dam was under construction, the Yunnan Dachaoshan Hydropower Company Ltd. was set up and hailed as the "first large-scale hydropower company in China organized according to modern corporate standards." The main goal of establishing these jointly invested companies was to move away from the path of the planned economy and secure funding for large-scale hydropower projects (Magee, 2006b: 141).

16 Hydrochina's counterpart, with responsibility for water resources instead of energy projects, is the MWR Water Resources and Hydropower Planning and Design Institute (*Shuilibu shuili shuidian guihua sheji zongyuan*).

17 A notification published by the NEA (2011, No. 361) governs the planning and design work for energy projects.

18 This tax policy differs from province to province. In Yunnan, for example, the tax is divided up by the provincial government according to how much land is flooded by dam construction (Wang & Li, 2011).

19 The regulations do not specify the circumstances under which a "hearing" mechanism is necessary.

20 Different sources state different numbers when it comes to the people resettled by each dam. On the one hand, this might depend on where the sources obtained the information about the numbers but on the other, one of the main factors influencing

the numbers stated is demographic change, which is included in the calculations for estimating the number of migrants. In the case of the Nuozhadu Dam, for example, Xu and Li stated, in 2005, that according to the calculations made in 2002, 41,315 people would have to be resettled, but originally, in 2002, this number had been expected to rise to 46,867 by 2013.

21 In China, large hydropower stations have an installed capacity of 25 megawatts, while the installed capacity of medium-sized dams lies between 5 and 25 megawatts. Hydropower stations with an installed capacity lower than 5 megawatts are considered small (NF Energy, n.d.).

22 For a detailed introduction to the rules guiding the process of assigning migrant status to villagers, see Chapter 5.

5 One dam, many policies

The resettlement experience of Green Mountain village

In 2004, the first of six villager small groups was informed that they would have to leave their homes by the summer of 2005 and move to Green Mountain, a village 200 kilometers away from their present location. Over the following eight years, all six villager small groups were relocated from their mountain village along the Lancang River to the plains near the urban center of Pu'er. Their home village had been designated as the future construction and inundation area of the Nuozhadu Dam, which would require the villagers' houses to be demolished and part of their fields to be washed away.

This chapter provides details of the resettlement processes of Green Mountain village, including the preparations for relocation, the actual relocation, and issues of contestation that ensued after the villagers had been resettled in their new homes.[1] The main focus of the analysis is on the complex relations that developed between flexible resettlement policy change at central and provincial government levels on the one hand and the detailed resettlement cum construction plan for the Nuozhadu Dam on the other. In the case presented here, the people from six different villager small groups, who used to reside in the vicinity of each other, were resettled in the same resettlement village over the course of eight years. The analysis shows how these groups that had previously considered themselves to be one large community were divided up into three different batches of migrants, a process that gave rise to social fragmentation and conflict. County and township government representatives, while trying to ease community tensions, have not been equipped with sufficient authority to solve the migrants' problems, the result of which has been a significant loss of trust by the local community.

One main theme that permeates this chapter is the juxtaposition of flexible policy change and the lives of local migrant communities as objects of this change. In the case of dam projects that are large both spatially and temporally, policy improvements can lead to social conflicts within communities, and construction processes that are far removed from the everyday lives of the migrants can arbitrarily divide local communities. This chapter traces the evolution of state-society relations during resettlement processes, in particular, grassroots government work, which has played a prevalent role in the resettlement processes of Green Mountain village and takes up a crucial part of local policy implementation.

The outline of the chapter is as follows: The first section illustrates the resettlement processes of Green Mountain village and the different resettlement experiences of the three batches of migrants. The problems encountered by the migrants that have resulted from both relocation itself and the dispersed resettlement mode applied to Green Mountain village are given particular prominence. The subsequent section looks at grassroots government work in the resettlement village with a special focus on the ways in which resettlement and power structures within the local resettlement bureaucracy have impacted on state-society relations and government work in Green Mountain village. Involuntary migration represents a deep interference with the lives of individuals, households, and communities.

Resettling Green Mountain village

In 2002, local governments at the prefecture and county levels in Pu'er together with the project developer, Hydrolancang, began to investigate the Nuozhadu reservoir region. This investigation included an analysis of the economic and social situation of the entire region to be inundated by the dam as well as the villages that were to serve as hosts for the displaced people (Simao Local History Committee, 2003: 163). The environmental capacity of the host villages also had to be assessed. The results of these investigations served as the basis for the resettlement plan and had to be submitted to the NDRC for approval.[2]

For the villagers who were about to be resettled, these investigations led to all their property being recorded in order to determine the future amount of compensation to be paid for land, houses, and crops. The number of people living in each village was also recorded in order to identify the precise number of people to be resettled. This identification process caused problems in a number of resettlement villages because, more often than not, the number of people officially identified as migrants tended to deviate from the perceptions of local communities.

According to the Nuozhadu resettlement plan, all those people who, at the time of investigation, were permanent residents of the respective village, legally owned a house, and had contracted land with the villager small group, would count as dam migrants. Furthermore, all those who had temporarily left the village to serve in the army, go to school, or had not yet found employment since graduating were considered to be dam migrants. In contrast, all those whose households were registered in the respective village but did not own a house and had not contracted land did not qualify as dam migrants; those who owned a house and had contracted land but were not registered in the village did not qualify as dam migrants; military officers, employees of government agencies, and those who had been allocated a job by the state did not qualify as migrants. As for people who had married into a jurisdiction outside the reservoir or construction region, only those who had not yet changed their household registration were counted as migrants (Pu'er Resettlement Bureau, 2011).

In cases where the number of people previously counted as migrants changed after the investigation and before the migrants had signed the official resettlement agreement with the government, the number of migrants could be adjusted under the following circumstances (Pu'er Resettlement Bureau, 2011):

- If people are born or marry into the new village, or if army veterans, and unemployed graduates return to the reservoir or construction region.
- If children are adopted by a family that is resident in the reservoir or construction region, and this adoption has been officially recognized by the Civil Administration Department.
- If villagers have died, or have left the village for other reasons.
- If villagers who previously qualified as migrants find employment with the government or a state-owned enterprise, or become active army personnel.
- If villagers marry, and therefore leave the village in the reservoir or construction areas.

As these strict regulations on the migrant identification process show, the government and hydropower companies have an inherent interest in keeping the official number of dam migrants low. This does not only decrease the perceived social impact of the construction project but also reduces the amount of compensation and land to be allocated to local communities.

With reference to local governments in this context, it should be noted that it is certainly in the interests of the provincial administration to keep migrant statistics low. As mentioned in Chapter 4, plans for the Nuozhadu Project were developed at the provincial level, where the Kunming Institute, the government, and Hydrolancang worked together to formulate the resettlement plan. In line with this plan, Hydrolancang has been disbursing the resettlement compensation, while the provincial Land and Resources Bureau has been overseeing the land allocation. County-level government organs, although tasked with executing decisions made by their superiors, have an inherent interest in raising the number of dam migrants because this increases the inflow of compensation into resettlement communities, which reduces social pressures.

Nevertheless, the incentive structure within the Chinese bureaucratic system leads county governments to implement migrant identification procedures on very strict lines. For example, Uncle Xu's daughter-in law did not qualify as a dam migrant because she only married into the family after the identification process had been completed. Although the wedding took place before the family was actually relocated, the daughter-in-law was not entitled to compensation or land. In other households, family members were working outside the village and therefore did not qualify as permanent residents of the village (Interview, ZW120805). In South Stream (see Chapter 6), a total number of forty-one villagers failed to be granted migrant status (Interview, NDH1208031).

As far as the construction project is concerned, it is necessary to limit the number of migrants in order to keep investment low, but for the households involved, the strict application of migrant identification procedures leads to substantial financial losses. At the same time, for those who continue to reside in the village but are not granted resettlement status, this differentiation can lead to the loss of group identification, since they do not enjoy the same rights as the officially recognized dam migrants.

It becomes apparent here that the formal requirements for being granted the status of dam migrant go beyond the oftentimes informal procedures prevalent in the everyday lives of Chinese villagers, who might cultivate land that they have not officially contracted or are able to prove that they have contracted land in another village where they do not reside (Hu, 2007). When formal procedures such as those listed above are introduced to a village in the course of dam construction, they often clash with the preexisting informal habits to the disadvantage of the potential migrants.

One particularly striking fact, in this context, is that preparations for resettlement are accompanied by several rounds of formal paperwork, two rounds of investigations of village and personal property, and resettlement agreements signed between the government and each household confirming that the assessment of the investigated property is correct and that the household is willing to resettle. However, once resettlement has been concluded, several years might pass before the migrants receive their new certificates of land use rights and their household registration is changed to the new village. In fact, in both Green Mountain and South Stream, as of February 2013, the majority of the villagers had not yet received their land use rights certificate nor had their household registration been changed. Although the county government is aware of this and – in the case of land allocation – is even responsible for the situation, the return to informality is silently tolerated (in the case of the change in *hukou*) or even promoted (in the case of issuing land use rights certificates).

Before reservoir investigations take place in the villages to be resettled, the provincial government has to issue an order that prevents villagers from undertaking any new construction work in the area to be inundated and – with the exception of brides – bans any new people from moving into the respective village. The local government is not able to control any of these activities, but new construction projects are not counted as property to be compensated, and new inhabitants are not identified as resettled people (*yimin*). In the case of Green Mountain village, although preliminary investigations had already begun in 2002, it was not until 2004 that the government announced the prohibition order (Lancang Government, n.d.).

Brother Wang was agitated when he told me that the government had informed some villagers that all construction projects built and crops planted before December 2003 would be included in the compensation to be paid to the resettled people but had told others that May 1, 2004 was set as the cut-off date. He was very upset about the fact that the government was obviously violating its own principle of "one dam, one policy (*yiku yice*)."[3] Brother Wang had studied the policies right from the start, when the resettlement work in their old home began in 2002, and had observed how the government frequently changed regulations and had applied different standards to different people:[4]

> The upper-levels hand down a document, but by the time it has reached the lower levels it's not valid anymore. By the time it has reached the lower

levels, the upper levels have already issued a new document. How can you call this "one dam, one policy"? The policy changes to frequently. If you say one then it should be one, and not two or three or four.

(Interview, ZW13021702)

The term "government" here refers to the resettlement bureaucracy at the prefecture level and above, but the officials who are ultimately responsible for policy implementation in the villages work in or below the county-level government. As already mentioned in Chapter 4, when the stocktaking first started in the village that was to be resettled, the resettlement bureaucracy at the county level had not yet been set up, and until the Resettlement Bureau in Wild Grass County was set up in 2003, the Bureau of Land Resource Administration within the district government was responsible for making the preparatory resettlement work. Only one year after being established, the Resettlement Bureau had to undertake the first relocations. "Back then," an official from the Wild Grass County Resettlement Bureau told me, "we didn't quite know how to do the work, there were hardly any policies to refer to, and we didn't have any experience of resettlement work" (Interview, SM130218).

Propaganda and thought work

Apart from the team that was responsible for the stocktaking work in the village, several other government teams were charged with preparing the resettlement work. As part of the government's efforts to improve "propaganda and thought work" during the resettlement process, one of the government teams was responsible for informing migrants about China's hydropower strategy, the Nuozhadu Project itself, and the current resettlement policy.

This increased attention on the part of the government with regard to informing migrants about the project that was the reason for their relocation. The relocation process itself should be seen in the context of the central government's recent rhetoric on guaranteeing the rights of those affected by large infrastructure projects, as briefly mentioned in Chapter 3 as well as by the need of the local government to resettle people whilst maintaining social order without making use of force (see also Deng & O'Brien, 2013).

According to a booklet handed out by the government to the migrants before resettlement, each migrant has the right to participation, information, choice, expression, and supervision throughout the resettlement process. First of all, migrants have the right to participate in the processes of preparing and revising the property investigation as well as the compensation and resettlement plans. They also have the right to choose their preferred mode of resettlement and to supervise the way in which the compensation paid out to the collective is used. Moreover, migrants are entitled to supervise and participate in the implementation of official policies by local cadres. In cases where policies are not implemented to the migrants' satisfaction or where other problems arise during the resettlement process, the migrants have the legal right to appeal against any decisions that are made (Pu'er Resettlement Bureau, 2011).

However, the booklet also spells out the responsibilities that accrue to the status of "dam migrant." First of all, the migrants have to comply with all laws, rules, and regulations related to their resettlement. They are also required to support national construction projects and follow all related requests to give up farmland and/or move out of their homes. During the entire resettlement process, migrants have to actively participate in resettlement work and support it. Once migrants have chosen their preferred mode of resettlement and have signed the resettlement agreement with the local government, they are not permitted to change the chosen resettlement mode or location for any reason (Pu'er Resettlement Bureau, 2011).[5]

The main problem with this list of rights and responsibilities listed in the booklet is that although migrants are now, more than ever before, able to make decisions concerning the way that they are resettled and where they are resettled, the degree of consultation and participation is limited by the fact that resettlement is a must, once a hydropower project has been approved. Furthermore, as will be shown below, despite the fact that migrants have the right to be informed about the resettlement process and the respective policies, local cadres control the information that is passed on to the migrants. The former have an inherent interest in manipulating this information in such a way that the resettlement process runs smoothly and the migrants are not given any reason to offer resistance. Although at first, this manipulated information might cause migrants to relocate without protest, once the truth comes to the surface, the conflicts are sometimes even more severe than they would have been had the cadres had been truthful in the first place.

In Green Mountain, about one year before the first batch of migrants was resettled, representatives from district, township, and village governments came to the village to introduce the national hydropower strategy, to explain why it was necessary to construct the Nuozhadu Dam, and to ask the future migrants to support the state's efforts. As is the case with most people who are informed that they will have to leave their homes and move to a new location, the villagers were at first reluctant to move and refused to sign the resettlement agreement with the local government. According to Group Leader (*zuzhang*) Wu, during the negotiations between the government and the migrants, the former employed a particularly skillful tactic to persuade the villagers to move; the Group Leader referred to this tactic as a "cheat, fool, threat (*pian, hong, xia*)":

> *Pian* refers to the fact that the government told us that the resettlement village we were about to move to was a particularly nice place where men would find beautiful women, and where it would even be possible for them to have more than one woman at a time. . . . All in all, they told us that the region around the resettlement village is a very exciting place to live [*hen haowan*]. . . . *Hong* means that, in the beginning, the government was very nice to us, and gave us a lot of benefits, which later on they deducted from our resettlement compensation. That is, before the move, in order to convince us that resettlement would be good for us, the government gave us 2,000 yuan per *mu* of contracted land, and told us that this was a special benefit that we were being granted. The cadres called this money "field input subsidy," and it was

paid out to the collective. The collective received a large amount of money, which made us very happy, and that's why we thought, it's not such a bad thing to move. However, later, after resettlement, the government deducted this field input subsidy from the compensation they still owed us. So in the end, it wasn't a special benefit at all. They simply paid it out early in order to persuade us to move. . . . *Xia* refers to the threats emanating from the government, if we refused to comply with their "request" to leave our homes. They threatened us, saying that, if we didn't move, they would simply drag us out of the buildings and move us by force. In the beginning, they were really nice, and used sweet words to persuade us to comply, but they always went on to say that, if we dared to resist, they would have no choice but to make us leave by other means.

(Interview, ZW13021701)

What is worth noting here is that, first, the local government emphasized the scale of the dam project, its importance for China as a country, and the fact that the project had been initiated by the central government. In this way, local governments tried to win the hearts of the migrants and to make them feel as if they were part of a larger undertaking designed to further the nation's future development. It can be assumed that the cadres deliberately emphasized the state's role in the dam project rather than that of the large energy corporations that are actually behind these schemes (Interview, KM130222), appealing in this way to the migrants' identity as citizens of the PRC, which they are now being given the opportunity to serve. The cadres also made an effort to be particularly friendly with the villagers and to establish good relations with them, in order to increase the trust of the people in the government and the Party as well as to persuade the villagers not to resist resettlement and the accompanying governmental demands. Thought work (*sixiang gongzuo*) is thus used as a tool "to pacify and 'transform' (*zhuanhua*)" migrants into abandoning any resistance towards resettlement (Deng & O'Brien, 2013: 534). Local cadres made use of tactics of "psychological engineering" to quite literally "move the masses" (Perry, 2002).

When propagating dam construction and resettlement, however, the local cadres refrained from mentioning the problems that had occurred in other resettlement villages, including insufficient and unproductive land, hostile host communities, and inappropriately low compensation standards. This is the kind of information that should have been provided for the future migrants in order to keep them fully informed of the possible consequences of resettlement, but the local cadres did not follow the official resettlement policies; they paid out compensation beforehand to encourage the migrants to agree to relocate and also to try to prevent any resistance on the side of the local communities.

2005: the first batch of villagers relocates

The Resettlement Bureau planned to relocate the villagers in different batches. The first to move were those who were living in the region that had been identified as the area needed for the preliminary construction work for the dam. Uncle Wu was one of the villagers officially referred to as construction area migrants (*shigong qu yimin*), who had to leave their homes first. This was in 2005, the year when the construction work in the reservoir area first started. Also in the same year, the district Resettlement Bureau issued the first measures governing resettlement and land compensation for the Nuozhadu and Jinghong Dam projects (Wild Grass County Government, 2005).

The measures stipulated that compensation was to be paid for the requisitioned land, for resettlement as such (in the form of the so-called production and livelihood compensation) as well as for plants and buildings belonging to the land in question. Depending on whether ownership was public or private, compensation was to be paid to the collective or to the head of the household. However, the district government would retain the money needed for allocating new land to the migrants in the villages they were moved to (Wild Grass County Government, 2005; Interview, ZW130217).

Uncle Wu received 39,600 yuan in compensation but complained that he had received a much smaller amount than the later batches of migrants who came to Green Mountain from Old Tree. According to Uncle Wu, one of the reasons his family and the other villagers relocated in 2005 received a lower amount was because they had had to move first – only one year after they had actually found out that they would have to leave their homes. Since the move was so sudden, and because the government had threatened to use force if the villagers refused to comply with the resettlement plan, the first group did not organize any protests. "In contrast," Uncle Wu says, "later groups protested and refused to act in accordance with government demands, which is why, in the end, they received more support" (Interview, ZW110811). During several other interviews with migrants, NGO representatives, and academics, this phenomenon of "big trouble leads to big solutions, small trouble leads to small solutions, no trouble leads to no solutions (*danao dajiejue, xiaonao xiaojiejue, bunao bujiejue*)" was repeatedly mentioned when differences in resettlement and land compensation were discussed.

This was not, however, the only reason why the first batch of migrants who moved to Green Mountain (perceived that they had) received less compensation[6] than subsequent groups. Group Leader Zhang told me that some of the sixty households relocated in 2005 did not yet have children, a factor that differed in families that moved later. This was because the second batch of migrants was relocated in 2008, and in the meantime, several members of the families had found spouses and had had children, all of whom counted towards the amount of per capita resettlement compensation.

Finally, policy change at central and local government levels also contributed to changes in compensation standards. In 2003–4, Hu Jintao introduced his concept of a harmonious society (*hexie shehui*) that together with the "scientific development concept" (*kexue fazhan guan*) represent the Hu administration's vision for China's future economic and social development. This new direction for development, despite being aimed at a variety of policy areas, had profound implications for rural and regional development strategies (Shambaugh, 2008). One of the main themes that President Hu introduced as part of the scientific development concept was "to put people first" (*yiren weiben*), one of the guiding principles for many policies to come, including the new resettlement regulations governing water resources and hydropower projects published in 2006 (State Council, 2006a, 2006b).

As explained in Chapter 3, these central-level policy changes were not only influenced by abstract themes introduced by the party leadership. The importance of paying attention to the social impact of hydropower development was made apparent by at least two incidents that occurred at the local level in Southwest China.[7] First of all, in 2003 and 2004, Yu Xiaogang of the Kunming-based NGO, Green Watershed, organized villagers to voice their grievances about the planned Xiaowan Dam and the Nu River Project in Yunnan. The NGO compiled a 180-page report on the negative effects of the dam on the local population and the environment. This report was handed to the State Council in order to increase awareness of the local issues surrounding hydropower development (Interview, TB120329). Second, in 2004, the biggest demonstrations since Tiananmen took place in Sichuan, where the people themselves organized a demonstration against the planned Pubugou hydropower project (Y. Sun & Zhao, 2007: 132–133; Mertha, 2008). According to an official from the Ministry of Water Resources, the Pubugou incident had a profound influence on resettlement policies (Interview, BJ120817).

The new regulations did not only feature the new guiding principles, such as the *yiren weiben* slogan, but also considerably increased the standards of land and resettlement compensation paid to the migrants. As a result of the policy update, the Yunnan provincial government and the corresponding Resettlement Bureau had to design more specific regulations that would render the broad central policies applicable to the local situation in Yunnan.[8] This is why, in 2008, the provincial government issued "Opinions" on implementing the new resettlement regulations published by the State Council. The "Opinions" stated that for all projects on which construction had begun before September 1, 2006, old regulations and industry standards could be applied, but that compensation should be dealt with according to the new regulations (Yunnan Government, 2008). These "Opinions" were then passed on to the lower-level governments responsible for implementing resettlement work. This is why, in 2008, the Pu'er government also issued new regulations governing resettlement work within its jurisdiction to replace the prefecture's former 2004 policy (Pu'er Government, 2008).

This publication coincided with an incident that occurred in Pu'er in July 2008 and attracted nationwide attention. In Menglian County, rubber farmers clashed with local police as the result of a disagreement over a contract between the farmers and a local rubber company. The confrontation involved five hundred rubber farmers, two of whom died, while many others were injured. Since many of the farmers had been relocated to Menglian from Zhaotong in northwest Yunnan in the course of the Xiluodu Dam project, this incident did not only attract the attention of public security organs but also caused governments at provincial and prefecture levels to rethink their resettlement work. The People's Court in Pu'er also carried out an investigation on social stability in the course of which the investigative team visited resettlement villages in the entire region (Fanwen, 2008; Interview, SM110812).

In the meantime, Uncle Wu and his fellow villagers were finding it difficult to adapt to their new lives in Green Mountain, mainly because insufficient land had been allocated to them and the little that they had was less fertile than they were used to, but also because the host population was anything but welcoming towards them, refusing to grant them access to communal paddy fields or to irrigation facilities. At the same time, Uncle Wu was arguing with the Resettlement Bureau of Wild Grass County about the compensation that had still not been paid out to him in full. In their home village, Uncle Wu and several other villagers had built houses close to their fields along the Lancang River. They had done this because their fields were four kilometers away from where they lived in the village, and the more elderly peasants, in particular, wanted to have a place to rest close to their fields. However, these houses were not on land that was going to be inundated in the course of the dam construction work and therefore did not count as property to be compensated for by the energy company.

2007: the second batch of villagers relocates

For the second batch of villagers who moved to Green Mountain in 2007, the process ran much more smoothly, at least in the view of the villagers in the first batch. According to Uncle Wu and his neighbor, the thirteen households that had newly arrived did not have to worry about meeting with hostility from the host population, since they had already grown used to the fact that new migrants would be living in their community, and conflict with the government did not arise, since the resettlement work was now being carried out much more efficiently. In addition, new resettlement regulations had been published that already applied to the new group of villagers. According to an official from the local Resettlement Bureau, the resettlement compensation was later also adjusted for the first group of villagers, but there were still other obvious differences between the two groups, the most apparent being their houses. The first group lived in simple and, for the most part, small brick houses with leaking roofs, while the houses of the second group were made of concrete and were much larger.

Uncle Xu belonged to the second batch of villagers, and he confirmed that the first group had indeed received less money. In his view, however, this had not been due to policy change but was rather related to the fact that less land belonging to the first batch had been flooded, which meant that they received less in compensation. He told me that the first batch also had advantages that his batch did not enjoy; his family, for example, had still not received all the compensation they were entitled to because the government had not counted his son's wife as a migrant. She had been working outside the village when the number of migrants was determined, she had therefore not been granted migrant status, and the family had received less compensation. In addition, his resettlement had not

Figure 5.1 Picture of houses built for first batch of migrants
Source: Author.

Figure 5.2 Picture of houses built for second batch of migrants
Source: Author.

proceeded particularly smoothly. Although he said that he was satisfied with the money he had received at that point, when he and his family had first arrived in Green Mountain, their houses had not been ready for them, and they had had to move in with families from the first batch and live with them for five months until their houses were finished.

2012: the third batch of villagers relocates

In 2012, Brother Wang's family, together with twenty other households, moved to Green Mountain. By the time they arrived, the first and the second batches of migrants had already lived in Green Mountain for seven and five years, respectively. During all this time, their families had become larger and the land that had originally been allocated to these two groups was no longer sufficient. The government had given them 1.5 *mu* of land (*di*) and 7 *fen* of paddy field, and since their families were growing, they started to cultivate the land around the plots allocated to them. However, when the Wangs and the other families arrived in 2012, it was precisely this additional land taken by the first two groups that the government had intended for the third batch of migrants.

Aunt Zhang, who belonged to the second batch and whose family had started to cultivate more land than that which they had been allocated, told me that by the time the third batch of villagers had arrived, the resettlement policies had improved to such an extent that the third group had many advantages and received

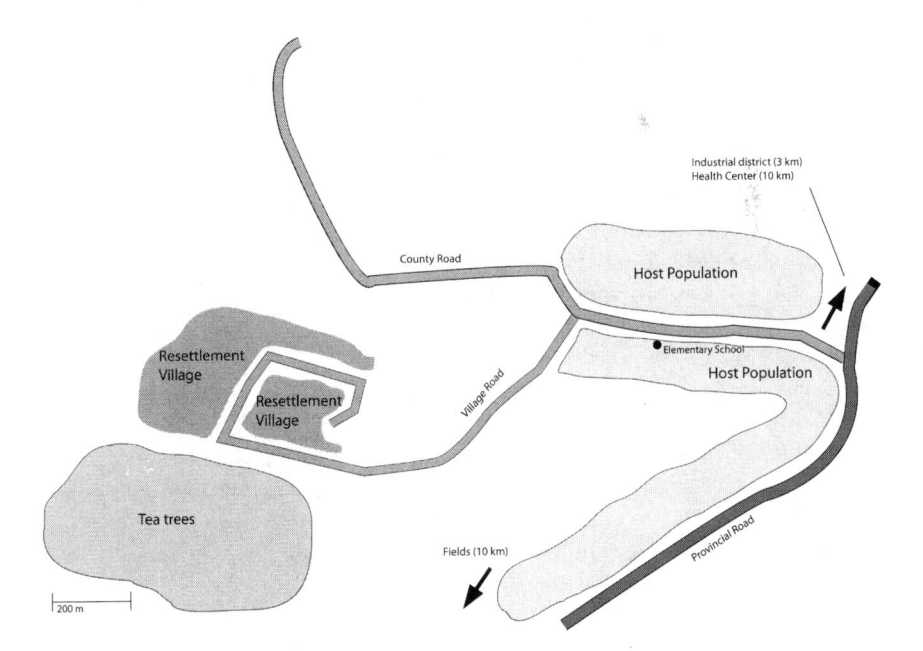

Map 5.1 Green Mountain resettlement village
Source: Author.

much more in compensation. A new resident fee (*juzhu fei*) had been introduced, which meant that every new migrant received 7,110 yuan, a sum of money that the first two batches had not been offered. In addition, by the time the third batch eventually moved, their children had grown up and established separate families, which had led to higher amounts of compensation. This is why the Zhangs and the other early arrivals had decided that it would be fair to continue to cultivate the land that the government had intended for the third batch of migrants.

Clearly, the Wangs and the other later arrivals were very unhappy about the current situation. They had spoken to the families occupying their land, and they had also reported the problem to the government, but so far without any results. The government had tried to persuade the first two groups to give up the land, but since they had already started to cultivate crops on this land, they were unwilling to do so. Uncle Wang told me that earlier groups had also had certain advantages as a result of policies that were not applicable in his case and that this had resulted in disadvantages for the third batch of migrants. He regarded it as unfair that, first of all, the policies were changed to their disadvantage and that, second, they were additionally being punished by their fellow villagers. "The problem is," he informed me,

> these families who are occupying our land are our kin [*qinqi*], we cannot simply use force. The government has to do this, but they have no means to do this either. The first two batches came to this village, divided their families [*fenjia*], and took the land that the government had never allocated to them. The government had provided land for one hundred households. But after the first batches had divided their families, and had more children there were more than one hundred households. So we now need more land, but there is none.
>
> (Interview, ZW13021702)

Due to the fact that rural land is collectively owned instead of state-owned, it is the collective that distributes the land among its members. And as the majority of its members belong to the first two batches, the vote on how to distribute the land benefits this majority instead of the households belonging to the third batch. Brother Wang complained that

> each of the groups has its own interests, and the government has to resolve this situation. Everybody has a different opinion on what is fair and what is unfair, and how the money should be allocated. Everybody makes their calculations according to their own interests [*ge shuo ge youli, ge ren suan ge ren de zhang*]. Can you really solve everything democratically? The interests of the minority cannot be protected by democracy. Land can only be distributed by force.
>
> (Interview, ZW13021702)

It becomes obvious here that each of the three batches of migrants has a different perception on who benefited and who lost the most in the course of resettlement.

Each of the three groups perceived themselves as being the most disadvantaged while the other two were regarded as having gained at their expense. When speaking to the Zhangs of batch number one about the land issue, they tell me that "the government had allocated land to batch three as well, but we decided not to give the land to them. We have been at a disadvantage (*chikui*), their policy is much better, they've received more money, so we've decided to keep the land" (Interview, ZW13021701).

Another problem encountered by the third batch of migrants is their former choice of resettlement mode. Dam-induced resettlement in China is categorized according to the distance involved in resettlement, by whom the resettlement is organized (by the local government or the migrants themselves), and whether migrants from the same community are resettled together or separately. The Chinese terminology that is generally used to refer to these different forms of resettlement is *waiqian* for outward resettlement, *houkao anzhi* for resettlement in the vicinity of migrants' former homes, *tongyi anzhi* for government-organized resettlement, and *zixing anzhi* for self-organized resettlement. Each household has the right to apply for the latter and, depending on the government's decision, to organize resettlement by themselves, including the choice of location for resettlement.

Furthermore, in recent years, the government has also introduced so-called long-term support resettlement (*changxiao buchang anzhi*), which, in contrast to the formerly dominant big agricultural resettlement (*da nongye anzhi*), provides only for the allocation of a small area of land after resettlement but then supports migrants financially over a period of up to fifty years depending on the number of years that the respective hydropower stations continue to operate. The long-term support mechanism was introduced because local governments were more and more frequently encountering difficulties when trying to allocate land after resettlement had taken place, due to the limited availability of such land. According to the detailed implementation guidelines published by local governments, programs were developed to train migrants for jobs outside agriculture and support them in finding employment in townships or cities (Du et al., 2011: 27).

It is up to each villager small group to choose which type of resettlement is to apply to them. In the case of the Nuozhadu Project, for those villager small groups that have decided on long-term support resettlement, the government uses part of the land compensation that is to be paid to the migrants towards the long-term support fund. The money deducted from the migrants' compensation is equivalent to the value of 1.21 *mu* of land per capita. In return, each migrant receives 187 yuan per month for the years during which the dam continues to operate. In addition, depending on the amount of land compensation remaining after this deduction, the local government allocates 0.3 *mu* of arable land to each migrant as well as a cemetery and an area of forest for cutting firewood to the collective. Compensation for the remaining land is paid out to the villager small group (Pu'er Resettlement Bureau, 2011).

Among the migrant families resettled in Green Mountain, fourteen households had chosen self-organized resettlement instead of government-organized resettlement. One of these were the Wangs, who had left their homes together with the first batch but, instead of moving to Green Mountain, had decided to stay in their original township and organize their own resettlement. In order to do this, they had to apply to the township government and were subsequently required to find a new place to live, build a new house, and negotiate with the local population over acquiring land from them. When asked why he had decided to organize his own resettlement, Uncle Wang replied that he had been "backward" (*luohou*) back then. He wanted to have the freedom to make decisions about his own life and not always have to follow the decisions made by the collective and the government (Interview, ZW13021702).

After the move, Uncle Wang realized that self-organized resettlement was not as good as he had thought it would be. Although the migrants had the freedom to choose where they wanted to move to, they also missed out on part of the compensation that they were entitled to, since not everything is paid out to individual households but given to the collective. Furthermore, after Uncle Wang and his family had organized their own resettlement, they realized that it was very difficult to negotiate with their host community over contracting land. Under the terms of the government-organized resettlement mode, the township and county governments are responsible for allocating land, but Uncle Wang had had to do this on his own, and as he explained,

> If one has problems, one can rely on the party and the government. We couldn't do this, because we had decided to leave the collective. So in the end, we wanted to return to the big family. However, by then, the other batches of migrants didn't want us anymore.
>
> (Interview, ZW130217202)

As early as 2006, Uncle Wang and his family had started to consider the possibility of applying for a transfer from self-organized resettlement to government-organized resettlement. His family recognized the fact that they had made a mistake by leaving the collective. Although, at first, the district government had told migrants that the resettlement mode could not be changed once the agreement had been signed, a representative from the local Resettlement Bureau explained that there were exceptions to this rule. In fact, the government has realized that in those cases in which migrants have chosen to organize relocation by themselves, the process of adaptation is more difficult than if the government organizes the resettlement. This is because in the former case, the migrants have to organize the land, housing, and schooling on their own, and they are excluded from their former community. Although the families decide on this for themselves, they oftentimes overestimate the advantage of being able to stay in the vicinity of their former homes and at the same time underestimate the difficulties related to finding land.

> If the households want to switch to government-organized resettlement, we have no choice but to at least look into the case, and see if it is reasonable for them to transfer. Although they have signed a contract with us, in the Chinese

countryside, these written arrangements don't mean anything. If the villagers want to move, they just move. This is why in 60 to 70 percent of cases, we allow them to transfer to government-organized resettlement, if they apply for it. This is better than not helping them at all, and causing more conflicts.

(Interview, SM130218)

This explanation, provided by a Resettlement Bureau representative, shows that self-organized resettlement does not only increase the burden for migrants who, after resettlement, realize that they have lost out by not staying with the collective, but also increases the workload of local governments who, after having approved self-organized resettlement, have to make arrangements for transfers to government-organized resettlement. This could be seen as a sign of flexibility on the part of the local cadres who are trying to limit the potential for social conflict after resettlement, but migrants are not allowed to deliberately change their place of residence until a transfer has been officially approved.

For two families, this ruling meant that their newly built houses were torn down by the government, after they had decided to leave their self-organized resettlement spot and relocate to Green Mountain. As in the case of Uncle Wang, these two families who had first moved further up the mountain close to the reservoir region of the Nuozhadu Dam, realized, after a while, that this move would only bring them disadvantages. For example, the government had agreed to provide their new places of residence with running water, electricity, and a road, but after a year had gone by, the government had still not fulfilled its part of the agreement, and the families therefore decided to join their former fellow villagers in Green Mountain. They each spent 35,000 yuan on constructing houses in Green Mountain, but even before they were able to finish them, the government informed them that they could not stay in their new homes, because this move had not been officially approved. As a result, the houses were demolished, and the two families had to move back to their former homes (see Figure 5.3).

These cases of self-organized resettlement and the problems that have ensued for migrants who have chosen this mode of resettlement illustrate the difficulties in communication between the local government and the migrants. Retrospectively, it is hard to prove whether the government had failed to fully inform migrants about the conditions for self-organized resettlement or whether the migrants had simply misunderstood or misperceived the information that they had been given. Nevertheless, the examples show that an increase in consultation and participation, as promoted by central resettlement policies has to be met with appropriate measures to ensure policy clarification at the grassroots level. The majority of migrants resettled in the course of the Nuozhadu Project have only been educated to the elementary school level and are not used to reading official policy documents, but this is not to follow the line of some Chinese bureaucrats and other experts in the field of rural development, who have claimed that Chinese peasants are of low quality (*di suzhi*) and lack culture (*wenhua*).[9] The intention of this analysis is to emphasize the problems that highly formalistic resettlement processes can lead to in the lives of people who are oftentimes far removed from formal bureaucratic procedures.

Figure 5.3 Torn down house of migrant household
Source: Author.

Grassroots government work after resettlement

Before, during, and after resettlement, street-level bureaucrats play a major role in the resettlement process. In particular, those villages that are considered to be more conflict-prone receive a higher degree of attention from local governments. Grassroots government and party work in resettlement villages take three different forms. First of all, local cadres employed in the resettlement bureaucracy are responsible for resettlement villages within their jurisdictions. Second, in order to strengthen political work in resettlement villages, local governments in Pu'er have begun to recruit dam migrants into the resettlement bureaucracy. Third, the system of sent-down cadres has been applied, referring to urban officials "adopting villages (*baocun*)" and helping them during the process of adaptation after resettlement.

The work of local Resettlement Bureaus has already been introduced in Chapter 4. What concerns us here is the way that dam migrants are used as intermediaries between state and society and how sent-down cadres attempt to help migrant communities rebuild their livelihoods after resettlement. The latter practice of sending down cadres (*xia pai*) stems from the Mao era, when educated young people were sent to the countryside to function as manual laborers or "thought workers." Since the Central Work Conference on Poverty Alleviation (*Zhongyang fupin gong-zuo huiyi*) was held in 1996, the central government has been calling on urban work units to adopt villages and send down cadres responsible for social and economic development and poverty alleviation in the respective villages (Rolandsen, 2012).

Work units and departments at all levels of the Chinese party state take part in village adoption, creating opportunities for economic development in poor village communities. Apart from fostering industrial development by improving the local infrastructure, the sent-down cadres also have the responsibility to bolster local Party organization. As such, the cadres are tasked with ameliorating the oftentimes antagonistic relationship between rural communities and local governments, and with "stitch[ing] up the torn garment that is Chinese [rural] society" (Rolandsen, 2012: 69).

Hostility between the local governments and the rural masses, as well as conflicts within local communities, are particularly prevalent in resettlement communities that are mainly dissatisfied with the resettlement work undertaken by local governments. In addition, dam migrants often find it difficult to rebuild their livelihoods in a new environment (see also Tilt, 2014). For these reasons, in Pu'er, government departments have adopted resettlement villages (*baocun*), and their officials have been given responsibility for a group of households within each village (*banghu*).[10] This means that these officials travel regularly to their respective resettlement village and speak to the households assigned to them. Their work mostly revolves around helping migrants adapt to their new environments, both socially and in the context of their productive activities. When these households report a problem, the official responsible has to resolve it or report it to higher government levels, if an immediate solution cannot be found.

In addition, county and township governments dispatch working groups (*gongzuo zu*) that are stationed in the villages for certain periods of time after resettlement. These working groups have a similar function to the sent-down cadres. However, while the latter, in addition, have to carry out their daily tasks within their work unit, the working groups are stationed in one village permanently and, during that time, are only concerned with this particular village. In Green Mountain, a working group stayed in the village from mid-2011 through August 2012. The group consisted of ten officials from various departments of the local government, who came to the village on a daily basis to talk to the villagers and monitor the process of adaptation. The accommodation for the officials was usually organized in the community hall of the village where a kitchen was available for their use, and there were beds for them to sleep in after lunch.[11] During their time of duty, the cadres made household-to-household calls to inquire about migrant problems and act as a mediator in intravillage conflicts.[12]

Problems were particularly prevalent when the third batch of migrants moved to Green Mountain. The task of the working group was to talk to the first two batches of migrants and to convince them of the need to give up part of the land that they had been cultivating so that the third batch of migrants would also have some land. However, due to the change in policy at the central and provincial government levels, the first two batches perceived the third batch to be far better off in terms of their overall resettlement situation and compensation. Accordingly, the first two batches refused to give up any of the land that they had been cultivating.

Although the working group attempted to negotiate between the different parties, there was nothing they could do, because the land was in the hands of the villager small group of which the majority of members had decided not to give up any of their land.

This was not the only time that the working group was unable to help the migrants with their problems. When some migrants complained about the fact that the resettlement policy was changing too frequently, leaving some migrants worse off than others, the cadres were unable to help. Although the working group reports these problems to the local government, which then reports problems further up, this does not alter the fact that resettlement policy has been changed while resettlement processes are being carried out. The migrants' comments on the working group in their village are therefore often worded as follows:

> The working group and the local government are incapable. We just laugh at them. We know that they have no power or influence at all, and they know it, too. We do not listen to them any longer, because we know they cannot solve our problems. The work they do is completely useless. Although the working group knows of the problems caused by frequent policy changes, they cannot do anything about it. They themselves do not like their work either. They have to come here every day, only to be scolded by us, the migrants. So when they come down [i.e., to the villages] they get scolded, when they go up [i.e., to their superiors] the get scolded as well [*xia lai bei ma, shang qu ye bei ma*].
>
> (Interview, ZW13021701)

There is even a hint of sympathy in the words of the migrants when speaking about the working group, at least among the migrants of the first and second batches. The third batch, which still has not received any land, is much more frustrated when it comes to the working group and the local government in general. Brother Wang from batch three commented the work of the government as follows:

> How can they still keep on coming to our village? Do they have any self-respect at all [*tamen zenme hai you lianmian lai*]? The working group is unable to do anything for us. We have talked to all kind of government representatives about our problems. We've called them more than twenty times, yet, nothing has happened. In the end it's not the government but the people themselves who are left with implementing the policies.
>
> (Interview, ZW13021702)

When I was attempting to conduct interviews for this research among the third batch, the migrants would frequently mistake me for a government representative and refuse to speak with me. Only after I had explained to them that I was an independent researcher were they willing to share their stories with me, but during the interview, they still frequently asked whether I was, in fact, really a government representative. When the migrants were asked why they refused to speak to government representatives, they explained that the inability of the working group had led them to refuse to speak to any government representative. In addition, the villagers had removed a signpost in their village that the government had set up to show the names and pictures of the cadres responsible for the resettlement work in the village. The group leader told me that this was in order to demonstrate the villagers' frustration with the local government and their refusal to be ruled by incapable officials.

The third method employed by the local government to gain better control of the migrant community was slightly more successful. For a few years, the local government had been recruiting village group leaders into their resettlement bureaucracy to make them directly responsible for social stability within their resettlement community. This was a method that was constantly used to try to prevent social instability and migrant protests. In Menglian County, for example, three dam migrants act as deputy township governor, deputy village party branch secretary, and assistant director of the resettlement village, respectively. Officially, this measure has been undertaken to resolve conflicts between local governments and migrant communities, since migrants themselves are supposed to act as intermediaries between the two groups and are expected to have a greater understanding of both government and migrant perspectives (Na, 2010).

In Green Mountain, all three village group leaders have been recruited by the local government as assistants to the working group. In return for paying each migrant 200 yuan per month, they have to work about five days each month. Their main tasks consist in supporting the working group with the implementation of resettlement work and facilitating communication between their fellow villagers and cadres. For the migrants-turned-cadres, such appointments mean that they come under heavy pressure from both the government and the migrant community; the working group requires the group leaders to calm down the migrant community and prevent them from staging any protests, but at the same time, their fellow migrants blame the group leaders for not resolving their problems. Furthermore, the fact that the group leaders receive money from the working group has led many migrants to accuse them of being part of the incapable government bureaucracy. This is why the group leaders were planning to give up their posts as working group assistants, arguing that while they could put up with the government scolding them, they could not deal with the animosity shown to them by their fellow villagers, because they had to live with them, every day, in the same community.

While government representatives from the county and township levels frequently visit resettlement villages, migrants rarely get to see provincial-level government officials who usually only travel to some of the villages to make inspections and ensure that policies are implemented adequately. Officials from the provincial government were in fact supposed to visit Green Mountain. Officials from the county and township government had informed the villagers about the visit and asked them to clean the streets and the yards in front of their houses so as to make everything look good to their superiors. After everything was cleaned, county and township representatives came to pre-inspect the village and make sure that Green Mountain was presentable to the provincial officials and the reporters who were expected to accompany the delegation. However, when pre-inspecting the village, county and township representatives decided that Green Mountain appeared too chaotic with its different types of houses, some of which had not even been finished. Thus, instead of taking the opportunity to show their superiors the problems caused by the resettlement plan designed at the provincial level and ask for financial support for addressing the migrants' demands, the grassroots officials decided to cover up their problems. Instead, they took their superiors to those villages where resettlement went smoother or at least where social divisions could not be observed by a single look at the houses. This strategy of covering up problems in order to not challenge performance evaluations is a frequently seen phenomenon in contemporary China (e.g., Heberer & Schubert, 2012; Zhou, 2010).

Community conflict and tensions

Chinese resettlement policy for water resources and hydropower projects has improved considerably over recent decades. This chapter has shown the effect that these changes in policy have had on local policy implementation in Pu'er. By contrasting the resettlement experience of Green Mountain village with developments that simultaneously took place at the prefecture, provincial, and central levels within China's water resources and hydropower bureaucracy, it has become apparent that especially in the case of dam projects that are large, both spatially and temporally, policy improvements may contribute to social conflicts within communities. In the cases presented here, resettlement policy divided the community into different batches of migrants depending on where they lived before relocation – in the construction area for the dam or in the area to be flooded by the dam.

Although for the construction process, this categorization might be deemed both useful and appropriate, these categories are detached from the lives of local people; being externally imposed, from the migrants' point of view, this categorization is arbitrary in the sense that it does not reflect social realities but instead merely reflects the criteria for "scientific planning." The villagers who happened to live in the dam construction area were turned into pioneers who had to move first. In contrast to the meaning of the term "pioneer" in migration studies, the agency to "pave their own way" was, in this case, denied to Uncle Wu and his peers (e.g., Bakewell, de Haas, & Kubal, 2011). Instead, from a planning point of view, the resettlement plan designed at the provincial level determined the way to move. With the local state lacking the ability to flexibly respond to migrants' demands, inhabitants of Green Mountain were left on their own when it came to dealing with any social repercussions.

From the time when the planning of the resettlement work began in the migrants' home village in 2002, ten years went by before the third batch of migrants was relocated. During this period of time, the entire country underwent tremendous upheavals in the context of social and economic development, which were reflected in the development paradigms designed by the central leadership as well as in the policies published by the water resources and hydropower bureaucracy. The changes in policies were intended to improve resettlement work and, ultimately, the migrants' lives, but for those who were resettled during the processes of policy change, as well as for the local officials who had to implement the changes, the burden of work increased.

Major issues of concern in Green Mountain and other resettlement villages visited for this research as well as for other studies (e.g., Tilt, 2014; Ying, 2005) are the amounts of land and resettlement compensation, the standards of the houses constructed in the new villages, and the quality and quantity of land provided for the migrants. The resettlement process of Green Mountain that was undertaken in three stages over the course of several rounds of policy change, visualized these different standards outlined in the policies to the local community. While the first batch of migrants had been equipped with old brick houses, the second and third batches were provided with much nicer homes. Although the houses had to be paid by the migrants themselves, requiring the first batch to pay much less than the subsequent two batches; nevertheless, having to see the new houses of their fellow villagers on a daily basis, members of the first batch felt disadvantaged. In fact, this feeling of being at a disadvantage was prevalent in all three batches, as each one of them had suffered some kind of loss that others were not perceived to having suffered.

Such kind of community tension also exacerbated the conflict over farmland, which was arguably the most severe conflict in the village. Tensions surrounding farmland is an increasingly hot issue in China where industrialization and urbanization take up large amounts of fertile land, causing farmers to abandon agriculture and find other means of employment. Even in a province like Yunnan where industrialization and urbanization are confined to a limited number of regions, farmland is scarce. This is mostly due the fact that much of the province is mountainous with areas suited for agriculture being limited. Hydropower stations and subsequent inundation of vast areas of land only aggravate this situation. The Nuozhadu Dam alone has caused the loss of $329.97km^2$ of land. Therefore, local governments find it increasingly hard to secure areas of land that are both suitable for resettlement and provide for sufficient amounts of farmland. As Chapter 6 shows, local governments try to secure additional land for migrant collectives from the host population, which, however, depends on their willingness to give up land. In Green Mountain, land allocation was undertaken when the resettlement plan was drawn up in 2004. While the amount of land was sufficient for the first and second batches; by the time batch number three arrived, newly established households from batches one and two had already begun to cultivate the entire area. Although it could have been anticipated by the local government that an increase in the population of Green Mountain would lead to conflicts over land, the resettlement plan did not foresee an increase in the amount of land for the communities. Dealing with these issues has been a strenuous process for the local government.

Despite of making use of skillful tactics of "soft coercion" (see Habich, 2015), for the local government, cooperation with migrants from Green Mountain has become almost impossible. This is because the migrants have lost faith in the abilities of the local cadres. The top-down hierarchy of the hydropower and resettlement bureaucracy has introduced changes in local resettlement processes that local government representatives are unable to implement in a way that satisfies both their superiors and the migrants. Although the county and township governments have dispatched a working group to Green Mountain in order to smooth the conflicts between the different migrant groups, the government lacks effective tools to solve public demands. The daily presence of powerless government representatives has only increased the antagonistic attitude of the migrant community.

Notes

1 Green Mountain here refers to the six villager small groups that were resettled to the same village during an eight-year period.
2 For an introduction to the complex planning and approval processes for dams and resettlement, see Hensengerth (2010). Hensengerth describes the processes as they are determined by the new resettlement regulations passed in 2006, but in theory, most of the content of these regulations had already been applied to the Nuozhadu Project, despite the fact that the official approval process had begun before 2006 (Interview, K120827).
3 "One dam, one policy" refers to the principle of resettling all the people involved according to the same policy. For this reason, a unified resettlement plan for each hydropower station is drawn up before relocation starts.
4 Brother Wang's family only moved to Green Mountain in 2012. Although he is not living in the village himself but working and residing in a nearby town, he is familiar with the resettlement situation because he has been trying to protect his family's rights throughout the entire process.
5 As another section in this chapter and the case study on South Stream will show, the local government does not consistently act in accordance with this last stipulation. Under certain circumstances, migrants are allowed to change their chosen mode of resettlement after they have signed the resettlement agreement.
6 It is very hard to obtain proof of the exact amounts that migrants have received in compensation, because oftentimes migrants themselves do not know how much compensation they are supposed to receive and how much they have actually received. Some of the migrants I spoke to are illiterate, and even if they are able to read, they are not always able to understand government documents. In addition, compensation is usually paid out in several installments, which, for many people, makes it difficult to trace the exact amount of compensation that has been paid out. One migrant reported that he receives varying amounts of money but that he has no idea what this is for or why the sum constantly changes. Furthermore, part of the compensation is not paid directly to the household but is instead transferred to the collective, which then either hands the money over to individual households or invests it in collectively owned equipment. Finally, policy changes during the resettlement process render it even more difficult to understand and trace the exact amounts of compensation paid.
7 For an analysis of the Chinese policy process and the complex interactions involved between actors in the political center in Beijing and between central and local governments across the country, see Heilmann (2008b).
8 Within the hierarchy of the Chinese institutional structure, the central government makes decisions and designs policies that local governments are subsequently supposed to implement. The central government passes policy mandates and directions down to local governments that, instead of providing detailed prescriptions on how to proceed with implementation, only offer general guidelines on how to address a

particular policy problem. Within these guidelines established by the central government, local governments set up their own, more detailed policies that reflect central provisions and specify them in such a way that they can be applied to local circumstances (e.g., Lieberthal & Oksenberg, 1988).

9   During interviews conducted for this research, government officials and other experts working in the field of resettlement frequently referred to the low cultural capacity of migrants as one of the greatest problems that street-level bureaucrats have to face.

10   Usually, one department is responsible for one village, and each cadre within that department is responsible for a certain number of households within the village.

11   According to the "new three together (*xin san tong*)" principle, sent-down cadres should not constitute a burden for villagers. They should therefore cook for themselves and organize their own lodgings (Rolandsen, 2012: 74).

12   In another example provided by Deng and O'Brien (2013), a working group is dispatched to maintain social order through relational repression.

6 One dam, many policies

The resettlement experience of South Stream village

In June 2008, the lives of 324 people in 70 households belonging to a villager small group changed irrevocably: Their home village close to the construction site of the Nuozhadu Dam was going to be partially flooded by the reservoir, and they were to be resettled in a village near the urban center of Pu'er, about 200 kilometers away from their original homes. This chapter provides a detailed description of the resettlement processes of South Stream village, including the preparations for relocation, the actual relocation, and issues of contestation that ensued after the villagers had been resettled in their new homes. A comprehensive picture of the impact of the government resettlement policy on the resettlement processes, including related changes and adaptations, is obtained by focusing on the issues directly related to these changes, namely, community reactions and strategies employed in response to policy change and local policy implementation. In the case presented here, a group of dam migrants attempted to actively shape policy-making in the area of dam-induced resettlement and succeeded in pressurizing the local government to implement policy more equitably. In detail, the migrants took action in order to obtain financial support to cover their living expenses, to pressurize the local government into paying out compensation for land as well as an increase in housing compensation, and to urge the government to implement the newly introduced, long-term compensation mechanism.[1]

Although successful in preventing any larger protests, the local government was exposed to repeated petitioning and resistance by the villagers. In order to prevent migrants from further obstructing the dam site, the county government paid out requested money to South Stream village. Although the entire amount of compensation has to be paid by the project developer, arguing that all stipulated funds had already been transferred to the provincial government, Huaneng refused to pay the sum additionally requested by the villagers. Instead, the county government had to pay additional compensation from their own pockets so as to pacify the migrants. From a legal standpoint, Huaneng's argument was probably correct. The company had most likely paid out the amount of compensation stipulated in the resettlement plan. However, first, it is unknown how much of this money had actually reached the county and township levels; second, the resettlement plan had been negotiated between the provincial government and Huaneng itself on the premise that the resettlement budget be kept low. Moreover, current bureaucratic structures prevent county and township governments to readily adapt the resettlement plan to local circumstances. While this has the potential to limit predatory behavior by local cadres, it simultaneously limits local state agency.

Three interrelated themes are dealt with here: First of all, the chapter is about the forms of resistance developed by migrant communities in response to dam-induced resettlement. Resistance, here, does not refer to the refusal of migrants to relocate *per se* but rather to the migrants' opposition to local policy implementation after relocation had already occurred, with reference to existing policies, those in the making and those propagated to the migrants before relocation.[2] Policy propagation and the methods employed by the government to prepare people, psychologically, for relocation and resettlement is the second theme of this chapter, and this, in turn, is closely related to the third theme: state-society relations and the ways in which these are mediated by dam construction and resettlement processes. This contextualization immediately increases the number of actors involved to include a third party, that is, the state-owned enterprises that construct, operate, and ultimately profit from dams. The aim is to show how migrant communities acknowledged the presence of this third actor in the processes of dam-induced resettlement and how they attempted to involve the Huaneng Corporation in their efforts to improve local policy implementation.

It should be noted that, although the forms of resistance that develop as result of resettlement are an important theme, the primary goal of my research is not to provide in-depth analyses of the dynamics underlying migrant protests but, rather, to show how resettlement policy change has empowered local migrant communities without providing local governments with sufficient authority to adequately address the migrants' claims.

Preparing the migrants for resettlement

Compared with the 1991 regulations for dam-induced resettlement, which focused on the actual process of relocation and respective compensation, the new policy introduced in 2006 goes into much more detail regarding the resettlement planning, post-resettlement support, and monitoring process. There is a separate section for each of these topics in the regulations, and this highlights the important role that pre- and post-resettlement phases now play (State Council, 1991, 2006a). In the case described here, the change in policy is reflected in the amount of time that county, township, and village governments spent in South Stream to prepare for the relocation of the villager small group. While earlier resettlement processes focused on resettlement itself in order to clear areas that had been identified as future construction sites, current resettlement work includes several years of preparatory work in the villages to be relocated (Interview, SM130218).

Taking stock

Preparations for the resettlement of the South Stream villager small group began in 2004, when the local government started to send out teams who were tasked with investigating the area and taking stock of the peasants' crops, houses, and other possessions in order to estimate the budget needed for compensation. In the same year, the government announced a ban on starting up any new construction projects in the village because, first of all, these would not be compensated and, secondly, they would hinder the process of clearing the area needed for dam construction.

The stocktaking process continued for several years, during which time government teams increased the accuracy of the property lists developed for the collective and the households. The process was eventually completed in 2007, when the government issued the final version of the list stating the villager small group's collective and individual households' compensation package. According to the government's calculations, the villager small group would receive a total amount of 56.3 million yuan in resettlement compensation and in compensation paid for land. Out of this amount, about 9.8 million yuan were to be paid to the collective, while the remaining 46.5 million yuan were to be paid to individual households, depending on the number of people officially recognized as dam migrants in each household as well as the proportion of flooded land of each household's contracted land. Accordingly, compensation packages varied immensely, with some households being entitled to 1.6 million yuan while others would only receive as little as 5,760 yuan.[3]

Propaganda and thought work

As in the case of Green Mountain, in addition to the team that was responsible for stocktaking in the village, another government team was charged with undertaking "propaganda and thought work" during the resettlement processes. This involved informing migrants about China's hydropower strategy, the Nuozhadu Project itself and also the current resettlement policy.

In South Stream, about a year before relocation started, a working group dispatched by the local government began to visit the future migrant community. The group consisted of twenty to thirty local cadres who frequently paid visits to the village during this year. It was their task to hold meetings with the village representatives as well as with the entire community. In addition, they went from door to door to speak to the householders individually. As the group leader, Mr. Liu, recalled:

> They informed us about this national project called Nuozhadu Hydropower Station that was being planned in order to ensure the future development of the country. They said that each of us would be asked to contribute our share to this very important project, and that our task consisted of leaving our homes to make way for the construction. They went from household to household to inform all of us about the advantages of resettlement and to tell us that we need not worry about anything, because the government would take care of us. They informed us about the date of our resettlement, which was set for the end of June, and also that they would begin to allocate land to

us on the first day after our arrival in the new village. To this day, they still haven't allocated the land that they promised us. . . . Back then, we believed what the government told us, and moved without resistance.

(Interview, NDH1302201)

Another villager added,

Before our move, the working group came to the village every day for at least two months. They held meetings every single day to tell us about the greatness of the new dam they were about to build. The government was especially warm [*reqing*] to us so we believed everything. They told us that everything would be fine after resettlement and that they would take care of all potential problems. They also explained that they could not tolerate any resistance, because this was a state project.

(Interview, NDH1208032)

This is a very similar description to the one provided by the group leader of Green Mountain. The government first introduced the hydropower project and the topic of hydropower development in general, describing it as extremely important. Moreover, the government, at least in the beginning, tried to be particularly friendly and to convince the villagers of the benefits of resettlement. Although the officials did not explicitly threaten the villagers, they strongly implied that resistance would be met with oppression.[4] In Green Mountain, the cadres even paid out compensation before resettlement in order to illustrate the financial benefits of the move, but the villagers in South Stream did not mention a similar strategy; this might have something to do with the fact that the villagers from the group that was moved to Green Mountain initially showed more resistance and refused to sign resettlement agreements. In the case of South Stream, the local government was somehow able to persuade the people to leave their homes and relocate.

Nevertheless, success in persuading a migrant community not to offer resistance before and during relocation has not been the only consequence of local government propaganda work: In two instances, the South Stream migrants made use of information provided by the local government to advance their own claims with regard to resettlement. The first instance refers to an issue related to the categorization of the migrants. The government informed the South Stream migrants about the details of the resettlement processes, including the date of resettlement and the category of migrant in which each of the South Stream villagers had been placed. As mentioned in Chapter 4, resettlement for large dams takes place in several stages depending on the location within the planned dam construction area of those villages that are to be resettled. However, as is often the case, the plans made by the engineers for the Nuozhadu Project did not fit the situation that local cadres were confronted with on the ground, which gave rise to disagreements between the dam migrants and the local Resettlement Bureau.

The future migrants of South Stream were informed of the fact that they were living in the cofferdam area of the Nuozhadu Project and that the construction plans required them to leave the area by June 2008. According to the construction plans, all the communities (290 households or 1167 people in total) living in the cofferdam area below the altitude of 656 meters were to be relocated in 2008 (Fanwen, 2008). The South Stream villager small group, however, was spread below and above this cutoff line, that is to say, only eight households belonging to the group were located below the altitude of 656 meters, while all the other group members lived above that line. When the migrants first heard about the cutoff line, they were relieved because they took it to mean that they might not have to move at all. This was why the village representatives took the opportunity to start negotiations with the government, asking the Resettlement Bureau to relocate only the eight households living below the altitude of 656 meters. The villagers asked the government to move them above the cutoff line and closer to the rest of the households belonging to the villager small group.

The Resettlement Bureau explained to the villagers that this was not what the engineers of the dam had had in mind when they set the primary area for relocation at below 656 meters. The plan had been for the migrants to relocate in different stages, with the households located below the altitude of 656 meters moving first. At a later stage, all households located below the altitude of 813 meters were to be moved, including all the industries below that level, and this would apply to all the households of the South Stream villager small group. This is why the local government decided to resettle all the households in one go instead of relocating the eight households first and the remaining members of the small group at a later stage.

Group Leader Liu was suspicious of the arguments presented by the local cadres, but he did not have any evidence to prove that they were lying. This is why the villagers eventually decided to give in and sign the agreement with the local government, guaranteeing that they would relocate according to the terms presented by the Resettlement Bureau. "We were hoping that they would allow us to stay in our homes," Liu told me,

> We thought that if only ten percent of our group members actually lived within the area needed for the cofferdam, then they could move them up the slope to live near us, and that would be it. The policy did not count us as cofferdam area migrants, but as inundation area migrants, and inundation area migrants were to move only later, so "Why move earlier, if we can still stay in our homes and cultivate our land?" we thought. But the working group did not accept our suggestion. They said that if we didn't move, we would negatively affect the construction of the hydropower station. So we thought we'd better move. It was not our intention to hinder the construction process of such a big national project.
>
> (Interview, NDH1302201)

The above example shows that, right from the start, the local community paid attention to the way that the local government was organizing their resettlement and stepped in as soon as they became aware of any inconsistencies. In this case, however, the villagers did not attempt to resist resettlement, they simply aimed to stay in their village as long as possible in order to continue cultivating their land. They had invested a lot of time and money in plowing their fields and planting crops and did not want their efforts to go to waste any earlier than necessary.

Since the local government had previously informed the villagers about the different areas (i.e., cofferdam, inundation area and construction area) and stages of construction and resettlement, the villagers had sufficient information on which to base their claims and therefore approached the working group with their demand to be resettled in line with the previously propagated policies. For the local government, however, the suggestion put forward by the villagers would have led to additional work, because the eight households concerned would have needed to be resettled twice: first further up the mountain and then again at a later stage when the inundation area was to be cleared and all the households belonging to the South Stream villager small group were required to leave. For this reason, the local cadres decided to move the group in one go.

The Resettlement Bureau frequently has to enter into such negotiations with dam migrants over inconsistencies between construction plans and the situation on the ground. On the one hand, these inconsistencies sow seeds of distrust among the dam migrants as soon as the migrants realize that resettlement is not being carried out in line with the policies handed down by the provincial government. On the other hand, such situations increase the workload of the Resettlement Bureau, because they have to deal with the accompanying complaints from the communities involved (Interview, SM130218). In addition, in this case, the migrants viewed their eventual agreement to resettle earlier as a concession granted by them, and they continued to use this as evidence of their willingness to comply with the government's requirements and as leverage for further claims.

For example, although the migrants eventually agreed to being resettled all together at one time and earlier than they had originally thought, they were still not ready to give up their land just yet. Instead, they informed the Resettlement Bureau that, after the move, they would continue to return to their land to cultivate it until the area was flooded for the dam. In fact, as of February 2013, some of the South Stream migrants were still cultivating their original land, which was considered an important source of income, mainly because land in the resettlement village was limited. In another instance, they used their compliance as leverage for a request regarding the long-term support mechanism that the migrants wanted to see implemented in their village.

This leads to the second instance when South Stream migrants made use of information provided by the local government to advance claims related to resettlement. In 2008, the deputy township head visited the village as part of an investigation into the current situation of resettlement preparation. During a meeting with the villagers, the deputy made sure that the overall feeling of the villagers towards resettlement was positive and also encouraged the villagers to comply with the local government's resettlement plans. In addition, he reassured the future dam migrants about the positive future that lay ahead of them, highlighting a new policy that central and provincial governments were currently working on, which was going to be implemented in the resettlement village of South Stream. The policy he was referring to was the long-term compensation mechanism (*changxiao buchang buzhu*) mentioned in Chapter 5. He introduced the mechanism and explained how it would serve as an additional source of income for those who continued to cultivate land or took up jobs in the prefecture's urban center and how it would be especially suitable for the older generation who might rather want to retire than continue to work on their fields.

However, at the time when the deputy was propagating this innovation of the government for resettlement villages, the long-term compensation mechanism had not yet become an official policy and was merely being discussed by the provincial government and hydropower companies in Yunnan. Even when the villagers were subsequently relocated, the mechanism was still only being implemented as an experimental program in certain resettlement villages along the middle reaches of the Jinsha River in northern Yunnan (Yunnan Government, 2007) and in one other county in Pu'er. In fact, the long-term support mechanism was part of a larger effort led by the Huadian Group and local governments along the Jinsha River to develop a more diversified resettlement and compensation mechanism that would go beyond the currently practiced rural resettlement based on land and would introduce resettlement to urban areas with future employment outside agriculture (Xinhua Net, 2013).[5]

Therefore, when the deputy township head was propagating the new policy in South Stream, the mechanism was only being implemented on a small scale, without any detailed guidelines on how the long-term compensation mechanism was going to be implemented in the area affected by the Nuozhadu Project in Wild Grass County. After hearing about the new policy, however, the migrants in South Stream wanted the policy to be implemented in their village, which is why they began to exert pressure on the local government. The details of the argument surrounding the long-term compensation mechanism in South Stream are discussed further below, but what is interesting at this point is the way in which the deputy township head used the long-term compensation mechanism as a tool to convince farmers of the advantages that would accompany resettlement without even knowing how or whether the mechanism would benefit the South Stream migrants at all. Little did he expect the perseverance with which the villagers have continued until this day to pressure the local government towards implementing the long-term compensation mechanism. The case presented here shows that the impact of the increased flow of information from the government to the South Stream migrants has been twofold.

On the one hand, the propagation of China's hydropower strategy, and the importance of the Nuozhadu Dam for Pu'er and China more generally, have lowered the resistance to resettlement among the South Stream migrants. The villagers that were interviewed all argued that they did not mind the resettlement as such but wished that the government would ensure the fair implementation of the resettlement policies that had been designed to help the migrants before, during, and after relocation. On the other hand, since they had been informed about the resettlement policies, the migrants were able to follow the implementation processes and make sure that the local government actually implemented the policies as they had originally promised. The intensification of "propaganda and thought work" in policy implementation may have cheated the migrants into leaving their homes without resistance, thereby undermining their right to know, but the limited information on resettlement policy that they were given, at the same time, increased the migrants' knowledge about how resettlement was supposed to be implemented. This even had other unforeseen consequences, for example, when some of the policy details given by the governmental working group were perceived to be incorrect, the migrants did not hesitate to remind the Resettlement Bureau of their previous promises.

Therefore, while the policy of the local cadres with regard to providing information for the migrants facilitated the relocation processes, the same policy rapidly gave rise to problems after relocation had taken place, when the migrants were able to use the information that they had been given about the existing policies to their own advantage and against the cadres, namely, by exerting pressure on the local government to fulfill the promises made earlier. The primary motive of the migrants in taking this action was not to expose local government wrongdoing but rather to ensure that they themselves were treated fairly and to limit the negative consequences that resettlement would have on their lives.

Choosing a new home

Before relocation took place, the Resettlement Bureau of the local government presented the villagers with three resettlement villages to choose from. Originally, the migrants had hoped to be resettled within the same township, not too far away from their former homes and land, and they asked the Resettlement Bureau to see whether this would be possible; later, however, the migrants were informed that resettlement within the same township was not possible and that, in their case, the provincial government would not grant approval. The reasons for this were rather practical: there was not enough land available in the vicinity of the villagers' former homes (Interviews, NDH1302202, SM130218).

As explained in Chapter 5, plans for the location of resettlement villages and for the allocation of land are first drawn up by the provincial government together with relevant experts from industry and academia. In the case presented here, the experts at the provincial level did not consent to the villagers' request to be resettled within their home township but made them choose from among three resettlement villages in a different neighboring township. The selection of villages that was presented to them included Green Mountain (see Chapter 4), South Stream, and a third village that was between one and two hours away from Green Mountain and South Stream, respectively, and was located about half-way between the migrants' home village and their new resettlement villages. Before relocation, the local government organized a tour to each of the three villages to allow representatives from each household to see the resettlement options for themselves and to help them decide which village they would like to move to (Interview, SM130218).

According to the Group Leader Liu, the household representatives considered several factors before making their decision, the most important of these being the quality of the land that they were going to be allocated in the resettlement village; the difference in climate between the resettlement village and their home village; and the location of the resettlement village in terms of distance from adjacent cities, schools, and hospitals. After considering all these factors, the majority of the household representatives belonging to the villager small group decided to move to South Stream because the land was of better quality than in the other two villages; because there was only a minor difference in the climate; and because the location was favorable in terms of schooling, nearby hospitals, and the urban center, which would provide them with more options for finding employment outside the village.

The third village was not chosen for relocation by any of the household representatives because the land on offer there was considered less fertile than that in the other two villages, but as mentioned in Chapter 5, ten households belonging to the villager small group decided to move to Green Mountain because of its proximity to a tea-processing district where the villagers were hoping to find work. Group Leader Liu, contended that these households failed to consider the long-term consequences because they disregarded the fact that the land available in Green Mountain was not as good as that in South Stream (Interviews, NDH1208031, NDH1302201). In retrospect, the situation did not develop as well as the South Stream migrants had hoped, mainly because the local government did not allocate them all the land that they were supposed to receive but also because finding jobs in the urban center was not as easy as the migrants had imagined.

Preparing the host population for resettlement

The local government did not only visit future migrants to prepare them for resettlement but also undertook to inform the future host community in the resettlement village of the fact that several hundred people would be moving to their village. By this means, the Resettlement Bureau hoped to prevent future conflicts from developing between the host population and the migrants and also to persuade the host population to sell some of their land to the local government. The Resettlement Bureau had to rely on the host community's being willing to sell part of its land holdings because otherwise there would not be enough land available in the area for the government to allocate to the migrants.

The resettlement village for the South Stream migrants is located about 500 meters down a slope from the Deep Forest villager small group. With a total population of 299 people (i.e., 69 households), this villager small group had an annual income of 1.7 million yuan in 2011, amounting to an average per capita income of 4,724 yuan. The villagers primarily depend on crop farming and animal husbandry for their livelihoods. The crops are cultivated on 300 *mu* of land that are in the possession of the small group. In addition, the group has 9,600 *mu* of forest land, 2,800 *mu* of which are categorized as economic forest used for growing tea and coffee trees (Wild Grass County Government, 2013).

In 2007, the Nanping Township government responsible for communicating with the host population first approached the group leader of the Deep Forest villager small group to inform him about the resettlement issue. The local cadres convened several meetings with the community to inform them about the hydropower project and the necessary processes of resettlement that would accompany the construction work. The cadres asked the villagers to support them in resolving the resettlement issue by selling part of their land to the local government who would then turn it over to the migrants. They tried to convince the host population of the advantages that immigration would have for the village economy: the construction of the resettlement village, the cadres argued, would bring investment into the area and an increase in the village population would foster overall development (Interview, SM120805).

As a result, most of the villagers agreed to sell part of their land to the government. With an average per capita availability of one *mu* before immigration, most of the households that decided to sell some land gave away two to three *mu*, depending on how much contracted land they had originally been allocated. Each household that sold land to the government for the migrants received 19,000 yuan, out of which 16,500 yuan went to the household that had provided the land and 3,500 yuan was paid to the collective.

At least on the surface, some of the households in the Deep Forest villager small group have benefited from resettlement and the subsequent sale of land to the government/migrants. While walking through the village in August 2012, numerous ongoing construction projects could be observed, most of which were new residential properties. The funding for these projects mainly stemmed from the money that villagers had received for selling their land to the government, and the projects would have not been possible without the land sales. However, as one villager told me, selling the land, at that time, had not really been so advantageous after all. Although he had been able to put the money he received towards financing his newly built house, he would have received much more money, had he kept the land and sold it a few years later. But the government did not leave him any choice, he claimed, the cadres told him that he would have to sell part of his land. Apart from putting pressure on him, government representatives visited the village regularly to invite the villagers for meals and to improve the village facilities in order to create a positive image of resettlement. "They did a lot of good things for the village, in order to convince us," the villager informed me. "That's their method of bringing [us] into line [*xietiao*]." This was why, in the end, he sold five of the eight *mu* he had previously contracted for crop cultivation. This interviewee received 82,500 yuan, in total, for the sale in 2007, but he remains convinced that had he sold the land in 2012, he would have received at least 100,000 yuan.

Although the local government again employed skillful methods of propaganda to convince the members of the Deep Forest villager small group of the advantages of resettlement and the necessity of selling their land, the villagers did not agree to sell any of the land used to cultivate coffee. The villagers had, at first, agreed to do so, but after the price of coffee rose sharply over a few years, they became reluctant to give up their increasingly profitable land to the migrants.[6]

According to the group leader of the Deep Forest villager small group, migration has not, on the whole, influenced their lives in any special way. One advantage has been the fact that several families in Deep Forest have been able to renovate or build new houses, because of the money pouring in from land sales. At the same time, however, several small incidents occurred between migrants and Deep Forest villagers. The former "thought they were better than us, because they had received so much resettlement compensation. For this reason, they treated some members of our group without much respect and this caused a few arguments" (Interview, NDH120803). The group leader was reluctant to speak about this topic. He pointed out that there were also a few drug addicts among the migrants and that the host community had been afraid that they would cause trouble. These people, however, made up only a minority among the dam migrants, and the host community was getting on well with the majority of them. He also emphasized the fact that, in his opinion, the local government had done a good job in resettling the people, repeating what I had already read and heard several times from local cadres, namely, that before resettlement, the migrants had been living in a very poor and underdeveloped area without much infrastructure, but now they were much better off with all the compensation they had received and the new infrastructure in their village (Interview, NDH120803).

Moving to a new village

In late June 2008, the migrants left their homes to move to South Stream. Compared with the resettlement processes for Green Mountain village, relocation in South Stream was not as clearly divided. Although the villagers were moved in different batches, the time frame for resettlement only covered a few months. This is why, when asked about their resettlement, the villagers referred to their community as being resettled together rather than in different batches. The location of each family's home, however, was chosen according to when the respective family arrived in the village. Those that moved first, chose plots for their houses along the national road on which the village is located, while households that moved later, live in rows that are further away from the street and closer to the forest (see Map 6.1). Within each of the rows, families chose their locations according to where their friends and relatives were moving. Although families living along the road have set up small shops and restaurants that profit both from customers from within the village as well as from people passing by on the road, the villagers claim that the selection of plots for their houses has caused neither conflict nor dissatisfaction among those who live in rows further away from the road (Interview, NDH 13022013).

As was the case in Green Mountain, several households did not join the resettlement organized by the government but instead organized their own resettlement (*zixing anzhi*), and again, as in Green Mountain, these households now wished to join the settlement in South Stream. However, according to the South Stream migrants, since these households had decided to leave the community in the first place, they now felt embarrassed about re-joining them. Only one household had

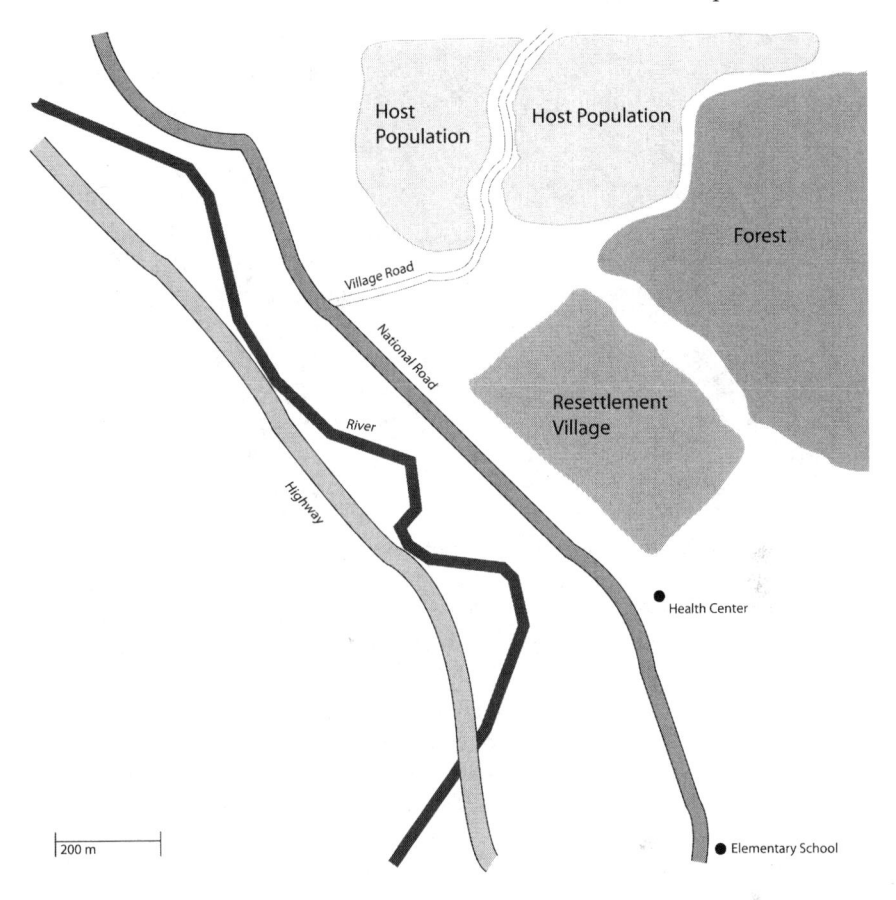

Map 6.1 South Stream resettlement village and host population
Source: Author.

had the courage to resettle to South Stream after they had become aware of the disadvantages incurred by self-organized resettlement in comparison with government-organized resettlement. As in the case of the two households who moved to Green Mountain, after becoming frustrated with their self-organized resettlement, one household had moved to South Stream and built a house there. Again, this move was considered illegal by the local government, because the family had originally signed an agreement stating that they would organize their own resettlement and move to a location further up the mountain close to their original home. While the local government had demolished the houses of the two families in Green Mountain, the family in South Stream had been left alone so far. Nevertheless, the household was now being subjected to pressure on two fronts, first of all, because they did not have government approval to move to South Stream, and this meant that they had to live with the fear that their new house, which they had just built in South Stream, would be demolished, and that they would be sent back to their former settlement in their home village. Second, they were to a certain extent alienated from the rest of the migrant community in South Stream, because they had originally decided to part from them.

Before the villager small group first moved to South Stream, the local government had promised to allocate land one day after the actual relocation had been completed, and this was scheduled for late June 2008. According to the original plan put forward by the local government, the per capita area of land that was supposed to be allocated to the South Stream resettlement village was the same amount of land that Green Mountain migrants were supposed to receive. Each villager was entitled to receive 0.7 *mu* of paddy field, 1.5 *mu* of dry land, 4 *mu* of forestland, and 0.1 *mu* of vegetable plot (Fanwen Net, 2011), but as of February 2013, the migrants had only received paddy fields and some land. This was due to the fact that there was not enough land available in the region for the migrants, and this was why the local government had to negotiate with the host population about selling land in the first place. The host community would only agree to sell some of the land needed for the migrants, however, which is why the increasingly profitable land for coffee cultivation could not be transferred to the migrants.

Since the cultivation of coffee was so profitable, and since they needed to make ends meet, the migrants began to cultivate coffee illegally in the forest adjacent to the village. In order to prevent the local government from finding out about their illegal methods of cultivation, the migrants primarily tended their coffee plants at night when local cadres were not visiting the village. It should be noted that when the new migrants first arrived in the new village, they did not know how to cultivate coffee; in their home village, the group had primarily planted tea, corn, and fruit trees. The migrants therefore decided to ask the host population in South Stream to teach them how to tend the coffee plants and to tell them where they could sell the beans.[7]

In order to make ends meet, as previously mentioned, some of the villagers continued to cultivate the fields that had not yet been flooded in the reservoir area. One particular reason for this was that the paddy fields of their home village were much more fertile than the paddy fields of South Stream. However, not everybody who still had land there actually returned. Travelling back was both time-consuming and expensive: The bus travelling between the urban center of Pu'er and their home village took about three hours and cost 30 yuan for a one-way ticket. This is why not everybody returned, and others intended to purchase more land in South Stream, once the local government had paid out all the compensation that was due. Unfortunately, the villagers did not know when the government would do this nor did they know whether the local population would be willing to give up any more land.

Although the migrants would have liked to continue to cultivate the land, the problems mentioned here have led 60 percent of the migrant adult population to find jobs outside the village. Some of the farmers-turned-workers have, in the meantime, left the village permanently, in order to live near their new places of employment closer to the urban center, while others are still living in the village and commute to their jobs on a daily basis. Transportation is now more convenient than had been the case in their home village, and this allows the migrants to work outside the new village. Nevertheless, they tend to argue that, on the whole, their income is now lower than it was before resettlement. This is mainly related to the decline in land availability. Although, on paper, there is no difference in average per capita availability of land between the migrants' home village and South Stream, there has been a de facto decline of more than 20 *mu* per person. This is due to the fact that in the region where their home village was located, the population density was very low, and the villager small groups used to live spread out in the mountains.[8] Although each household had officially been allocated only a few *mu*, there was still enough land in the area for every family to cultivate much more.

Issues of contestation

Dam-induced resettlement in China has been frequently accompanied by protests on the part of those who have to leave their homes or those who have already left and feel that they have been neglected by the government after resettlement. Two of the starkest examples occurred in 2003 and 2004, when first, the Kunming-based NGO Green Watershed organized villagers to express their grievances about the planned Xiaowan Dam and the Nu River Project in Yunnan, and second, when the protesters organized themselves to protest against the planned Pubugou hydropower project in Sichuan, which led to the biggest demonstrations since Tiananmen (Sun & Zhao, 2007: 150; Mertha, 2008).

Apart from these large-scale protests, migrants frequently vent their frustration on a much smaller scale by visiting the local Resettlement Bureau and submitting formal complaints and requests through the letters and visits system. This has also been the case in South Stream, where dissatisfied migrants frequently call upon the township and county governments to help them resolve the problems caused by resettlement. Issues of contestation in the present case have been related to the registration process of migrants, their living expenses, land compensation, housing compensation, and the long-term compensation mechanism. The migrants in South Stream have complained about many further issues related to resettlement, but in order to study the strategies and reactions of the migrants to policy change and policy implementation, this chapter focuses on those problems that migrants regard as grave enough for them to file official letters of complaint or to even take to the streets.

Living expenses

Migrants frequently cite lack of or limited compensation as one of the problems related to resettlement (e.g., Yardley, 2007; Ying, 2008). In China, this is caused either by inadequate policies (although these have been modified in recent years, to allow considerable increases in compensation standards) or, more often, by the corrupt behavior of local officials who tend to divert part of the compensation money into their own pockets or use it for other purposes deemed more necessary or urgent (on the latter, see e.g., Takeuchi, 2013).

After resettlement, the South Stream migrants received their compensation in several installments. The local government told the villagers that this was because of the negative experiences with migrants resettled in the course of the construction of the Dachaoshan Dam, further north along the Lancang River. In that case, the local government had paid out large sums of money in compensation, which had led the migrants to neglect their work and live off the compensation. The migrants had subsequently spent all their money, with the result that several communities fell into poverty, and this caused social instability. In order to avoid a repetition of these events, the government in Pu'er decided to pay out compensation in small sums of several thousand yuan only (Interviews, SM130218, NDH1302201).

However, the payment of compensation in small installments did not prevent migrants in South Stream from living precariously. Although compensation was paid out during and after resettlement, the money was barely enough to complete the construction of the new houses for the migrants. For each person, 60 square meters of land was available, on which the house was to be constructed. As was the case in Green Mountain, instead of letting the villagers decide for themselves about the kind of houses they would like, the construction

Figure 6.1 Picture of houses in South Stream
Source: Author.

of each building was based on a specific standard and design determined by the local government. A construction company was made responsible for building the houses,[9] and the villagers had to pay for them. Although the land on which the houses were constructed was free of charge, the houses cost around 200,000 yuan, and since the compensation that many families had received was not enough to cover all the expenses, many families had to take out a loan in order to cover the shortfall.

Some families received only a few thousand yuan as compensation for their land, either because they had only contracted small plots in their home village or because parts of their land were not yet flooded. In addition, the compensation standard for their original houses was calculated according to the structure, age, and quality of each house. In 2007, the responsible county government set compensation for houses between 951 yuan and 53 yuan per square meter. This is why some of the households in the village received as little as 40,000 yuan in total compensation, which led them to incur large debts in order to be able to pay for the housing to be built to the high standard set for the new housing by the local government.[10] The family of the group leader, who is considered as relatively better off, received 60,000 yuan and 190,000 yuan in compensation for their former house and land plus crops, respectively. With the construction costs for the new house amounting to 200,000 yuan, the household had only 50,000 yuan left with which to buy the new land they needed to compensate for the loss of land that they had incurred through resettlement (Interview, NDH1302201).

In late 2010, the group leader convened a meeting of all household representatives in order to find a way to combat the spread of poverty among village households. The villagers knew that given the absence of any official policy, there was nothing on which they could base their claim to specific financial entitlement, but since their livelihoods were at risk, they did not see that they had any other option but to act. The migrants were, however, aware that one official guideline for resettlement was to "move migrants out, let them have a stable lifestyle, and give them the ability to become rich" (*bandechu, wenduzhu, nengzhifu*), which gave them a point of reference when approaching the local government (Interview, NDH1302201).

During the meeting, the migrants decided on the strategy for action that is depicted in Figure 6.2. The group leader explained it as follows:

> First, five people go to the local government together to talk to the officials. There cannot be more than five people, because according to the letter and visits regulations, if a group of more than five people goes to visit the government, this is considered as making trouble [*naoshi*]. Then we wait and see what the government tells us, and if we are not satisfied with the response, then we write an official document in which we explain our problem to the government. After we have submitted the document [to the local government], we wait for two to four weeks. If the government doesn't respond, we go to protest at the power station.
>
> (Interview, NDH1302201)

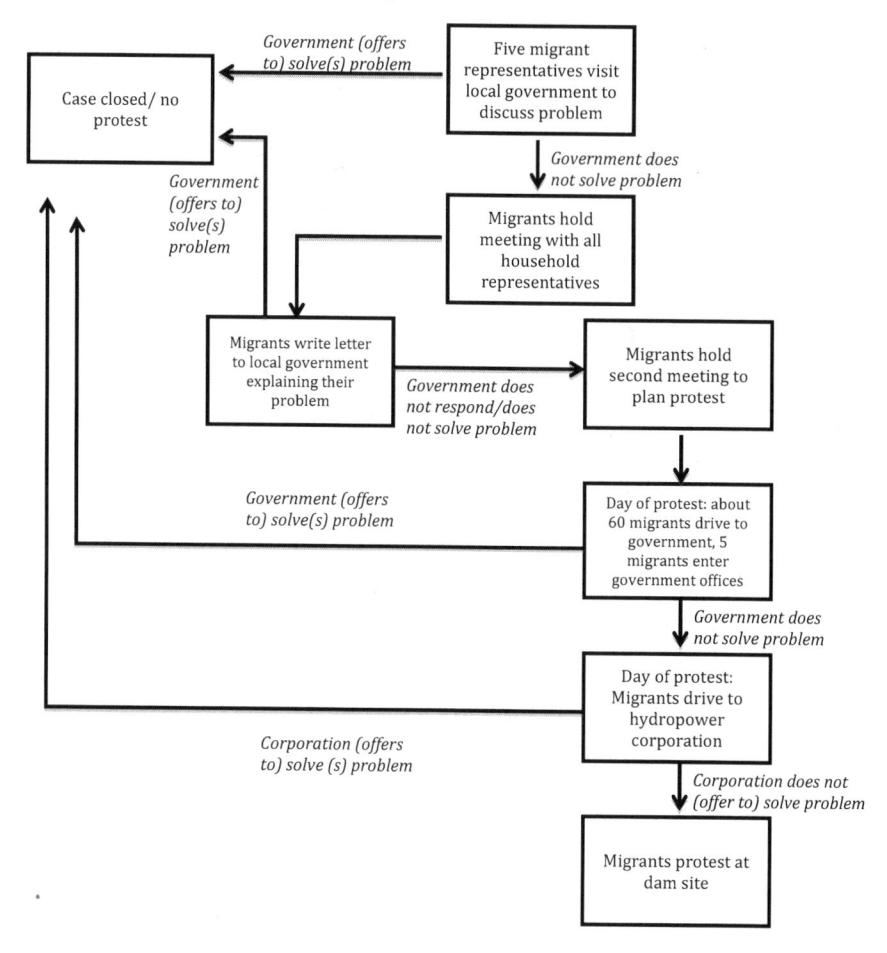

Figure 6.2 Problem-solving strategy employed by South Stream migrants
Source: Author.

When the five migrant representatives visited the local Resettlement Bureau, the officials informed them that compensation was paid out according to official policies and that no changes could be made, meaning that the local government did not intend to help the migrants resolve their financial problems. This was why, after returning to the village, the five representatives convened a meeting of all the villagers to discuss the issue again. During this meeting, the household representatives decided to write an official letter and hand it over to the local government. However, according to the group leader, the villagers were not in the position to write such official letters themselves. Most of the migrants had not received any education, and those who had – including the group leader – had only been educated up to the elementary school level. This is why the villagers decided to approach one of their friends from outside the village who would be able to help them write the letter.

When the letter was ready, they submitted it to the district Resettlement Bureau and waited for an official response, but after a month had passed without any reaction from the Resettlement Bureau, the migrants decided to hold another meeting to discuss their next steps. At this meeting, the migrants decided that their only option was to go to talk directly to the energy company, and, should this not prove successful either, the migrants would have to drive to the hydropower station to block the road. "The hydropower station is now on our land, so if the local government cannot do anything, we have to talk to those people who took our land," one villager explained to me. The next stage was to decide on the best place to block access to the station. Some of the migrants were familiar with the roads surrounding the power station and suggested blocking one of the streets outside the construction area but within one kilometer of the dam. In this way, they would not actually be on the construction site of the dam itself but would still be close enough to gain the attention of the people responsible. They hoped, as a result of this action, that a political leader from the provincial government or even from the central government would come down and see exactly how local governments in Pu'er were treating the migrant population.

Before setting off for Simaogang, where the headquarters of the Huaneng Lancang Corporation were located, the villagers first drove to the district Resettlement Bureau in Pu'er, in order to make sure that the local government knew what they were planning to do and to draw attention to their protest. Once again, to show that they were complying with the regulations, only five people went into the Resettlement Bureau office to talk to the officials, while the other fifty-five protesters waited outside. The five representatives informed the officials about their plan, pointing out that this protest seemed to be the only option open to them, if the government would not offer them financial support. The officials tried to prevent the migrants from driving to the energy company headquarters, but since they would not be bound to any firm agreements on the compensation issue, the villagers set off in their cars again, in the direction of the Huaneng Lancang Corporation.

The district government officials had no choice but to follow them, to try to prevent the situation from escalating near the hydropower station. This is why, for the 1.5 hour drive to the energy company, the ten cars in which the migrants were sitting were followed by several more cars filled with government and Party representatives. By the time the migrants reached the company's premises, more local officials had already arrived at the compound. When the five migrant representatives went into the building to speak to the staff of the energy company, they were followed by local officials from the district, the township, and village governments; the director of the district Resettlement Bureau; public security personnel; and officials from the local People's Court, the People's Procuratorate, and the Party Organization Department, all of whom had arrived in the meantime.

Inside the building, the villagers started to argue with representatives from the government, the Party, and the power station. The migrants declared their intention of blocking access to the hydropower station and added that they would not leave until they had received a satisfactory answer regarding the financial support they had requested. In return, the government officials threatened the villagers, claiming that any losses incurred by the power station as a result of the obstruction would have to be made good by the migrants. Huaneng representatives informed the villagers that the company had already transferred all the funds to the government and that the amount paid was based on the official resettlement plan for the Nuozhadu Dam. They explained that compensation was to be paid in stages, according to the progress of construction and resettlement and that, if there were any inconsistencies with regard to the amount of money that the migrants received, these were a matter to be negotiated with the local government, not with the hydropower company.

The discussions continued for half an hour but without any satisfactory results for the migrants, who then left the company and went on, as planned, to obstruct access to the power station. They drove to the road that they had previously decided on at the village meeting and blocked it so that no cars and construction vehicles could pass through; they also set up a banner on which they highlighted their plight in bold letters for passersby. Shortly after the migrants arrived, the military personnel (*wujing*) responsible for maintaining the security of the dam tried to persuade the migrants to leave, but they maintained their position for twenty-four hours at which point, the local cadres who had followed the migrants to the dam caved in. The head of the People's Congress of the responsible county, the director of the county Resettlement Bureau, and the director of the county Party Organization Department agreed to pay out 900 yuan to every South Stream migrant. The migrants considered this concession a success and left the power station.

Land compensation

The villagers were not dissatisfied merely because they were not going to receive larger sums of money, which they could use to make meaningful investments. In 2011, they had also heard from their friends in other resettlement villages that the local government in Wide River County had paid out more in compensation to these villagers than it was giving to South Stream at that time. This is why the group leader together with four other representatives of the villager small group went to the county Resettlement Bureau to check the official documents regarding land compensation.

At first, the officials in the Resettlement Bureau were reluctant to provide them with the documents, but in the end, the group of migrants did not only manage to have a look at the documents but was even able to make copies. When talking to me about the issue, the group leader handed out some of these copies and showed me that the local government had, in fact, cheated the villagers by providing them with a lower estimate of the land to be inundated than was officially recorded: After the government had examined the forestland in their home village, the migrants were told that the entire area encompassed 7000 *mu*. However, according to the copy made by the group leader, the actual area of the forestland belonging to the villager small group in the home village amounted to 7800 *mu*.

During their visit to the local Resettlement Bureau, the five representatives talked to the cadres about the issue and asked them for prompt payment of the money that was due to them. However, the local government argued that they had already paid out everything they had received from the energy company and that further installments could only be provided after the energy company had disbursed the next round of payments. The migrants were not satisfied with this response. They knew that the local government had cheated them in the case of the forestland, and they had also learned that other resettlement villages were receiving higher amounts of compensation than they were.

As a result, after the five representatives had returned from their trip to the Resettlement Bureau, they again called for a meeting of household representatives to discuss the issue. During this meeting, which was held in March 2011, they decided to write another letter to the local government. In this letter, the villagers asked the Resettlement Bureau to pay out 50 percent of the land compensation that the government still owed them for their farmland, garden plots, and part of their forestland that they had lost to the Nuozhadu Dam.[11] In the document, the villagers argued that all the land compensation should be paid out and that the members of the small group would take care of the money and make sure that it would mainly be used for the purpose of industrial development. In total, the villagers asked the local government to pay them for 3098.78 *mu* of land, which would amount to 10.4 million yuan.

One month after the meeting in the village, in April 2011, the migrants submitted the letter to the Resettlement Bureau of the district government; once again, however, the local government did not respond. After another month, the villagers called for a second meeting to discuss their subsequent action. As in the previous year, they believed that their only option was to block the road near the power station. The group leader informed me that the subsequent events were very similar to those that had taken place in 2010. On the day that they had picked for the protest in May 2011, the villagers first drove to the local government bureau, before moving on to the power company, and eventually to the power station. The only difference was that this time, their protest did not last for one full day and one night but instead ended after four hours when the government officials decided to give in. The officials agreed that within a month of the protest – before June 15 – they would pay the money to the migrants. The officials told the migrants that, in fact, they did not have the money, but in order to calm down the migrants and support them in their efforts to settle down in South Stream, the government would take the risk and divert the money from other channels to give it to the migrants for their land compensation. And in fact, the local government did pay out the money within the stipulated period of time. In total, the South Stream villager small group received 10.4 million yuan, which was distributed among migrant households according to the amount of inundated land they had contracted in their home village.

Increase of housing compensation

A little more than one year after the government had paid out part of the land compensation that the migrants had requested, in June 2012, the migrants learned from relatives in other resettlement villages that the compensation paid for houses had been increased and that the local government was already paying out this increase in a few resettlement villages that were being resettled at that time. The migrants were furious that they had had to learn about the policy change from their relatives instead of from the local government, which had been so very active in propagating its policies before resettlement started, but had left the migrants on their own afterwards.

This is why the group leader called for a village meeting to discuss the issue. During the meeting, the migrants again decided to send five representatives to the local Resettlement Bureau to discuss the issue with the officials responsible. The latter confirmed that there had indeed been an increase in housing compensation but that it was impossible for the local government to pay this to every migrant household immediately. The migrants were not satisfied with this response and continued to discuss the issue with the Resettlement Bureau, threatening to block access to the hydropower station again, if officials refused to pay out the money that the migrants were entitled to. "They design a policy, and then they break the policy. So in effect, they are breaking their own rules," the group leader told me when speaking about the increase in housing compensation. The migrants had already decided that if the local government did not give a satisfactory response to their request, they would simply employ the same strategy that they had used the previous year: write a document, present it to the officials, wait for about a month, and then block access to the hydropower station.

On this occasion, however, the local government officials even wanted to prevent the villagers from getting as far as blocking the road in the first place. Every protest has the potential to draw attention from higher government levels, and this can pose a threat to the political future of local cadres. For this reason, the government decided to pay the increase in housing compensation, which amounted to 40,000 yuan for each household in South Stream. This figure was based on an official policy guideline published by the prefecture government, a fact that might have led the district government to give in more quickly than in the previous cases of contestation involving South Stream migrants.

Long-term compensation mechanism

When I visited the South Stream resettlement village in February 2013, one constant theme and problem raised by the migrants was the long-term compensation mechanism that was mentioned in Chapter 4. As explained previously, the deputy township head had mentioned the long-term compensation mechanism during a visit to the migrants' home village even before resettlement started, but despite the fact that the long-term compensation mechanism had been intensely studied by the time the South Stream migrants had been resettled, the government in Pu'er had still not published any specific guidelines for its implementation. The resettlement scheme employed in South Stream therefore followed the conventional pattern of "big agricultural resettlement" including the allocation of land for migrants as their basic livelihood asset.

In 2010, the Pu'er government finally adopted the long-term compensation mechanism but still only with reference to the reservoir area of the dam and not to every area affected by the construction of the dam. Since the South Stream migrants had previously lived in the cofferdam area, the mechanism did not apply to them. The fact that the local government had first advocated the policy in the village but then failed to implement it later gave rise to great frustration among the migrants in South Stream, with the result that they decided to continue to put pressure on the government to implement the long-term compensation mechanism in their village (Interview, NDH1302203).

Another reason why the villagers wanted to apply for long-term compensation was the fact that they had not yet been allocated all the land they had been promised according to the resettlement plan: The "big agricultural resettlement" scheme entitled each villager to 0.7 *mu* of paddy field, 1.5 *mu* of dry land, 4 *mu* of forestland, and 0.1 *mu* of vegetable plot; however, as of February 2013, the migrants had only received paddy fields and part of the land that they were entitled to. This is why the villagers decided to raise the issue of the long-term compensation mechanism with the local government. Specifically, the villagers wanted the government to implement the mechanism in their village. Although they had originally been resettled according to the "big agricultural resettlement" scheme, the villagers argued that since they had not yet been allocated all the land they were promised, they wanted to transfer to the long-term compensation mechanism, which entitled them to monthly financial support and could therefore at least partly make up for their loss of land.

Over the past four years, the villagers had visited the local government regularly to express their concerns on this issue but had not yet achieved a satisfactory outcome. This is why they once more decided to write an official letter and present it to the prefecture government – the lowest level of government that has published an official regulation regarding the long-term compensation mechanism in their jurisdiction. In this document, which was signed by all household representatives in January 2013, the migrants requested that the government implement the long-term compensation mechanism in South Stream in order to foster development and improve the lives of the migrant population. This letter represented the migrants' latest efforts to have the policy implemented, and this issue was the most bothersome for the villager small group. As of February 2013, the villagers had still not received a reply from the local government, and they were undecided about their subsequent action. Although their request was not in line with government policy, which does not entitle cofferdam migrants (i.e., South Stream migrants) to apply for long-term compensation, migrants still saw taking action to block access to the hydropower station as an option.

Migrant reactions

This chapter has highlighted the resettlement experiences of the South Stream migrants as well as their reactions to the perceived unfairness that has resulted from resettlement itself, policy change during resettlement, and uneven policy implementation by local governments. Uneven policy implementation here refers not only to the partial implementation of resettlement policy in South Stream, such as deficiencies in allocating land, but also to the unequal implementation of policy, such as the housing compensation that was paid out in some resettlement villages but not in others. In this context, three interdependent themes have been considered: First of all, the forms of resistance developed by migrant communities in response to dam-induced resettlement. Although, in this case, the migrants did not attempt to change broader structures of the law and the state, they did more than just "work . . . the system . . . to their minimum disadvantage" (Hobsbawm, 1973: 12); on the contrary, while accepting the current state of affairs regarding hydropower development and resettlement, they made use of existing (and constantly changing) resettlement policies to improve their current situation as a displaced group.

This is not intended to imply that dam migrants find themselves in an advantageous position due to resettlement – quite the opposite is the case. The forms of resistance presented here, however, show that the migrants do not simply accept their fate as displaced people and their corresponding treatment at the hands of the local government, nor do they openly revolt against displacement. Their forms of resistance cover a middle ground, where they make use of existing rules governing dam-induced resettlement to minimize their losses. The reactions of migrants toward local policy implementation depart from what J. Scott (1985) has termed "everyday forms of resistance" in that they formally and overtly voice claims to the state and hydropower companies. At the same time, migrants do not contest formal definitions of power but rather accept them as given and attempt to improve their situation within the existing structures.

Four issues of contestation in South Stream have been described here, as well as the ways in which the migrants dealt with them. The migrants were driven to protest for several reasons: to gain financial support to cover their living expenses, to pressure the local government into paying out land compensation and the increase in housing compensation, and also to urge the government to implement the long-term compensation mechanism. In at least two of the cases, the migrants decided to protest in order to obtain fair treatment, because they discovered that other resettlement villages had received better treatment than South Stream. This was possible because many of the migrants had been acquainted with each other from before resettlement, when they used to live in neighboring hamlets. After they had been moved to different resettlement villages, the migrants continued to stay in touch and compared the processes and outcomes of relocation in their respective communities.

The South Stream migrants developed a specifically staged strategy for their protests: First, the migrants wanted to avoid breaking the law, wherever possible, and therefore referred to official policies when formulating their complaints. This applied to their negotiations with government representatives as well as to the letters that they wrote to the local government. In these letters, the migrants frequently cited both official policies and the statements made by local cadres who had propagated resettlement policy in their village before relocation. Second, as soon as they realized that the local government was not going to help them resolve their problems, the migrants aimed to attract attention from government representatives higher up in the hierarchy than the representatives they had originally approached for help. Normally, once the first stage of the strategy based on an appeal to the official policies had failed (because the government would not help to resolve the problems), the migrants followed with the second stage of their strategy, that of attracting attention.[12] In two of the above cases, the presence of Party and government representatives from the county Party Organization Department and other bureaus is likely to have encouraged the officials from the Resettlement Bureau to relent.

As one of the most important organs of the CCP, the Organization Department controls all personnel assignments in the national system. While the Ministry of Personnel under the State Council and corresponding Personnel Bureaus at the local level is also responsible for managing Chinese cadres, the Organization Department is far more influential for it being responsible for dealing with leadership positions (Shambaugh, 2008: 141; Zhong, 2003: 107).[13] Since the early 2000s, Organization Departments at all levels have stepped up their efforts in evaluating state and party cadres through a variety of methods including individual interviews, questionnaires, and assessments by the populace (Shambaugh, 2008: 142).[14] Representing one of the main organs responsible for party discipline, it does not come as a surprise that officials of the Organization Department have been present during these incidents of protest organized by South Stream villagers. Over recent years, the relationship between the masses and the Party has become a key concern for the CCP especially in rural areas. Those cadres who are able to handle protests well in the eyes of the Organization Department will receive a better evaluation, and vice versa.

The role played by the district Resettlement Bureau in the protests is of interest as well, because the state itself contributed to raising awareness in the resettlement village. Although an NGO had visited the village in 2011 to speak about the resettlement issue and to raise awareness among the migrants of their right to protest, ultimately, it was the local state itself that informed the migrants about the existing policies and even about the policies that were merely in the making and had not yet been published. This increased flow of information for the migrants gives them more power vis-à-vis the local state, since it allows them to check on the performance of local cadres and to base their claims on the information provided. However, the information provided by the local government in advance is not always accurate or comprehensive. At the same time, the provision of information can lead to increasingly tense relations between the local state and society, if the former does not follow up with adequate policy implementation.

Apart from introducing new disclosure methods for policy implementation, policy change at the central and provincial government levels in the area of dam-induced resettlement over the past few years has also been accompanied by new mechanisms for consultation with migrant communities. In the case presented here, this has led to migrant household representatives being consulted over the choice of resettlement villages available and the method of resettlement itself, be it unified and government-organized or dispersed and self-organized. These measures of enhanced consultation merely provide migrants with the ability to steer resettlement in a direction that, at least at first, seems to be most suitable (or for that matter least unfavorable) to the households without giving the migrants the ability to control the resettlement processes. Nevertheless, such policy concessions empower migrants vis-à-vis the local government, by providing them with reference points for their negotiations with local officials, and even if they cannot base their claims on any particular existing policy, the migrants still have the impression that the central government is on their side, encouraging them to make their voices heard. This is in line with what O'Brien and Li (2006) refer to as "rightful resistance" where protesters employ the officials rhetoric of the state, make use of divisions within the state, and mobilize as much support from the community as possible in order to make their voices heard.

The case presented in this chapter has shown how changes in resettlement policy have empowered local migrant communities by granting them more rights and by providing them with more information before they are relocated. This empowerment, however, has gone hand in hand with increased demands on local governments that must now implement new and more demanding policies handed down from above, while at the same time responding to the claims of the empowered migrants. Local governments (in particular those at the county level and below) now have to deal with an increase in pressure from below and above but have not been granted the authority to address these pressures adequately. In other words, the new and improved resettlement policies have widened the gap between theory (i.e., what the policy stipulates) and practice (i.e., what the local government implements) while at the same time empowering the migrants and encouraging them to raise their voices whenever they perceive any inconsistencies in policy implementation.

Notes

1 Compared with "big agricultural resettlement," which was being implemented in most resettlement villages in Yunnan, the long-term compensation mechanism is another type of resettlement strategy altogether that either does not provide for the allocation of land, or provides only for the limited allocation of land to the villagers, but instead provides migrants with long-term compensation for the time of the operation of the respective hydropower station. In addition, depending on the detailed implementation guidelines published by local governments, programs are developed to train migrants for jobs outside agriculture and assist them in finding employment in townships or cities. Currently, there is no single strategy for implementing the mechanism, for example, in the case of some dam projects, migrants are compensated in kind; in others, the migrants are paid long-term support in cash (see Du et al., 2011: 27).

2 This type of protest is in line with what O'Brien (1996) and O'Brien and Li (2006) have termed "rightful resistance," see also Chapter 2 of this study.

3 This information is based on a list that was handed to me by the villager small group leader. The list states the exact amount of compensation to be paid to each household and the collective.

4 See also Stern and O'Brien (2011) on state signaling in China.

5 The official name for this locally developed mechanism is the "16118 Resettlement Compensation Method" (16118 *yimin buchang anzhi fangshi*), where the numbers

"16118" refer to one long-term compensation mechanism; six different methods of resettlement (urban resettlement, urban and township integrated resettlement, agricultural resettlement, dispersed resettlement, monetary resettlement, and employment resettlement); one reservoir development fund; a unified post-resettlement support policy; and eight resettlement measures (including measures such as properly managing resettlement funds, carrying out resettlement in line with local conditions, and appropriately identifying the resettlement population as well as the property to be compensated) (China Energy News, 2013).

6 During the time that the Deep Forest villagers were discussing whether to sell land for coffee cultivation, the price for Arabica beans (the type of bean cultivated by the Deep Forest villager small group) more than doubled, with 1 pound (lb) of beans selling for US$1.15 in 2005 and US$3.00 in early 2011 (International Coffee Organization, 2013).

7 In recent years, the prefecture government has begun to expand the cultivation of coffee in the region. As of 2011, there were four coffee farms in South Stream that occupied an area of more than 5,000 *mu*. Government officials argue that, for some households, cultivating and selling coffee beans makes up 70 percent of their income, with some of the wealthiest households earning about 300,000 yuan per annum. In early 2012, the coffee giant, Starbucks Coffee Company, signed an agreement to develop a joint venture with Ai Ni Group – one of Yunnan's largest coffee operators and agricultural companies. The joint venture began to operate in early 2013 (Pu'er News, 2013; Starbucks Newsroom, 2012).

8 The South Stream migrants belong to the Bulang minority nationality group who tend to live high up in remote forested mountains (Hattaway, 2004: 14).

9 Although I do not have any information on the company that built the migrants' houses, according to the records of construction works in the village provided for me by the group leader, roads in the resettlement village were not built by a local enterprise but rather by a construction company from Chongqing.

10 Tilt (2014: 134) reports similar situations of indebtedness among resettled households along the Lancang River.

11 The villagers asked for only 50 percent of the money that the government still owed them, first of all because they did not want to seem to be making unreasonable claims and, second, because they hoped the local government would put the outstanding 50 percent toward their application for the long-term support mechanism.

12 For a recent study on how villagers created a "protest spectacle" in order to make their voices heard in an incident of environmental activism in Zhejiang, see O'Brien and Deng (2014).

13 For example, at the township level, officials below the rank of deputy section chief (*fu keji*) are handled by the government Personnel Bureau at the county level whereas the county Organization Department is charged with appointing officials above this rank (Smith, 2015: 600).

14 Between 2001 and 2004, the Central Committee and the State Council have adopted a range of regulations, designed to improve the quality of party and state cadres including the methods for their selection. As a result, evaluation of party personnel has become much more rigorous, including annual assessments of professional accomplishments, moral integrity, and acceptance by the population (Shambaugh, 2008: 141–142).

7 Conclusion
Policy, power, and mediation

The Chinese regime has been described as one that is continuously evolving and adapting to a changing national and international environment, thereby ensuring its continued stability. The key question of this book is how the adaptive capacity of the central state plays out at the local level in China. It examines local processes of policy implementation to clarify the extent to which local state actors are able to shape these processes and to ensure that resettlement is completed without endangering social stability and possibly their own political careers.

Past studies have painted a mixed picture of the ways in which local states come to terms with demands by their superiors and their local constituencies. In particular, work by O'Brien and Li (1999) on *selective policy implementation* sparked a series of studies that highlighted the dysfunctional elements of the Chinese policy process. O'Brien and Li sought to explain why beneficial central policies were frequently turned into harmful policies by local state actors. In contrast, other studies have found that local cadres are in fact willing to experiment, innovate, and adhere to central policy directives (Heilmann, 2008a, 2008b, 2009; Heilmann & Perry, 2011; Wang, 2008, 2009; Ahlers & Schubert, 2014), using their room to maneuver in ways that are favorable towards their local constituencies. Ahlers and Schubert (2014) argue that in the case of the "Building a New Socialist Countryside" (*shehui zhuyi xin nongcun jianshe*, BNSC) initiative, the local state has proven its willingness to follow central policy guidelines while simultaneously responding to public demands and achieving positive policy outcomes.

Compared with the BNSC policy, which was designed to foster local initiatives in the sphere of rural development, China's resettlement regulations are part of the country's hydropower policy – a centrally mandated development strategy aimed at increasing clean energy provision. Dam-induced resettlement by itself is a coercive process that, only if implemented well, does not leave dam migrants worse off than before relocation. In comparison, BNSC has the aim of improving the socioeconomic situation of the Chinese countryside and is therefore much more likely to be well received among local cadres and communities.

Thus, this book analyzes local policy implementation in a policy field that is characterized by powerful political actors aiming to achieve energy security as well as by influential energy companies striving to reap the financial benefits of

China's strategy to increase the provision of electricity generated by hydropower. This new focus on renewable energy, and the decision to stick to the construction of large dams despite the high social and environmental costs that this entails, has brought with it a number of policy changes designed to minimize these costs for local communities or at least to prevent potentially negative social consequences from undermining the country's hydropower policy. The amended resettlement regulations published in 2006 have to be regarded in this context.

Their publication is also illustrative of a more general shift in focus from economic development towards social development that has occurred under the Hu-Wen administration. The leadership's quest for a harmonious society was spurred by the need to prevent so-called "software failures," which were seen to threaten the legitimacy of the current regime (Woo, 2007: 17). As studies on "authoritarian resilience" in China have shown, in various policy fields, the Chinese state has been successful in its pursuit of adaptation. In the case of dam-induced resettlement, Chapter 3 highlights the adaptive capacity of the central government, which over the past decades has responded to diverse national and international demands and has continuously upgraded resettlement regulations. These adaptive processes have direct bearing on the local state where local policymakers and implementers have to react and adapt accordingly. This book scrutinizes these local processes of adaptation and the ways in which policy adjustments react with local socioeconomic circumstances and institutional constraints to form new patterns of state-society relations.

Central government policy change means much more than just a potential improvement in migrant lives. Not only do the results of local policy implementation feed into central-level policy change, but in line with the findings of O'Brien and Li (2006), central-level policy change and the introduction of socially oriented resettlement policies create a space for local communities to engage with and directly affect local policy implementation. In order to obtain a full picture of the Chinese policy process surrounding dam-induced resettlement, it is therefore necessary to make the connection between the different administrative layers involved in this process right down to the grassroots level at which local cadres and migrant communities come together to shape policy outcomes.

The past six chapters show how the introduction and continuous renewal of more socially oriented resettlement policies together with the underlying power structures enshrined in the hydropower and resettlement bureaucracies induce the local state to employ a method that this book suggests be called *fragmented mediation under hierarchy*. Three main arguments have provided the framework for this study: First of all, the Chinese policy process is defined by elements of democratic centralism, which allow the Chinese government sufficient flexibility to integrate a variety of voices into public policies and to adapt these to a constantly changing environment while ensuring strict adherence once the policy has been fixed. However, in the case of dam-induced resettlement, there is an imbalance between democracy and centralism throughout the policy process. Although different opinions are considered from all levels of government while the policy and resettlement plan are being formulated, after the resettlement plans have been fixed at the provincial level, strict adherence is required by lower-level implementing agents. This inflexibility during policy implementation paired with frequent policy change at the central level tends to undermine local state agency.

It is therefore clear that, despite the fact that opinions emanating from lower levels seem to be listened to, the Chinese policy process is organized in a top-down manner so that county and township governments act as service providers rather than as active agents in dam-induced resettlement. The main actors in China's power sector are large state-owned enterprises that enjoy strong political backing from Beijing when it comes to constructing large and oftentimes controversial power stations. Officially framed as a clean and efficient way to produce energy, hydropower is one area in which China's power companies have invested great sums to reap even greater benefits. When it comes to making decisions about resettlement in the course of dam projects, a top-down command structure can also be observed: the larger the dam, the more top-down the decision-making process. At the same time, with each increase in dam size, the number of dam migrants increases, meaning that there is a strong negative correlation between the decision-making authority and the workload of governments at the county level and below.

It has furthermore been argued that, in the field of hydropower development, rule-guided market relationships and top-down bureaucratic interactions have come together to produce a situation in which local governments at county and township levels are unable to find efficient ways to resolve problems that occur during the resettlement processes. Local governments are caught in a double bind, forced to obey orders issued by their superiors who are subject to the profit margins of hydropower companies but also placed under pressure to satisfy the demands made by local resettlement communities. The latter have been empowered by the newly introduced resettlement policies, which are more socially oriented than previous regulations and – at least on paper – provide more space for migrants to participate in resettlement processes. This new pressure on the local state means that local cadres have to mediate society in such a way that social unrest among dissatisfied migrants is prevented while, at the same time, trying to fulfill the requirements of the resettlement plans fixed at higher levels of the government bureaucracy. Compared with the local corporatist state that has developed as a result of the economic reform policies that have been implemented, the local state is now adapting to newly introduced policies that are more socially oriented and require local cadres to accommodate migrants' demands more than ever before. In this study, the resultant emerging phenomenon has been referred to as fragmented mediation under hierarchy. It could be argued that the local state attempts to mediate society in such a way that social unrest among dissatisfied migrants is prevented, while at the same time the requirements of the resettlement plans fixed by higher levels of the government bureaucracy are met. Seen from the perspective of the central level, adaptation has been successful, because its hydropower policy is being implemented without causing regime threatening social instability or a loss in central state legitimacy. However, looked at from the perspective of the local government, adaptation has been a much more strenuous process that has, on the one hand, led to migrants being resettled on time without severe social unrest but, on the other hand, brought with it a loss of local state legitimacy.

In the case of Green Mountain, policy change led to social fragmentation and deep frustration of the migrant community. During the course of the resettlement implementation for the Nuozhadu Dam, resettlement policy has changed continuously and has, in addition, affected state-society relations on the ground. In detail, the flexible adaptation of central-level resettlement policies and their subsequent reversal at lower government levels has two consequences: First, the local state faces a situation of *policy overload*, meaning that, while existing policies are being implemented, either the local cadres are faced with the task of changing implementation for all the migrants who are resettled after a certain date or the local state has to adjust implementation in such a way that migrants who have already been resettled also have the opportunity to enjoy the potential benefits of the newly introduced regulations. In the first case, the migrants who have been resettled at an earlier date are likely to protest against being excluded from new policies (as has happened in Green Mountain); in the second case, the resettlement budget has to be increased, which again depends on decisions made at the provincial level. No matter what the policy stipulates, the workload of the local Resettlement Bureau is significantly increased, which results in *fragmented mediation*. As the local state does not have either the organizational or the financial capacity to satisfy all the demands of higher-level policies, local cadres implement new policies when these are deemed necessary, for example, in response to threats of protest action by a local community or when they see fit. However, due to the increasing efficiency of the connections among the migrant community, information about inconsistencies in policy implementation now travels quickly from one village to the next, which again results in dissatisfaction among those who have not benefited from the latest policies.

In the cases presented above, county and township governments have tried to exploit newly introduced policies to their own advantage (increased policy propagation) in order to satisfy the demands of higher government levels and to succeed in moving the migrants out of their homes. However, once the demands of their superiors have been satisfied and local communities have been relocated to make room for project construction, local cadres have to face the demands of migrant communities who, after being resettled, have realized that the picture of resettlement that had been painted for them was overly rosy. The ensuing contestations require the local state to coordinate community interests within the provisions of the resettlement plans as well as within the limits of their own organizational and financial capacities.

As for the increase in policy propagation, the South Stream case has shown that an increase in the provision of information may turn into a disadvantage for local cadres. On the one hand, the propagation of China's hydropower strategy and the importance of the Nuozhadu Dam for Pu'er and China, more generally, have lowered resistance against resettlement among South Stream migrants. On the other hand, this provision of information has caused migrants to follow up on the process of implementation and to ensure that the local government actually suits the action to the word. Although the increased intensity of "propaganda and thought work" in policy implementation may cheat migrants into leaving their homes without resistance, thus undermining their right to know, the pieces of information provided on resettlement policy have, at the same time, also increased the migrants' knowledge about how resettlement is supposed to be implemented.

Finally, it has been argued that the top-down politicized nature of hydropower politics in China leaves little space for civil society organizations to influence policymaking. Although, under certain circumstances (see Mertha, 2008), NGOs and the media have successfully cooperated to overturn policy decisions, this study contends that these instances are merely episodic and do not mark a general trend towards more open policymaking. This book has shown that NGOs and the media, by taking action to expose problems during the resettlement process, contributed to the introduction of more socially oriented resettlement policy in 2006. This process confirms the finding that the Chinese policy process has become increasingly pluralized, but it has also been shown that, due to the perceived need to build dams and the more regularized construction and resettlement processes that have partly resulted from this, actors within the bureaucracy regard NGOs not only as a threat to hydropower development but also as redundant organizations. Thus, NGOs that were previously active in protecting the rights of resettled people are slowly being pushed out of the policy process, first, because government actors have taken on the task of improving resettlement policies on their own and, second, because several large protests related to resettlement work have led the government to frame dam-induced resettlement as an issue that can directly affect social stability. Third, in a political environment like China, NGOs are granted room only to supplement the work of an underfinanced government (Teets, 2015). In the case of dam-induced resettlement, NGOs have not only threatened the positive investment environment that provincial governments promise to provide for energy companies but they have at times even increased the cost of resettlement. In the eyes of the government, the NGOs have thus failed to fulfill the function that had legitimized their existence in the first place.

When society is granted a say in the policy process of dam-induced resettlement, this is only in the case of affected communities rather than civil society groups. The former rely on political changes that have been taking place in the context of improved resettlement regulations and societal consultations. These improvements have indirectly empowered migrant groups to make use of their newly granted rights to exert a direct influence on policy implementation (see O'Brien & Li, 2006).

Outlook and directions for further study

Although this study has made a series of contributions to research in the field of hydropower development and resettlement in China and, in particular, to research on local processes of policy implementation, a few shortcomings remain. First of all, the fact that this study has applied qualitative research methods limits the scope to generalize from the findings. Resettlement does not only vary from province to province, but also shows significant differences within one province (here, Yunnan). Due to the reasons already mentioned in Chapter 1, this study has focused only on Pu'er and resettlement villages created during the course of the Nuozhadu Project. Further research is needed on resettlement policy implementation in other localities within and also beyond Yunnan. This would allow for a comparison of the coping strategies employed by local governments in response to flexible policy change by central government and to the introduction of more socially oriented resettlement regulations. In order to further conceptualize local state flexibility, additional research in different policy fields with variations in bureaucratic structures and pressures resting on county and township governments are necessary. These policy fields can be studied in isolation, however, as local states see themselves confronted with the task of simultaneously implementing various different and potentially conflicting policies, the interrelationships between different processes of implementation should be highlighted. This allows us to not only discern top-down and bottom-up pressures resting on local cadres but also those constraints emanating from power structures and policy priorities endogenous to the government level under scrutiny. Longitudinal studies about the modes of cooperation between local cadres and local communities furthermore have the potential to lay bare the impact of failed attempts at cooperation (as described in Chapter 5) on the processes of implementation in other policy fields.

Second, this book has focused exclusively on hydropower development. Resettlement is also necessary, however, in the case of water resources projects, such as dykes and the South-North Water Transfer Project. Although such projects are governed by the same central-level resettlement regulations introduced in 2006 (see Chapter 3), the power structures underlying resettlement work for water resources and hydropower projects differ. While water resource projects are initiated and funded by the state with the aim of enhancing public provision, hydropower plants are funded by energy companies that are increasingly subject to market forces (Interview, NJ130304). Hence, a comparison between these two types of projects has the potential to provide further knowledge on the role played by local states in project construction and resettlement as well as on the impact of different types of interest structures on this role.

Furthermore, it remains to be seen to what extent political developments under the new administration headed by Xi Jinping will impact resettlement policymaking and implementation. So far, observers of Chinese politics have had their difficulties in characterizing the new president. At first, Xi's initiatives to strengthen Party rule have been compared to Mao-era campaign-style politics. Later, Xi was regarded as just another ineffectual Hu Jintao who failed to implement substantial economic reforms. However, since the adoption of the "Decision on Major Issues Concerning Comprehensively Deepening Reforms" at the Third Plenary Session of the 18th CPC Central Committee in November 2013, Xi is referred to as the "New Deng" who aims to fundamentally reform the Chinese system (Miller, 2014; Martin & Cohen, 2014). It has indeed been hard to characterize Xi and the potential impact of his reforms on different policy fields. However, looking at the anticorruption campaign, recent moves towards institutional recentralization, and increased Party dominance, it appears that the Xi administration will reinforce the situation of local state inflexibility presented here. While in the field of dam-induced resettlement, policy changes have not been introduced so far, the above-mentioned institutional reforms as well as the anticorruption drive are having a deep impact on the political atmosphere in China, influencing cadres at every administrative level. Thus, the research presented here sheds light not only on local state behavior with regards to dam-induced resettlement. Instead, the study presents an example of what we are about to observe in other policy fields of local governance as well.

Appendix: research methods

The data for this research was drawn from a number of different sources. First of all, secondary data was compiled, in the form of information and statistics, including reports by NGOs, the results of past research in the field and statistics collected by government agencies. Although secondary data is often uneven in coverage and availability and might at times be unreliable, it nevertheless provides information that might not be available elsewhere and cannot be collected in the communities.

Second, semistructured interviews were conducted with key informants to assess their knowledge of policy change in the field of dam-induced resettlement. The key informants who were interviewed included government officials, representatives from industry, academics, and NGO activists, and they therefore represent a variety of opinions on policy evolution and implementation. This proved to be an effective method of gaining a basic understanding of policy change and implementation within a relatively short period of time.

Third, interviews were also conducted with individuals and households in resettlement villages. According to official definitions, a household is a unit that undertakes land contracts and that – until 2006 – had to pay taxes and collective levies. It makes up the basic unit of organization in production and runs its own economic activities (Guo, 2008: 197–198). The questions for these interviews were based on the information collected during the key informant interviews and made it possible to gain a detailed picture of the resettlement experiences of individuals and households. Semistructured interviews were employed in order to enhance our understanding of the resettlement processes and the way that resettlement policies were being implemented on the ground.

Between August 2011 and March 2015, five consecutive field visits were carried out. A preliminary field visit was carried out in August 2011. In the course of this field trip, representatives from the major institutions involved in hydropower development in Yunnan were interviewed, including private and public sector representatives, university researchers as well as NGOs in the provincial capital, Kunming. Through this, firsthand information on dam construction projects in Yunnan as well as the major points of contention surrounding the issues of electricity generation and supply and the social consequences of hydropower development could be gained. In addition, I visited four villages affected by flooding and resettlement in the course of the construction of the Nuozhadu Dam. The majority of interviewees approached during this first field trip were revisited during subsequent stays. In line with the most-similar-cases design developed by Przeworski and Teune (1970), I chose two resettlement villages for in-depth study. The two villages have been resettled from the same home village (Old Tree) to two different resettlement villages (Green Mountain and South Stream) within the same county (Wild Grass). By selecting these two villages, the socioeconomic situation as well as the local cadres who have organized the move remain constants. The major difference between the two villages has been the fact that Green Mountain started resettlement before the major policy change in 2005 and was resettled in three batches until 2012. In contrast, South Stream moved in 2007. The comparison drawn between the two communities can help to explain the impact of flexible policy change on ongoing processes of local policy implementation and what this means for state-society relations on the ground. Despite similar socioeconomic conditions, resettlement proved to be an intervention that had strikingly different effects on both communities.

A second field visit was carried out over a period of two months in July and August 2012. The trip started in Pu'er where I spoke to officials from various government departments (including representatives from the local Development and Reform Commission, the Resettlement Bureau, the Policy Research Office, the Water Supplies Department, and the Policy Research Office); met with local informants who knew a great deal about the Nuozhadu Dam; travelled to a village at the Lancang River that was affected by the Nuozhadu Dam; and revisited the resettlement villages that I had been to in 2011. In addition, I visited and conducted interviews in two other resettlement villages in different counties in Pu'er. This allowed me to get a more comprehensive picture of how resettlement processes are undertaken all over the prefecture. In order to gain a better understanding of villagers' attitudes towards the dam, resettlement, and land inundation in the region, I also visited villages that had not been resettled. This allowed me to ask the villagers about their attitudes towards the dam and the ways in which it has impacted on the local society and economy. Although these villagers had not been resettled, they had lost land as a result of inundation.

In addition to conducting interviews in these villages, I visited the project site of the Nuozhadu Dam and talked to families who were directly involved in the construction process of the dam. For these families, the dam had had a profoundly different impact on livelihoods because they had gained employment and a stable income throughout the construction process. Some of them had moved to the region as a direct result of their gaining employment at the power plant. Most of them had previously worked in agriculture but had certain skills that were needed during the preliminary construction phases. In one case, the father of the family worked on the construction site, while the rest of the family continued to cultivate land that they had newly contracted near the reservoir. When the preliminary construction phase ended, the whole family once more started to concentrate on land cultivation. Only a short while later, several villages around the reservoir region had to be relocated, including this family, and thus, although the family had benefitted from the dam project during the early construction phases, these same people were clearly disadvantaged during the later phases. In addition to these conversations at the local level in Yunnan, interviews were undertaken with government and industry representatives in Beijing, as well as with academics concerned with development-induced resettlement in China. Altogether forty interviews were conducted in resettlement villages and eighteen interviews in other villages affected by the dam. Each interview comprised one to four interviewees. An additional thirty-two interviews were conducted with industry representatives, academics, NGO activists, and government representatives at the central, provincial, county, and township.

The quality of the data collected was influenced by several factors. First, interviews were mainly conducted in Mandarin or in the local dialect spoken in Pu'er. Therefore, some information might have been lost in translation. This applies, in particular, to the interviews conducted in the local dialect. In these cases, however, a colleague of mine from Pu'er accompanied me to all the interviews, interpreting between Mandarin and the local dialect. Second, the fact that dam-induced resettlement is a sensitive topic (see Chapter 1) also limited the scope of my research, at least during the early stages. Although questions asked were as specific and factual as possible, some people might have felt too constrained to talk openly about their experiences. Due to the sensitivity of the topic, the recording of interviews was only possible to a limited extent. Particularly during the preliminary research trips, although contacts were forged at central and local levels, the sensitivity of the project was a constant theme throughout the conversations and interviews.

Documents have been collected from all actors working on dam-induced resettlement within China's bureaucracy, including the State Council, the Ministry of Water Resources (MWR), the National Development and Reform Commission (NDRC), the National Energy Administration (NEA), the Ministry of Land Resources (MLR), and the Hydrochina Corporation, a government agency that is responsible for water resources and hydropower projects in China. The majority of these documents were collected online. In 1998, the Chinese government adopted a "government online" policy. According to the "Management Measures for Governmental Affairs Publicity of Environmental Agencies," all formal documents, with the exception of those containing state secrets, should be made available to the public (Huang et al., 2010: 227).

Hydropower development in itself, as well as resettlement, are highly sensitive topics in China. As for large dams, detailed information on construction processes are considered to be state secrets, whereas resettlement touches upon the issue of social stability, posing great challenges for researchers and those being researched alike. In order to protect the anonymity of my interview partners, the names of the resettlement villages have been changed, and personal names omitted.

Bibliography

Ahlers, A. L. (2014). *Rural Policy Implementation in Contemporary China: New Socialist Countryside*. London: Routledge.

Ahlers, A. L., & Schubert, G. (2014). Effective Policy Implementation in China's Local State. *Modern China, 41*(4), 372–405.

Alpermann, B. (2010a). State and Society in China's Environmental Politics. In J. Kassiola & S. Guo (Eds.), *China's Environmental Crisis: Domestic and Global Political Impacts and Responses* (pp. 123–151). New York: Palgrave Macmillan.

Alpermann, B. (2010b). *China's Cotton Industry: Economic Transformation and State Capacity*. London: Routledge.

Angle, S. C. (2005). Decent Democratic Centralism. *Political Theory, 33*, 518–546.

Bakewell, O., de Haas, H., & Kubal, A. (2011). Migration Systems, Pioneers and the Role of Agency. *International Migration Institute* (Working Paper No. 48). Retrieved from: www.imi.ox.ac.uk/pdfs/imi-working-papers/WP-11-48

Bao, M. (2009). Environmental NGOs in Transforming China. *Nature and Culture, 4*(1), 1–16.

Berman, P. (1978). The Study of Macro- and Micro- Implementation. *Public Policy, 26*(2), 157–184.

Biba, S. (2012). China's Continuous Dam-Building on the Mekong River. *Journal of Contemporary Asia, 42*(4), 603–628.

Blecher, M. (1991). Developmental State, Entrepreneurial State: The Political Economy of Socialist Reform in Xinji Municipality and Guanghan County. In G. White (Ed.), *The Chinese State in the Era of Reform: The Road to Crisis* (pp. 265–291). Houndmills: Macmillan.

Blecher, M., & Shue, V. (1996). *Tethered Deer: Government and Economy in a Chinese County*. Stanford: Stanford University Press.

Blecher, M., & Shue, V. (2001). Into Leather: State-Led Development and the Private Sector in Xinji. *The China Quarterly, 166*, 368–393.

Brady, A.-M. (Ed.). (2012). *China's Thought Management*. London: Routledge.

Bragg, C. K. (2003). "Crossing a River by Groping for Stones": Factors Reshaping the Policy Innovation Process for Chinese Water Policies. *Public Administration Quarterly, 27*(3/4), 243–273.

Brint, S., & Karabel, J. (1991). Institutional Origins and Transformations: The Case of American Community Colleges. In W. W. Powell & P. J. DiMaggio (Eds.), *The New Institutionalism in Organizational Analysis* (pp. 337–360). Chicago: University of Chicago Press.

Brødsgaard, K. E. (2002). Institutional Reform and the *Bianzhi* System in China. *The China Quarterly, 170*, 361–386.

Brødsgaard, K. E. (2012). Politics and Business Group Formation in China: The Party in Control? *The China Quarterly, 211*, 624–648.

Brown, P.H., Magee, D., & Xu, Y.L. (2008). Socioeconomic Vulnerability in China's Hydropower Development. *China Economic Review, 19*, 614–627.

Burns, J.P. (1994). Strengthening Central CCP Control of Leadership Selection: The 1990 *Nomenklatura*. *The China Quarterly, 138*, 458–491.

Büsgen, M. (2006). NGOs and the Search for Chinese Civil Society: Environmental Non-Governmental Organisations in the Nujiang Campaign. *Working Paper Series* Retrieved from: www.eu-china.net/upload/pdf/materialien/michael%20buesgen-diplom_08-08-19.pdf

Cai, Y. (2003). Collective Ownership or Cadres' Ownership? *The China Quarterly, 175*, 662–680.

Cai, Y. (2008). Local Governments and the Suppression of Popular Resistance in China. *The China Quarterly, 193*, 43–64.

Chamberlain, H. (1998). Civil Society with Chinese Characteristics? *The China Journal, 39*, 69–81.

Chan, H.S. (2004). Cadre Personnel Management in China: The Nomenklatura System, 1990–1998. *The China Quarterly, 179*, 703–734.

Chau, K. (1995). The Three Gorges Dam Project of China: Resettlement Prospects and Problems. *Ambio, 24*(2), 98–102.

Chen, K. (1998). Administrative Decentralisation and Changing State-Society Relations in China. *International Journal of Public Administration, 21*(9), 1223–1255. doi:10.1080/01900699808525346

Chen, S., Han, Z., Liu, L., & Zhao, P. (1998). 水库移民社会风险预警系统初探 [First Exploration of a Risk Warning System for Dam Migrants]. 水电能源科学 [*Hydropower Energy Science*], *3*, 9–15.

Chien, S.-S., & Zhao, L. (2008). The Kunshan Model: Learning from Taiwanese Investors. *Built Environment, 34*(7), 427–443.

Child, J., Yuan, L., & Tsai, T. (2007). Institutional Entrepreneurship in Building an Environmental Protection System for the People's Republic of China. *Organization Studies, 28*, 1013–1034.

China Energy News. (2013). 对"16118"移民长效补偿安置方式的思考 [Thoughts on the "16118" Long-term Support Resettlement Mode]. *People*. Retrieved from: http://paper.people.com.cn/zgnyb/html/2013–03/18/content_1213150.htm

China Huaneng Group. (2011). 中国华能 [China Huaneng Newsletter], *6*, 157.

China New Energy Net. (2011). 十二五规划: 水电是能源发展主攻方向之一 [The 12th Five-Year Plan: Hydroelectric Power Is One of the Major Directions of Resource Development]. Retrieved from: www.newenergy.org.cn/html/0114/4111139614.html

China Power. (2007). 中国水力发电学会水库经济专委会成立20周年大会召开 [Conference on the 20-Year Anniversary of the Formation of the Reservoir Economics Committee by the Chinese Association for Water Resources and Electricity Generation]. Retrieved from: www.chinapower.com.cn/article/1099/art1099260.asp

China Society for Hydropower Engineering (CSHE). (2012). 澜沧江水电站首台机组发电 [First Turbine of Lancang River Hydropower Stations Generates Electricity]. Retrieved from: www.hydropower.org.cn/info/shownews.asp?newsid=8303

Christensen, T., Dong, L., & Painter, M. (2008). Administrative Reform in China's Central Government: How Much "Learning from the West"? *International Review of Administrative Sciences, 74*(3), 351–371.

Chung, J.H. (2000). *Central Control and Local Discretion in China: Leadership and Implementation during Post-Mao Decollectivization*. Oxford: Oxford University Press.

Cook, S. (2015). The Risks of Expanding Repression in China. *The Diplomat*. Retrieved from: http://thediplomat.com/2015/04/the-risks-of-expanding-repression-in-china/

Cooper, C.M. (2006). "This Is Our Way In": The Civil Society of Environmental NGOs in Southwest China. *Government and Opposition, 41*(1), 109–136.

CPC Central Committee. (2013). 中共中央关于全面深化改革若干重大问题的决定 [Decision on Major Issues Concerning Comprehensively Deepening Reforms]. Retrieved from: http://cpc.people.com.cn/n/2013/1115/c64094–23559163.html

CPC Central Committee. (2014). Communique of the 4th Plenary Session of the 18th Central Committee of CPC. Retrieved from: www.china.org.cn/china/fourth_plenary_session/2014–12/02/content_34208801.htm

Cronin, R.P., & Hamlin, T. (2010). Mekong Tipping Point: Hydropower Dams, Human Security and Regional Stability. *Stimson.* Retrieved from: www.stimson.org/print.cfm?pub=1&ID=980

Cunningham, E.A. (2015). The State and the Firm: China's Energy Governance in Context. *Global Economic Governance Initiative, 1.* Retrieved from: www.bu.edu/pardee school/files/2014/12/Chinas-Energy-Working-Paper.pdf

d'Hooghe, I. (1994). Regional Economic Integration in Yunnan. In D.S.G. Goodman & G. Segal (Eds.), *China Deconstructs: Politics Trade, and Regionalism* (pp. 286–321). London: Routledge.

Deng, Y., & O'Brien, K.J. (2013). Relational Repression in China: Using Social Ties to Demobilize Protesters. *The China Quarterly, 215*, 533–552.

Diamant, N.J., & O'Brien, K.J. (2015). Veterans' Political Activism in China. *Modern China, 41*(3), 278–312.

Ding, X. (2010). Policy Implementation in Contemporary China: The Making of Converted Schools. *Journal of Contemporary China, 19*(64), 359–379.

Donaldson, J.A. (2011). *Small Works: Poverty and Economic Development in Southwestern China*. Ithaca: Cornell University Press.

Du, J., Zhong, Z., Gong, H., & Bian, B. (2011). 水电工程移民长效补偿研究 [*Research on Long-term Compensation for Dam-induced Resettlement*]. Beijing: Waterpub.

Dwivedi, R. (2002). Models and Methods in Development-Induced Displacement. *Development and Change, 33*(4), 709–732.

East China Investigation and Design Institute. (2006). 云南省澜沧江苗尾水电站可行性研究勘测设计科研大纲 [Yunnan Province Lancang River Miaowei Hydropower Station Feasibility Research and Design Outline]. Hangzhou: East China Investigation and Design Institute.

Edin, M. (2000). *Market Forces and Communist Power: Local Political Institutions and Economic Development in China*. Uppsala: Acta Universitatis Upsaliensis.

Edin, M. (2003). State Capacity and Local Agent Control in China: CCP Cadre Management from a Township Perspective. *The China Quarterly, 173*, 35–52.

Environmental Impact Assessment (EIA). (2010). China Energy Data – Statistics and Analysis – Oil, Gas, Electricity, Coal. Retrieved from: www.eia.doe.gov/cabs/China/Electricity.html

Fanwen. (2008). 移民局工作总结 [Summary of Resettlement Bureau Work]. Retrieved from: www.zk168.com.cn/fanwen/zongjie/zongjie_264150_2.html

Fanwen Net. (2011). 移民开发局安置建设工作调研报告 [Research Report Resettlement and Construction Work by Resettlement Development Bureau]. Retrieved from: http://fanwen.glzy8.com/view/69504.html

Farid, M. (2014). China's Grassroots NGOs and the Local State: Catalysts for Policy Entrepreneurship. In J.C. Teets & W. Hurst (Eds.), *Local Governance Innovation in China: Experimentation, diffusion, and defiance* (pp. 117–140). London: Routledge.

Fitzgerald, J. (2002). *Rethinking China's Provinces*. New York: Routledge.

Frolic, M. (1997). State-Led Civil Society. In T. Brook & M. Frolic (Eds.), *Civil Society in China* (pp. 46–67). Armonk, NY: Sharpe.

Göbel, C. (2011). Uneven Policy Implementation in Rural China. *The China Journal, 65*, 53–76.

Goodman, D.S.G. (1997). *China's Provinces in Reform: Class, Community, and Political Culture*. London: Routledge.

Gore, L. (2011). *The Chinese Communist Party and China's Capitalist Revolution: The Political Impact of Market*. London: Routledge.

Guo, P., & Li, J. (1998). 世界银行贷款云南环境项目中的移民问题 [Migration in the Yunnan Environmental Projects of World Bank Landing]. *Yunnan Environmental Science, 17*(3), 25–28.

Guo, X. (2001). Land Expropriation and Rural Conflicts in China. *The China Quarterly, 166*, 422–439.

Guo, X. (2008). *State and Ethnicity in China's Southwest*. Leiden: Brill.

Habich, S. (2015). Strategies of Soft Coercion in Chinese Dam Resettlement. *Issues and Studies, 51*(1), 165–199.

Han, Z. (2015). Party Building in Urban Business Districts: Organizational Adaptation of the Chinese Communist Party. *Journal of Contemporary China, 24*(94), 644–664.

Harding, H. (1981). *Organizing China*. Palo Alto: Stanford University Press.

Harwood, R. (2013). *China's New Socialist Countryside: Modernity Arrives in the Nu River Valley*. Washington: University of Washington Press.

Hattaway, P. (2004). *People of the Buddhist World: A Christian Prayer Diary*. Carlisle: Piquant Editions.

He, Y. (2011). 云南省山区移民与发展研究 [Analysis on Mountain Migration and Development Research of Yunnan Province]. *Resource Development & Market, 27*(9), 838–841.

Heberer, T., & Schubert, G. (2012). County and Township Cadres as a Strategic Group: A New Approach to Political Agency in China's Local State. *Journal of Chinese Political Science, 17*(3), 221–249. doi:10.1007/s11366–012–9200–8

Heberer, T., & Trappel, R. (2013). Evaluation Processes, Local Cadres' Behaviour and Local Development Processes. *Journal of Contemporary China, 22*(84), 1048–1066. doi: 10.1080/10670564.2013.795315

Heggelund, G.M. (2004). *Environment and Resettlement Politics in China: the Three Gorges Project*. Aldershot: Ashgate.

Heilmann, S. (2008a). From Local Experiments to National Policy: The Origins of China's Distinctive Policy Process. *The China Journal, 59*, 1–30.

Heilmann, S. (2008b). Policy Experimentation in China's Economic Rise. *Studies in Comparative International Development, 43*(1), 1–26.

Heilmann, S. (2009). Maximum Tinkering under Uncertainty: Unorthodox Lessons from China. *Modern China, 35*, 450–462.

Heilmann, S., & Perry, E.J. (2011). *Mao's Invisible Hand: The Political Foundations of Adaptive Governance in China*. Cambridge, Mass: Harvard University Asia Center, distributed by Harvard University Press.

Hendrischke, H.J., & Feng, C. (1999). *The Political Economy of China's Provinces: Comparative and Competitive Advantage*. New York: Routledge.

Hensengerth, O. (2010). Sustainable Dam Development in China between Global Norms and Local Practices. *Discussion Paper*. Retrieved from: www.die-gdi.de/uploads/media/DP_4.2010.pdf

Hillman, B. (2014). *Patronage and Power: Local State Networks and Party-State Resilience in Rural China*. Stanford: Stanford University Press.

Ho, P. (2001). Greening Without Conflict? Environmentalism, NGOs and Civil Society in China. *Development and Change, 32*, 893–921.

Ho, P. (2007). Embedded Activism and Political Change in a Semiauthoritarian Context. *China Information, 21*(2), 187–209.

Hobsbawm, E. (1973). Peasants and Politics. *Journal of Peasant Studies, 1*(October).

Hoffman, A. J. (1999). Institutional Evolution and Change: Environmentalism and the US Chemical Industry. *Academy of Management Journal, 42*, 351–371.

Hohai University (Producer). (2012). 水利部水库移民经济研究中心 (National Research Center for Resettlement). June 14. Retrieved from: www.hhu.edu.cn/kxyj/deptintro.asp?ID=KB008

Holbig, H. (2007). Demokratie Chinesischer Prägung: Der XVII. Parteitag der Kommunistischen Partei Chinas [Democracy, Chinese Style: The 17th Party Congress of the Chinese Communist Party]. *China Aktuell – Journal of Current Chinese Affairs, 2*, 32–55.

Holbig, H. (2013). Ideology after the End of Ideology: China and the Quest for Autocratic Legitimation. *Democratization, 20*(1), 61–81.

Hsing, Y.-T. (2010). *The Great Urban Transformation: Politics and Property in China.* New York: Oxford University Press.

Hsu, J.Y.J., & Hasmath, R. (2012). The Changing Faces of State Corporatism. In J.Y.J. Hsu and R. Hasmath (Eds.), *The Chinese Corporatist State: Adaption, Survival and Resistance* (pp. 1–9). London: Routledge.

Hu, B. (2007). *Informal Institutions and Rural Development in China.* Oxon: Routledge.

Huaneng. (2013). Huaneng's Ranking in Fortune 500 Companies Rises to 231st. Retrieved from: www.chng.com.cn/eng/n75863/n75941/c1035468/content.html

Huang, P.C.C. (2009). *Chinese Civil Justice: Past and Present.* Lanham: Rowman & Littlefield Publishers.

Huang, Y., & Yang, D. (2002). Bureaucratic Capacity and State-Society Relations in China. *Journal of Chinese Political Science, 7*(1/2), 19–46.

Huang, X., Zhao, D., Brown, C.G., Wu, Y., & Waldron, S.A. (2010). Environmental Issues and Policy Priorities in China: A Content Analysis of Government Documents. *China: An International Journal, 8*(2), 220–246.

Huntington, S.P. (1970). Social and Institutional Dynamics of One-Party Systems. In S.P. Huntington and C.H. Moore (Eds.), *Authoritarian Politics in Modern Society: The Dynamics of Established One-Party Systems*, (pp. 3–47). New York: Basic Books.

Hydrochina. (2012). 集团简介 [Introduction of Corporation]. Retrieved from: www.hydrochina.com.cn/jtgk/jtgk.jsp

Hydrolancang. (2001a). 糯扎渡水电站可行性研究阶段勘测设计合同正式签订 [Contract Signed for Feasibility Study Phase of Survey and Design Work for Nuozhadu Hydropower Station]. Retrieved from: www.hnlcj.cn/shownews.asp?newsid=783

Hydrolancang. (2001b). 糯扎渡水电站可研阶段选坝报告通过审查 [Feasibility Study Phase on Selecting Dam Type for Nuozhadu Hydropower Station Passes Investigation]. Retrieved from: www.hnlcj.cn/shownews.asp?newsid=799

Hydrolancang. (2003a). 中泰就澜沧江景洪及糯扎渡水电站开发事宜达成共识 [China and Thailand Reach Consensus on Development of Jinghong and Nuozhadu Dams]. Retrieved from: www.hnlcj.cn/shownews.asp?newsid=1165

Hydrolancang. (2003b). 云南省澜沧江糯扎渡水电站可行性研究报告在京通过审查 [Yunnan Province Lancang River Nuozhadu Hydropower Station Feasibility Research Report Undergoes Investigation in Beijing]. Retrieved from: www.hnlcj.cn/shownews.asp?newsid=1273

Hydrolancang. (2011b). 华能糯扎渡水电站通过国家核准 [Huaneng's Nuozhadu Hydropower Station Passes National Investigation]. Retrieved from: www.hnlcj.cn/shownews. asp?newsid=2092

International Coffee Organization. (2013). ICO Indicator Prices. Retrieved from: www.ico. org/prices/p2.htm

Jackson, S., & Sleigh, A. (2000). Resettlement for China's Three Gorges Dam: Socio-Economic Impact and Institutional Tensions. *Communist and Post-Communist Studies, 33*(2), 223–241.

Jacobs, A. (2015). Taking Feminist Battle to China's Streets, and Landing in Jail. *The New York Times*. Retrieved from: www.nytimes.com/2015/04/06/world/asia/chinese-womens-rights-activists-fall-afoul-of-officials.html

Jinghong Government. (n.d.). 橄榄坝水电站移民安置工作动态 [Development of Ganlanba Hydropower Station Resettlement Work]. Retrieved from: http://jhs.gov.cn/home/bn_jhsymkfj/newshow.aspx?id=44053

Jun, J. (2000). Displacement, Resettlement, Rehabilitation, Reparation and Development – China Report. *World Commission on Dams Thematic Review 1.3.*

Kennedy, J.J. (2007). The Implementation of Village Elections and Tax-for-Fee Reform in Rural Northwest China. In Elizabeth J. Perry and Merle Goldman (Eds.), *Grassroots Political Reform in Contemporary China* (pp. 48–74). Cambridge: Harvard University Press.

Kennedy, S. (2005). *The Business of Lobbying in China*. Cambridge: Harvard University Press.

Kennedy, S., & Deng, G. (2010). Big Business and Industry Association Lobbying in China: The Paradox of Contrasting Styles. *The China Journal, 63*, 101–125.

Kong, B. (2010). *China's International Petroleum Policy*. Santa Barbara: Praeger Security International.

Kostka, G., & Hobbs, W. (2012). Local Energy Efficiency Policy Implementation in China: Bridging the Gap between National Priorities and Local Interests. *The China Quarterly, 211*, 765–785. doi:10.1017/S0305741012000860

Lam, W. (2006). *Chinese Politics in the Hu Jintao Era: New Leaders, New Challenges*. London: Routledge.

Lampton, D.M. (1987a). Chinese Politics: The Bargaining Treadmill. *Issues and Studies, 3*, 11–41.

Lampton, D.M. (1987b). Water: Challenge to a Fragmented Political System. In D.M. Lampton (Ed.), *Policy Implementation in Post-Mao China* (pp. 157–189). Berkeley: University of California Press.

Lampton, D.M. (1992). *A Plum for a Peach: Bargaining, Interest, and Bureaucratic Politics in China*. Los Angeles and London: University of California Press.

Lancang Government. (2008). 糯扎渡水电站澜沧县移民搬迁安置实施细则 [*Details for Implementing Migrant Relocation and Resettlement for Nuozhadu Hydropower Station in Lancang County*]. Retrieved from: www.ynf.gov.cn/ynczt_model/article. aspx?id=826631

Lancang Government. (n.d.). 澜沧县糯扎渡水电站和景洪水电站库区实物指标分解细化工作实施细则 [Lancang County Details on Material Index Survey for Reservoirs of Nuozhadu and Jinghong Hydropower Stations]. Retrieved from: http://wenku.baidu. com/view/fa9de93f376baf1ffc4fad5d.html

Landry, P.F. (2008). *Decentralized Authoritarianism in China: The Communist Party's Control of Local Elites in the Post-Mao Era*. Cambridge: Cambridge University Press.

Law110. (n.d.). 国家建设征用土地条例 [Regulations for Land Appropriation in National Construction]. Retrieved from: www.law110.com/law/guowuyuan/2113.htm

Le Mons Walker, K. (2006). "Gangster Capitalism" and Peasant Protest in China: The Last Twenty Years. *Journal of Peasant Studies, 33*(1), 1–33.

Li, C. (2012). The End of the CCP's Resilient Authoritarianism? A Tripartite Assessment of Shifting Power in China. *The China Quarterly, 211*, 595–623.

Li, D., & Bai, Y. (2007). Reservoir Resettlement in China: Past Experience and the Three Gorges Dam. *The Geographical Journal, 167*(3), 195–212.

Li, G. (2010). 解读水电工程建设移民安置长效补偿政策 [Reading the Policy on Long-term Compensation for Dam-induced Migrant Resettlement]. Retrieved from: http://xxgk.yn.gov.cn/ZT_SZ/newsview.aspx?id=157671&departmentID=6149

Li, H., Waley, P., & Rees, P. (2001). Reservoir Resettlement in China: Past Experience and the Three Gorges Dam. *The Geographical Journal, 167*(3), 195–212.

Li, L., & O'Brien, K. J. (2008). Protest Leadership in Rural China. *The China Quarterly, 193*, 1–23.

Li, L. C. (1998). *Centre and Provinces: China 1978–1993: Power as Non-Zero-Sum*. Oxford: Clarendon Press.

Li, L. C. (2006). Differentiated Actors: Central-Local Politics in China's Rural Tax Reforms. *Modern Asian Studies, 40*(1), 151–174.

Li, L. C. (2010). Central-Local Relations in the People's Republic of China: Trends, Processes and Impacts for Policy Implementation. *Public Administration and Development, 30*, 177–190.

Li, W., & Wang, Q. (2011). 水电提速困局 [Problems Surrounding the Quick Development of Hydropower]. *Caijing Magazine*. Retrieved from: http://magazine.caijing.com.cn/2011–04–24/110700987.html

Liang, C. (2010). China Launches Mekong River Basin Flood Control Training. Retrieved from: www.chinadaily.com.cn/china/2010–06/20/content_9993260.htm

Lieberthal, K. G., & Lampton, D. M. (1992). *Bureaucracy, Politics, and Decision Making in Post-Mao China*. Berkeley: University of California Press.

Lieberthal, K. G., & Oksenberg, M. (1988). *Policy Making in China: Leaders, Structures, and Processes*. Princeton: Princeton University Press.

Lin, C., & Lee, Y.-T. (2013). The Constitutive Rhetoric of Democratic Centralism: A Thematic Analysis of Mao's Discourse on Democracy. *Journal of Contemporary China, 22*(79), 148–165.

Lin, N. (1995). Local Market Socialism: Local Corporatism in Action in Rural China. *Theory and Society 24*(3), 301–354.

Lin, T.-C. (2007). Environmental NGOs and the Anti-Dam Movements in China: A Social Movement with Chinese Characteristics. *Issues and Studies, 43*(4), 149–184.

Liu, Y.-L. (1992). Reform from Below: The Private Economy and Local Politics in the Rural Industrialization of Wenzhou. *The China Quarterly, 130*, 293–316.

Lü, X. (2000). *Cadres and Corruption: The Organizational Involution of the Chinese Communist Party*. Palo Alto: Stanford University Press.

Luo, A. (2013). 云电送粤突破2000亿千瓦时大关 [Power Transmission from Yunnan to Guangdong Exceeds 200 Billion Kilowatt Mark]. *Renminribao*. January 16.

Magee, D. (2006a). Powershed Politics: Yunnan Hydropower under Great Western Development. *The China Quarterly, 185*, 23–41.

Magee, D. (2006b). "New Energy Geographies: Powershed Politics and Hydropower Decision Making in Yunnan, China." PhD dissertation, Department of Geography, University of Washington.

Manion, M. (1991). Policy Implementation in the People's Republic of China: Authoritative Decisions versus Individual Interests. *The Journal of Asian Studies, 50*(2), 253–279.

Mao, T. (1943). "Some Questions Concerning Methods of Leadership" (June 1). *Selected Works*, Vol. III. Beijing: Foreign Languages Press.

Martin, P., & Cohen, D. (2014). Mao and Forever. *Foreign Affairs*. Retrieved from: www.foreignaffairs.com/articles/china/2014–06–03/mao-and-forever

Mazmanian, D. A., & Sabatier, P. A. (1989). *Effective Policy Implementation*. Lanham: Lexington Books.

McAllister, D. E., Craig, J. F., Davidson, N., Delany, S., & Seddon, M. (2000). Biodiversity Impacts of Large Dams. *Background Paper No. 1 prepared for IUCN/UNEP/ WCD*.

McCartney, M. P., Sullivan, C., & Acreman, M. C. (2001). Ecosystem Impacts of Large Dams. *International Union for Conservation of Nature and Natural Resources and the United Nations Environmental Programme* (Background Paper No. 2). Retrieved from: http://climatechange-asiapac.com/system/files/resource/Ecosystem Impacts of Large Dams.pdf

McNally, A., Magee, D., & Wolf, A. T. (2009). Hydropower and Sustainability: Resilience and Vulnerability in China's Powersheds. *Journal of Environmental Management, 90*, 286–293.

Mertha, A. (2005). China's "Soft" Centralization: Shifting Tiao/Kuai Authority Relations. *The China Quarterly*, 791–810.

Mertha, A. (2008). *China's Water Warriors: Citizen Action and Policy Change*. New York: Cornell University Press.

Mertha, A. (2009). "Fragmented Authoritarianism 2.0": Political Pluralization in the Chinese Policy Process. *The China Quarterly, 200*, 995–1012.

Mertha, A., & Lowry, W. R. (2006). Unbuilt Dams: Seminal Events and Policy Change in China, Australia, and the United States. *Comparative Politics, 39*(1), 1–20.

Mill, J. S. (1843/1974). *A System of Logic*. Toronto: Toronto University Press.

Miller, A. (2014). How Strong Is Xi Jinping? *China Leadership Monitor, 43*. Retrieved from: www.hoover.org/sites/default/files/research/docs/clm43am.pdf

Ministry of Finance and Ministry of Electric Power Industry. (1981). 关于从水电站发电成本中提取库区维护基金的通知 [Notification on Extracting a Reservoir Maintenance Fund from Hydropower Station Electricity Prices]. *Ministry of Electric Power Industry and Ministry of Finance Document, No. 56*.

Ministry of Water Resources (MWR). (2011). 水利部水库移民开发局主要职责内设机构和人员编制 [Main Functions, Departments, and Staff of Resettlement Development Bureau under the Ministry of Water Resources]. Retrieved from: http://sym.mwr.gov.cn/zzjg/ymkfj/200903/t20090306_5006.htm

Montinola, G., Qian, Y., & Weingast, B. R. (1995). Federalism, Chinese Style: The Political Basis for Economic Success in China. *World Politics, 48*, 50–81.

Na, F. (2010). 普洱市水电移民安置情况调研报告 [Pu'er City Dam-induced Resettlement Situation Research Report]. Pu'er Municipal Party Committee Policy Research Office.

Nathan, A. J. (1976). Policy Oscillations in the People's Republic of China: A Critique. *The China Quarterly, 68*, 720–733.

Nathan, A. J. (2003). Authoritarian Resilience. *Journal of Democracy, 14*(1), 6–17.

National People's Congress. (1988). 中华人民共和国水法 [Water Law of the People's Republic of China].

National People's Congress. (2004). 中华人民共和国土地管理法 [Land Administration Law of the People's Republic of China].

National People's Congress. (2015). 境外非政府组织管理法（草案二次审议稿）[Law on Governing Foreign Non-Governmental Organizations (Second Draft)].

National Development and Reform Commission (NDRC). (2007). 水电工程建设征地移民安置规划设计规范 [Regulations for Planning and Designing Land Expropriation and Resettlement for Hydropower Project Construction]. *NDRC Document, No. 42.*

National Development and Reform Commission (NDRC). (2012). 国家发展改革委关于做好水电工程先移民后建设有关工作的通知 [National Development and Reform Commission Notification on Completing Tasks Surrounding the "First Resettle then Construct" Effort of Hydropower Construction Projects]. *NDRC Document, No. 293.*

National Energy Administration (NEA). (2011). 国家能源局关于印发水电工程勘察设计管理办法和水电工程设计变更管理办法的通知 [National Energy Administration Notification on Management Measures for Hydropower Project Design and Project Revision]. *National Energy Administration Document, No. 361.* Retrieved from: www.nea.gov.cn/2011–12/22/c_131321131.htm

News of the Communist Party of China. (2006). Three Represents. Retrieved from: http://english.cpc.people.com.cn/66739/4521344.html

NF Energy. (n.d.). 小水电 [Small Dams]. Retrieved from: www.nfenergy.com/cn/Relation.asp?id=8

O'Brien, K. J. (1994). The Impact of Union Political Activities on Public-Sector Pay, Employment, and Budgets. *Industrial Relations: A Journal of Economy and Society, 33*(3), 322–345.

O'Brien, K. J. (1996). Rightful Resistance. *World Politics, 49*(1), 31–55.

O'Brien, K. J., & Deng, Y. (2014). Repression Backfires: Tactical Radicalization and Protest Spectacle in Rural China. *Journal of Contemporary China, 24*(93), 457–470.

O'Brien, K. J., & Li, L. (1995). The Politics of Lodging Complaints in Rural China. *The China Quarterly, 143,* 756–783.

O'Brien, K. J., & Li, L. (1999). Selective Policy Implementation in Rural China. *Comparative Politics, 31*(2), 167–186.

O'Brien, K. J., & Li, L. (2006). *Rightful Resistance in Rural China.* Cambridge: Cambridge University Press.

O'Toole, L. J. (1995). Networking Requirements, Institutional Capacity, and Implementation Gaps in Transitional Regimes: The Case of Acidification Policy in Hungary. *Journal of European Public Policy, 4*(1), 1–17.

Oi, J. C. (1992). Fiscal Reform and the Economic Foundations of Local State Corporatism in China. *World Politics, 45*(Oct), 99–126.

Oi, J. C. (1995). The Role of the Local State in China's Transitional Economy. *The China Quarterly, 144*(Dec), 1132–1149.

Oi, J. C. (1999). *Rural China Takes Off: Institutional Foundations of Economic Reform.* Berkeley: University of California Press.

Oster, S. (2007). China Dam Project to Uproot Millions More. *The Wall Street Journal.* Retrieved from: www.wsj.com/articles/SB119212305140656176

Pei, M. (1998). Chinese Civic Associations: An Empirical Analysis. *Modern China, 24*(3), 285–318.

Pei, M. (2006). *China's Trapped Transition: The Limits of Developmental Autocracy.* Cambridge, MA: Harvard University Press.

People. (2001). 西电东送：西部大开发的标志性工程 [Sending Electricity from West to East: The Symbolic Project of the Western Development Strategy]. Retrieved from: www.people.com.cn/BIG5/jinji/31/179/20010810/531961.html

Perry, E. J. (1994). Trends in the Study of Chinese Politics: State-Society Relations. *The China Quarterly, 139,* 704–713.

Perry, E. J. (2002). Moving the Masses: Emotion Work in the Chinese Revolution. *Mobilization: An International Journal, 7*(2), 111–128.

Pressman, J., & Wildavsky, A. (1973). *Implementation: How Great Expectations in Washington Are Dashed in Oakland; Or Why It's Amazing That Federal Programs Work at All*. Berkeley: University of California Press.

Przeworski, A., & Teune, H. (1970). *The Logic of Comparative Social Inquiry*. New York: John Wiley.

Pu'er Government. (2007). 明确任务增强责任 扎实推进全市水电移民工作 [Clarify Tasks, Strengthen Responsibilities, Solidly Moving Forward the Whole City's Hydropower Resettlement Work]. Retrieved from: www.puershi.gov.cn/gov/ShowArticle. asp?ArticleID=1891

Pu'er Government. (2008). 普洱市人民政府办公室关于执行"云南省澜沧江糯扎渡水电站建设征地及移民安置规划报告补偿费用概算"（审定）的通知 [Pu'er People's Government Office Notice on Implementing the (Approved Edition) of the "Compensation Budget for Land Appropriation and Resettlement Plan Report of Yunnan Province Lancang River Nuozhadu Hydropower Station"]. *Pu'er People's Government Document, No. 39*. Retrieved from: www.puershi.gov.cn/gov/ShowArticle.asp?ArticleID=17186

Pu'er Government. (2009). 普洱市人民政府办公室关于成立普洱市移民工作领导小组的通知 [Pu'er Municipal People's Government Office Notification on Establishing Pu'er Municipal Resettlement Work Leading Small Group]. *Pu'er Government Document, No. 127*. Retrieved from: http://xxgk.yn.gov.cn/canton_model57/newsview. aspx?id=304464

Pu'er Government. (2010). 普洱市人民政府办公室关于印发普洱市移民开发局主要职责内设机构和人员编制规定的通知 [Pu'er Municipal People's Government Office Notification on Publication of Main Functions, Departments and Staff Regulations of Pu'er Municipal Resettlement Development Bureau]. *Pu'er Government Document, No. 220*. Retrieved from: http://xxgk.yn.gov.cn/canton_model57/newsview.aspx?id=309625

Pu'er Resettlement Bureau. (2011). 普洱市糯扎渡水电站建设征地补偿和移民安置 [*Compensation for Land Appropriation Compensation and Resettlement in Course of Nuozhadu Hydropower Station Construction in Pu'er Municipality*]. Handbook for Propagation.

Pu'er News. (2013). 星巴克爱伲咖啡有限公司正式投入运营 [Starbucks Ai Ni Coffee Company Officially Starts Operations]. Retrieved from: www.puernews.com/Dispaly_News.asp?N_FileID=201318164315

Qian, Y., & Weingast, B. R. (1996). China's Transition to Markets: Market-Preserving Federalism, Chinese Style. *Journal of Policy Reform, 1*(2), 149–185.

Read, B. L., & Michelson, E. (2008). Mediating the Mediation Debate: Conflict Resolution and the Local State in China. *Journal of Conflict Resolution, 52*(5), 737–764.

Remick, E. J. (2004). *Building Local States: China during the Republican and Post-Mao Eras*. Cambridge, MA: Harvard University Press.

Renmin Ribao. (1996). 三峡工程移民暨对口支援工作会议强调确保三峡截流顺利进行 [Working Conference on Three Gorges Resettlement Mutual Assistance Stresses the Need to Guarantee a Smooth Damming Process]. *Renminribao*. October 23.

Renmin Ribao. (2001). 水利部提出"十五"水库移民工作目标 [The Ministry of Water Resources put forth its "10th Five-Year Plan" Reservoir Resettlement Work Goals]. *Renminribao*. May 24.

Robinson, C. W. (2003). Risks and Rights: The Causes, Consequences, and Challenges of Development-Induced Displacement. The Brookings Institution – SAIS Project on Internal Displacement, Occasional Paper. Retrieved from: www.brookings.edu/fp/projects/idp/articles/didreport.pdf

Rolandsen, U.M.H. (2012). Stitching It All Back up: The Role of Sent-down Cadres in Rural Community Building. In A. Bislev & S. Thøgersen (Eds.), *Organizing Rural China, Rural China Organizing* (pp. 69–84). Lanham: Lexington Books.

Saich, T. (1996). *The Rise to Power of the Chinese Communist Party: Documents and Analysis.* Armonk: M. E. Sharpe.

Saich, T. (2000). Negotiating the State: The Development of Social Organizations in China. *The China Quarterly, 161,* 124–141.

Saich, T., & Hu, B. (2012). *Chinese Village, Global Market: New Collectives and Rural Development.* New York: Palgrave.

Schwartz, J. (2004). Environmental NGOs in China: Roles and Limits. *Pacific Affairs, 77*(1), 28–49. doi:10.2307/40022273

Scott, J. (1985). *Weapons of the Weak: Everyday Forms of Peasant Resistance.* New Haven, CT: Yale University Press.

Scott, W. R. (1995). *Institutions and Organizations.* London: Sage.

Shambaugh, D. (2008). *China's Communist Party: Atrophy and Adaptation.* Berkeley: University of California Press.

Shi, F., & Cai, Y. (2006). Disaggregating the State: Networks and Collective Resistance in Shanghai. *The China Quarterly, 186,* 314–332.

Shi, G., Su, Q., & Yuan, S. (2001). 小浪底水库移民风险及其规避 [Xiaolangdi Resettlement Risks and how to Avoid them]. *Xuehai, 2,* 44–51.

Shirk, S. L. (1993). *The Political Logic of Economic Reform in China.* Berkeley: University of California Press.

Simao Local History Committee. (2003). 思茅年鉴 [*Simao Almanac*]. Simao: Dehong Minzu Chubanshe.

Simao Water Resources & Hydropower Bureau. (1997). 思茅地区水利志 [*Simao District Water Resources Records*]. Kunming: Yunnan Minzu Chubanshe.

Sina. (2010). 华能水电开发被疑违规–深陷未批先建困局 [Huaneng Hydropower Development Suspected to be Illegal–Trapped in the "Construction without Approval" Dilemma]. Retrieved from: http://finance.sina.com.cn/chanjing/gsnews/20100417/12367771400.shtml

Sinohydro. (2012). fl接挑战 提升品牌 – 水电十四局功果桥水电站机电安装施工纪实 [Meeting a Challenge, Upgrading the Brand Name – Documentation of Sinohydro Bureau 14 Machinery Installation at Gongguoqiao Hydropower Station]. Retrieved from: www.sinohydro.com/664–999–604978.aspx

Smith, G. (2009). Political Machinations in a Rural County. *The China Journal, 62,* 29–59. doi:10.2307/20648113

Smith, G. (2015). Getting Ahead in Rural China: The Elite-Cadre Divide and Its Implications for Rural Governance. *Journal of Contemporary China, 24*(94), 594–612.

Solinger, D. J. (1992). *Urban Entrepreneurs and the State: The Merger of State and Society.* Boulder: Westview Press.

Spires, A. J., Tao, L., & Chan, K.-m. (2014). Societal Support for China's Grass-Roots NGOs: Evidence from Yunnan, Guangdong and Beijing. *The China Journal, 71,* 65–90.

Starbucks Newsroom. (2012). Starbucks to Partner with Ai Ni Group to Bring China's Yunnan Coffee to the World. Retrieved from: http://news.starbucks.com/article_display.cfm?article_id=617

State Council. (1991). 大中型水利水电工程建设征地补偿和移民安置条例 [Regulations for Land Appropriation and Resettlement Induced by Large- and Medium-Sized Water Conservancy and Hydropower Projects]. *State Council Document, No. 74.* Retrieved from: http://law.51labour.com/lawshow-59851.html

State Council. (1992). 关于加强水库移民工作的若干意见 [Opinions on Strengthening Reservoir Resettlement Work]. *State Council Document, No. 20.*

State Council. (2006a). 大中型水利水电工程建设征地补偿和移民安置条例 [Regulations for Land Appropriation and Resettlement Induced by Large- and Medium-Sized Water Conservancy and Hydropower Projects]. *State Council Document, No. 471.*

State Council. (2006b). 国务院关于完善水库移民后期扶持政策的意见 [State Council Opinions on Improving Post-Reservoir-Resettlement-Support Policies]. *State Council Document, No. 17.*

State Council. (2006c). 国务院关于同意建立全国水库移民后期扶持政策部际联席会议制度的批复 [State Council Reply Regarding the Establishment of a Nation-wide Inter-Departmental Conference on the National Reservoir Post-Resettlement Support Policy]. *State Council Document, No. 54.* Retrieved from: http://210.73.66.144:4601/law?fn=chl352s334.txt

State Planning Commission. (2002). 关于印发水电工程建设征地移民工作暂行管理办法的通知 [Notification on the Distribution of the Provisional Measures Governing Land Appropriation in the Course of Hydropower Construction Projects]. *State Planning Commission Document, No. 2623.*

Stein, M. (1997). *The Dispossessed: Victims of Development in Asia.* London: Earthscan.

Stern, R. E., & O'Brien, K. J. (2011). Politics at the Boundary: Mixed Signals and the Chinese State. *Modern China, 38*(2), 174–198.

Sun, F. (2011). 当代中国政府垂直管理存在问题及对策研究 [Centralized Management in the Government of Contemporary China: Existing Problems and Countermeasures]. 改革研究 *[Reform Research], 5,* n.p.

Sun, Y., & Zhao, D. (2007). Multifaceted State and Fragmented Society: Dynamics of Environmental Movement in China. In D. L. Yang (Ed.), *Discontented Miracle: Growth, Conflict, and Institutional Adaptations in China* (pp. 111–160). Singapore: World Scientific Publishing.

Svensson, M. (2012). Media and Civil Society in China: Community Building and Networking among Investigative Journalists and Beyond. *China Perspectives, 3,* 19–28.

Takeuchi, H. (2013). Survival Strategies of Township Governments in Rural China: From Predatory Taxation to Land Trade. *Journal of Contemporary China, 22*(83), 755–772.

Tan, Y., Hugo, G., & Potter, L. (2005). Rural Women, Displacement and the Three Gorges Project. *Development and Change, 36*(4), 711–734.

Tang, S.-Y., & Zhan, X. (2008). Civic Environmental NGOs, Civil Society, and Democratisation in China. *Journal of Development Studies, 44*(3), 425–448.

Teets, J. C. (2013). Let Many Civil Societies Bloom: The Rise of Consultative Authoritarianism in China. *The China Quarterly, 213,* 19–38.

Teets, J. C. (2014). *Civil Society under Authoritarianism: The China Model.* New York: Cambridge University Press.

Teets, J. C. (2015). The Evolution of Civil Society in Yunnan Province: Contending Models of Civil Society Management in China. *Journal of Contemporary China, 24*(91), 158–175.

Teets, J. C., & Hurst, W. (2014). Introduction: The Politics and Patterns of Policy Diffusion in China. In *Local Governance Innovation in China: Experimentation, Diffusion, and Defiance* (pp. 1–24). Abingdon: Routledge.

Tilt, B. (2014). *Dams and Development in China: The Moral Economy of Water.* New York: Columbia University Press.

Van Meter, D. S., & Van Horn, C. E. (1975). The Policy Implementation Process: A Conceptual Framework. *Administration & Society, 6*(4), 445–488.

Vogel, E. (2011). *Deng Xiaoping and the Transformation of China.* Cambridge, MA: Harvard University Press.

Walder, A. (1995). Local Governments as Industrial Firms: An Organizational Analysis of China's Transitional Economy. *American Journal of Sociology 101*(22), 263–301.

Wang, J.-H., Tseng, S.-W., & Zheng, H. (2015). The Paradox of Small Hydropower: Local Government and Environmental Governance in China. *Journal of Development Studies*.

Wang, M. (2015). China's New Foreign NGO Law Will Help Silence Critics. *The Interpreter*. Retrieved from: www.lowyinterpreter.org/post/2015/04/08/Chinas-new-foreign-NGO-law-will-help-silence-critics.aspx?COLLCC=2956191377&

Wang, Q., & Li, W. (2011). 水电地方帐 [Local accounts of hydropower]. *Caijing Magazine*. Retrieved from: http://magazine.caijing.com.cn/2011–04–24/110700966.html

Wang, S. (2008). Changing Models of China's Policy Agenda Setting. *Modern China, 34*(1), 56–87.

Wang, S. (2009). Adapting by Learning: The Evolution of China's Rural Health Care Financing. *Modern China, 35*(4), 370–404.

Wang, T., & Guo, C. (2006). 水库移民风险及规避策略 [Strategies to Avoid Dam-induced Resettlement Risks]. *Contemporary Manager, 12*, n.p.

Wang, Y. (2010). *中国水利水电工程移民问题研究* [*Study of the Resettlement Question in China's Water Conservancy and Hydropower Projects*]. Beijing: Waterpub.

Webber, M., & McDonald, B. (2004). Involuntary Resettlement, Production and Income: Evidence from Xiaolangdi, PRC. *World Development 32*(4), 673–690.

White G., Howell J. and Shang X. (1996). *In Search of Civil Society in China*. Clarendon Press: Oxford.

Wild Grass County Government. (2005). "Wild Grass" 县征地补偿和移民安置实施办法 ["Wild Grass" County Implementation Measures for Land Expropriation and Resettlement].

Wild Grass County Government. (2013). "Old Tree" 村民小组 ["Old Tree" Villager Small Group].

Wilmsen, B., Webber, M., & Duan, Y. F. (2011). Development for Whom? Rural to Urban Resettlement at the Three Gorges Dam, China. *Asian Studies Review, 35*, 21–42.

Wong, C.H. (2015). China Aims to Soothe Labor Unrest. *The Wall Street Journal*. Retrieved from: www.wsj.com/articles/china-aims-to-soothe-labor-unrest-1428478396

Woo, W. T. (2007). The Origins of China's Quest for a Harmonious Society Failures on the Governance and Environmental Fronts. In R. Sanders & Y. Chen (Eds.), *China's Post-Reform Economy – Achieving Harmony* (pp. 15–29). London: Routledge.

World Bank. (1993). *China Involuntary Resettlement*. Washington, DC: World Bank, Environment Department.

World Bank. (2012). Recent Experience with Involuntary Resettlement: Overview. Retrieved from: http://lnweb90.worldbank.org/oed/oeddoclib.nsf/b57456d58aba40e585256ad400736404/136789097aa33192852567f5005d6203?OpenDocument

World Commission on Dams. (2000). *Dams and Development: A New Framework for Decision-Making*. London: Earthscan.

Xinhua. (1992). 水库移民干部培训中心成立 [Cadre Training Center for Reservoir Resettlement established]. *Renminribao*. April 9.

Xinhua. (2003). 三峡工程背景资料 [Background Material to the Three Gorges Project]. Retrieved from: http://news.xinhuanet.com/ziliao/2003–05/30/content_894678.htm

Xinhua. (2011). China Vows to Curb Environmental Deterioration in Three Gorges Project Areas by 2020. May 18. Retrieved from: http://news.xinhuanet.com/english2010/china/2011–05/18/c_13881197.htm

Xinhua. (n.d.). 国家建设土地办法 [Measures for Land Appropriation in National Construction]. Retrieved from: http://news.xinhuanet.com/ziliao/2005–01/06/content_2423639.htm

Xinhua Net. (2013). 國有企業改革發展 華電集團破解水庫移民難題 [State-Owned Enterprise Reform Development – Huadian Group's Unraveling of Dam-Induced Resettlement Problem]. *China News*. Retrieved from: http://big5.chinanews.com:89/ ny/2012/01–04/3581031.shtml

Xinhua Net. (2014). 溪洛渡水电站大坝全线浇筑到顶 [Xiluodu Hydropower Reservoir Pours to the Top]. Retrieved from: http://news.xinhuanet.com/fortune/2014–03/06/c_ 119646678.htm

Xu, S., & Chen, W. (2006). The Reform of Electricity Power Sector in the PR of China. *Energy Policy, 34*, 2455–2465.

Xu, Y., & Li, H. (2005). 糯扎渡水电站农村移民安置 [Rural Resettlement of Nuozhadu Hydropower Station]. *Water Power, 31*(5), 20–22.

Xu, Y., & Mu, S. (2012). 先看移民安置妥没妥（政策速递） [First See whether Resettlers have been Resettled Appropriately or Not (Policy Delivery)]. *Renminribao*. April 10.

Yang, D. L. (1996). Governing China's Transition to the Market: Institutional Incentives, Politicians' Choices, and Unintended Outcomes. *World Politics, 48*(April), 424–452.

Yang, D. L. (2004). *Remaking the Chinese Leviathan: Market Transition and the Politics of Governance in China*. Stanford: Stanford University Press.

Yang, G. (2005). Environmental NGOs and Institutional Dynamics in China. *The China Quarterly, 181*, 46–66. doi:10.1017/S0305741005000032

Yang, Z., Liu, Y., Hu, P., Zhong, Y., Jiang, Z., & Zou, Z. (2006). 云南省大中型水电建设移民安置用地规划研究 [*Research on Land Usage for Resettlement Due to Construction of Large and Medium-sized Hydropower Station in Yunnan Province*]. Beijing: China Science and Technology Publishing House.

Yang, Z., Wang, H., Milliman, Y. D., Xu, K., Qiao, S., & Shi, G. (2006). Dam Impacts on the Changjiang (Yangtze) River Sediment Discharge to the Sea: The Past 55 Years and after the Three Gorges Dam. *Water Resources Research, 42*. doi:10.1029/2005WR003970

Yardley, J. (2007). Chinese Dam Projects Criticized for Their Human Costs. *The New York Times*. Retrieved from: www.nytimes.com/2007/11/19/world/asia/19dam.html?_r=2& hp=&pagewanted=print

Yeh, E. T., & Lewis, J. I. (2004). State Power and the Logic of Reform in China's Electricity Sector. *Pacific Affairs, 77*(3), 437–465.

Ying, X. (2005). 大河移民上访的故事——从"讨个说法"到"摆平理顺" [*From "Asking for a Statement" To "Balancing Relations (baiping lishui)" — A Story of a Hydroelectric Station Area in Southwest in China*]. Retrieved from: http://journal.probeinternational. org/2008/06/20/story-dahe-dam-chapter-1/

Ying, X. (2008). Critique of a New Trend in Villager Self-Government Studies. *Chinese Sociology & Anthropology, 41*(1), 43–56.

Yunnan Daily. (2009). 景洪水电站5台机组全部建成投产（图） [The Fifth Generator of the Jinghong Hydropower Station Is Fully Operational (Picture)]. Retrieved from: www. hydropower.org.cn/info/shownews.asp?newsid=1517

Yunnan Government. (2007). 云南省人民政府办公厅关于印发云南金沙江中游水电开发移民安置补偿补助意见的通知 [Yunnan People's Government Office Notification on Publishing the Opinions on Resettlement Compensation for Hydropower Development along the Middle Reaches of the Lancang River in Yunnan]. *Yunnan People's Government Document, No. 159*. Retrieved from: www.ynsym.cn/html/2012/sheng zhengfuzhengce_0712/17.html

Yunnan Government. (2008). 云南省人民政府关于贯彻落实国务院大中型水利水电工程建设征地补偿和移民安置条例的实施意见 [Yunnan People's Government

Opinions on Implementing the Regulations for Land Appropriation and Resettlement Induced by Large- and Medium-Sized Water Conservancy and Hydropower Projects]. *Yunnan People's Government Document, No. 24.* Retrieved from: www.jhs.gov.cn/home/bn_jhsymkfj/newshow.aspx?id=40790

Yunnan Net. (2010). 小湾水电站简介 [An Introduction to the Xiaowan Hydropower Station]. Retrieved from: www.hydropower.org.cn/info/shownews.asp?newsid=3526

Yunnan Net. (2011). 省政府与大唐集团签署战略合作框架协议 [The Provincial Government and Datang Group Sign a Framework Agreement on Strategic Cooperation]. Retrieved from: http://yn.yunnan.cn/html/2011–03/09/content_1525214.htm

Yunnan Net. (2012). 我省境内最大水电项目投产运营 – 华能糯扎渡水电站首台机组发电 [Our Province's Largest Hydropower Project Is Operational – First Turbine of Huaneng Nuozhadu Hydropower Station Generates Electricity. Retrieved from: http://yn.yunnan.cn/html/2012–09/07/content_2391944.htm

Yunnan Resettlement Bureau. (2012). 云南省移民开发局简介 [Introduction to Yunnan Resettlement and Development Bureau]. Retrieved from: www.ynymw.cn:8080/Article/Article.asp?nid=102

Yunnan Xinhua Net. (2011). 云南最大电站 – 糯扎渡水电站明年7月投产 [Yunnan's Largest Hydropower Station – Nuozhadu Dam Starts Electricity Generation in July Next Year]. Retrieved from: www.yn.xinhuanet.com/newscenter/2011‐05/27/content_22871816.htm

Zhang, Y. (2008). 我经历的重大转折 – 水利部农村水利司原司长 张岳 [The Big Transition I Have Experienced – Former Bureau Chief of the Rural Water Resources Bureau in the Ministry of Water Resources, Zhang Yue]. Retrieved from: www.cahee.org.cn/show.aspx?id=1116&cid=82

Zheng, R., & Shi, G. (2011). 西部水电移民风险管理 [*Study on the Risk Management of the Western Hydropower Resettlement*]. Beijing: Social Science Academic Press.

Zheng, Y., & Brødsgaard, K. E. (Eds.). (2006). *The Chinese Communist Party and China's Capitalist Revolution.* London: Routledge.

Zhong, Y. (2003). *Local Government and Politics in China: Challenges from Below.* Armonk: M. E. Sharpe.

Zhou, X. (2010). The Institutional Logic of Collusion among Local Governments in China. *Modern China, 36*(1), 47–78.

Zhu, D., & Shi, G. (2011). 水利水电移民制度研究:问题分析, 制度透视与创新构想 [*Institutional Research on Resettlement-Induced by Water Resources Projects: Issues Analysis, Institutional Perspectives & Innovation Constructing*]. Beijing: Social Science Academic Press.

Zhu, X. (2008). Strategy of Chinese Policy Entrepreneurs in the Third Sector: Challenges of "Technical Infeasibility." *Policy Sciences, 41*(4), 315–334. doi:10.1007/s11077–008–9070–2

Zhu, X. (2011). Government Advisors or Public Advocates? Roles of Think Tanks in China from the Perspective of Regional Variations. *The China Quarterly, 207,* 668–686. doi:10.1017/S0305741011000701

Index